Happiness and the Good Life

Happiness and the Good Life

Mike W. Martin

OXFORD
UNIVERSITY PRESS

OXFORD
UNIVERSITY PRESS

Oxford University Press, Inc., publishes works that further
Oxford University's objective of excellence
in research, scholarship, and education.

Oxford   New York

Auckland   Cape Town   Dar es Salaam   Hong Kong   Karachi
Kuala Lumpur   Madrid   Melbourne   Mexico City   Nairobi
New Delhi   Shanghai   Taipei   Toronto

With offices in

Argentina   Austria   Brazil   Chile Czech Republic   France   Greece
Guatemala   Hungary   Italy   Japan   Poland   Portugal   Singapore
South Korea   Switzerland   Thailand   Turkey   Ukraine   Vietnam

Published by Oxford University Press, Inc.
198 Madison Avenue, New York, New York 10016

www.oup.com

Oxford is a registered trademark of Oxford University Press

Library of Congress Cataloging-in-Publication Data
Martin, Mike W., 1946–
Happiness and the good life / Mike W. Martin.
p.   cm.
Includes bibliographical references (p.   ) and index.
ISBN 978-0-19-984521-7 (hardcover : alk. paper)
1. Happiness. 2. Well-being. 3. Conduct of life. I. Title.
BJ1481.M38   2012
170.44—dc23   2011019584

3 5 7 9 8 6 4 2

Printed in the United States of America
on acid-free paper

For Shannon, Sonia, and Nicole.

CONTENTS

PREFACE

How does happiness enter into good lives? Is it perhaps the highest good, and hence the most important feature of desirable ways of living? Is it instead only one aspect of worthwhile lives, and if so how is it related to other aspects? The answers to these questions are deeply personal and yet invite dialogue. They turn on how we understand happiness, good lives, and a host of practical, psychological, and philosophical issues. In my view, we are happy insofar as we love our lives, valuing them with ample enjoyments and a robust sense of meaning. As such, happiness is one vital dimension of good lives, but only one. My aim is to explore how happiness interacts with other aspects of good lives, in particular moral decency and goodness, authenticity, self-fulfillment, mental health, and meaningfulness in terms of a wide array of justified values. Here is a brief overview.

Chapter 1: Loving Life. What is happiness? The question calls for a concise definition rather than a compendium of things that make us happy. Plato and Aristotle began a tradition of defining happiness in terms of the virtuous life, which in turn they understood in narrow canonical terms. Today, however, most of us understand happiness as subjective and define it entirely in terms of emotions, attitudes, and other mental states. Psychologists aptly call it "subjective well-being." In tune with this subjective emphasis, I define happiness as loving one's life, valuing it in ways manifested by myriad enjoyments and a robust sense of meaning, regardless of whether the enjoyments and sense of meaning are rooted in justified values. I also understand "the good life" as shorthand for a wide diversity of admirable ways of living, ways that embody the virtues and other values in myriad ways.

Chapter 2: Valuing Happiness. How does happiness relate to morality? Happy lives are not always morally good, and morally good lives are not always happy. Nevertheless, happiness and morality are interwoven in myriad ways. Happiness is among the basic goods for a human being. In addition to being a self-interested good, it is a moral good, assuming it is not based directly on immorality. Its worth increases as it intertwines with moral values: Loving our lives has greater moral worth insofar as our lives are worth loving, and our enjoyments and sense of meaning have greater worth insofar as they are rooted in justified values. As affirmed in the Declaration of Independence, there is a human right to pursue happiness, which is implied in the basic right to liberty. There is even a limited responsibility, rooted in self-respect, to pursue happiness as an aspect of a good life. Of most interest in subsequent chapters, the virtues tend to promote happiness, and happiness often contributes to the virtues.

Chapter 3: Betting on Virtue. How do the virtues contribute to happiness? As Rosalind Hursthouse and others suggest, the virtues are a good bet in pursuing happiness. Specific virtues contribute to happiness in vastly many ways. As a preliminary sampling, I discuss nine virtues grouped in three categories: (1) virtues of the heart, centered on valuing what is good (gratitude, self-respect, love), (2) virtues of the will, centered on strength in pursuing what is good (courage, self-control, hope), and (3) virtues of reason, centered on wisdom (moral understanding, humility, mindfulness). Positive psychologists study how these and many other virtues contribute to happiness, and vice versa, and I draw on their insights while registering some cautions about their procedures.

Chapter 4: Authenticity. Is authenticity a reliable guide to happiness? Be yourself, we are told, and happiness will follow. Discovering and developing our "true self," the self that expresses our deepest aspirations and talents, does indeed contribute to happiness by tapping into wellsprings of enjoyment and meaning. Yet authenticity is neither a simple nor a sure guide to happiness. It is not even an independent guide, for what makes us happy is itself an important indicator of our deepest desires and hence of our authentic selves. Moreover, authenticity has multiple aspects that can be in tension with each other: wholehearted caring, self-honesty, self-acceptance, self-creation, and self-realization. In addition, authenticity connects with other values that might be in tension with happiness. These complexities are illustrated with decisions about whether to use biomedical enhancements.

Chapter 5: Happily Self-Deceived. Does illusion promote or diminish happiness? It might do either, depending on the situation. We are frequently mistaken about what makes us happy, and we can deceive ourselves about how happy we are. Within limits, many of these illusions augment happiness by bolstering hope and confidence. Yet honesty is even more important in pursuing happiness. Honesty helps us identify what we want most; it helps us appreciate what we enjoy most and find meaning in; it keeps our expectations realistic; and in general it keeps us in touch with reality as we pursue our vision of a good life.

Chapter 6: Suffering in Happy Lives. Is happiness compatible with suffering? Once again the answer is complicated. Nothing can protect us from tragedies that destroy what we cherish most and thereby undermine happiness. Yet much suffering can be integrated into happy lives, depending significantly on our attitudes. As is often said, suffering can deepen joy and meaning. Not surprising, philosophical perspectives on the value of suffering in good lives both reflect and shape conceptions of happiness.

Chapter 7: Paradoxes of Happiness. Should happiness be pursued directly and deliberately, with an eye on the prize? Doing so is self-defeating, according to the paradox of happiness, for it fosters self-absorption and undermines meaning and even enjoyment. Instead we should participate in activities and relationships that we find inherently meaningful, rather than solely because of the happiness we hope to find in them. Then, with any luck, happiness comes indirectly. This paradox expresses an important truth, albeit with a dollop of hyperbole. Indeed, it expresses a number of truths that are highlighted by dividing the paradox of happiness into a dozen more specific paradoxes concerning aims, success, freedom, and attitudes. These paradoxes form the backdrop for discussions of philanthropy, love, and work in the following chapters.

Chapter 8: Happy to Help. How is happiness related to helping others? Specifically, how is happiness connected to philanthropy, that is, voluntary giving of time or money for public purposes? Psychologists confirm commonsense beliefs that there are noteworthy correlations, and they see causation moving in two directions. On the one hand, helping tends to contribute to the helper's happiness, although not always. On the other hand, being happy tends to motivate happiness. This happiness-promoting aspect of giving is important in understanding the motives of philanthropists, which, as in most areas of life, typically mix self-interested and social-oriented motives. Yet there are also philosophical issues concerning how happiness, interacting with other aspects of good lives, enters into justifying.

Chapter 9: Shared Pursuits in Love. What does it mean to pursue happiness together within marriage and other committed relationships? Marriages are happy insofar as both partners are happy with and within the marriage, and happy marriages contribute to the overall happiness of each partner. Yet these ideas do not fully capture how marriages are shared pursuits of happiness. To that end, we need to invoke the ideas of shared agency, personal identity, and intimacy between partners who share the pursuit of a happy life together. Happiness plays a major role in justifying decisions to marry and to sustain or abandon marriages, as does a wider array of moral values. Although shared pursuits of happiness are singularly intimate, they illustrate how the pursuit of happiness is not as highly individualistic as we tend to think. Nowhere is the interplay of happiness and the virtues more complex than in love and marriage.

Chapter 10: Balancing Work and Leisure. What does it mean to live a balanced life, and in particular to balance work and leisure? Balance is often celebrated as a mark of wisdom and as a source of happiness. Yet happiness is also one of the main criteria for telling what balance is. Hence, as with authenticity and happiness, balance and happiness are interwoven in both their meaning and value. Additional criteria for balance include health and moral responsibility. As elsewhere, the criteria for balance are multifaceted and sometimes conflicting in good lives.

Chapter 11: Simplicity. What is voluntary simplicity, and does it increase happiness? The contribution of simplicity to happiness is emphasized from Buddha to Thoreau, and from Socrates to contemporary self-help books. As a virtue, however, simplicity is not a simple idea. If it is merely reducing complexity by cutting back on the number of our concerns, then it might be prudent or foolish. If instead it is the virtue of identifying and living by what is most important, removing undesirable distractions in order to stay focused on essentials, then it is a large part of practical wisdom—in all its nuance and subtlety. Happiness is one of the important values that enters into understanding simplicity (once again paralleling authenticity and balance). The question then arises how happiness relates to familiar "simplicity themes" such as greater mindfulness, frugality, and conservation. Simplicity is best subsumed under the wider rubric of coping with complexity in good lives.

Chapter 12: Felicity in Frankenstein. Does happiness promote virtue, and does unhappiness produce vice? Mary Shelley dramatizes the issue in *Frankenstein*. Reminiscent of Rousseau, her articulate monster argues that happiness does indeed advance goodness and misery causes malice. Victor Frankenstein largely shares this "happiness principle," and this agreement between creator and creature is central to the novel's plot. Shelley and her novel, however, convey a more nuanced perspective. The unqualified belief in the happiness principle easily becomes a source of moral evasion, for her protagonists and perhaps for us.

Chapter 13: Personal and Political. Should laws and government policies be guided by what positive psychologists are discovering about happiness? A number of distinguished thinkers contend that they should. Their main contention is that increasing personal wealth and the Gross Domestic Product are very limited ways to increase happiness. These advocates of a politics of happiness are right about the need to take the science of happiness seriously in public policy, but they are wrong when they sometimes elevate happiness above all other dimensions of good lives and good societies. Even when wealth does not contribute to happiness it can still have great importance in bringing economic security and creating opportunities for self-development. I conclude by summarizing my themes about happiness in good lives by drawing parallels with Goethe's insights into happiness.

I thank the publishers who permitted me to draw on my earlier articles, in revised form:

"Happiness and Virtue in Positive Psychology," *Journal for the Theory of Social Behaviour* 37:1 (2007): 89–103.

"Paradoxes of Happiness," *Journal of Happiness Studies* 9:2 (2008): 171–184.

"Happily Self-Deceived," *Social Theory and Practice* 35:1 (2009): 29–44.

"Suffering in Happy Lives," in *Philosophy and Happiness*, Lisa Bortolotti, ed. (New York: Palgrave Macmillan, 2009), pp. 100–115.

"Balancing Work and Leisure," in *The Value of Time and Leisure in a World of Work*, Mitchell Haney and David Kline, eds. (Lanham, MD: Lexington Books, 2010), pp. 7–24.

I thank Peter Ohlin for his superb editorial guidance, with this book as with my two previous books with Oxford University Press, and Lisa Bortolotti and Valerie Tiberius for serving as Oxford University Press reviewers and making insightful comments on the penultimate draft. I benefited from discussions with Carolyn Brodbeck, Robert A. Cummins, Don Gabard, Shari Kuckenbecker, Alfred R. Mele, Michael Pace, Amy Rudometkin, and Virginia Warren. I read an earlier version of chapter 10 at the conference "Work, Leisure, and Quality of Life," held at the University of North Florida (November 2008), where I learned from Kevin Aho, Robert Audi, Charles Guignon, Mitch Haney, Marcia Homiak, David Kline, Bert Koegler, and Valerie Tiberius. Chapman University provided a one-semester sabbatical that facilitated completion of the book, and my students provided an invaluable stimulus.

Above all, I thank my wife Shannon, and our daughters Sonia and Nicole for their gifts of love—and happiness.

Happiness and the Good Life

1

LOVING LIFE

I was troubled, abstracted, dreamy; I wept, I sighed, I longed for a happiness of which I had not the first notion, and yet whose absence I felt keenly.[1]
—Jean-Jacques Rousseau

What is happiness? The question calls for a definition rather than a laundry list of things that make us happy. A good definition will be concise, reasonably clear, attuned to ordinary language, and useful for the purposes at hand. It will not appeal to everyone, if only because the word "happiness" is ambiguous and can be defined with different purposes in mind. For example, motivational speakers prefer value-laden definitions of "true happiness" centered on virtuous and spiritually enlightened living. In contrast, psychologists employ value-neutral definitions of happiness as "subjective well-being," understood exclusively in terms of emotions (especially pleasurable ones), attitudes (satisfaction with one's life), beliefs (for example that one's life is going well), and other mental states. I follow the lead of the psychologists, primarily because they are closest to predominant understandings of happiness but also in order to draw upon their studies. In my view, we are happy insofar as we love our lives, valuing them in ways manifested by ample enjoyments and a robust sense of meaning. I explore how happiness, in this sense, functions as one dimension of good lives interacting with other dimensions, in particular with authenticity, health, self-fulfillment, moral decency and goodness, and meaningfulness in terms of justified values.

HAPPY PERSONS

Mike Leigh portrays an exceptionally happy person in his film *Happy-Go-Lucky*.[2] Poppy (played by actress Sally Hawkins) is an irrepressibly upbeat elementary schoolteacher who finds her life greatly enjoyable and deeply meaningful. She is bubbly, witty, and fun to be around. By temperament, she is not given to extended bouts of depression, anxiety, and anger. When her bike is stolen she can joke about it, and soon makes plans to learn how to drive. She is also kind, compassionate, a good friend, and strongly motivated in her career. When one of her students bullies another child on the playground, she comes to the aid of both children. After protecting the child who is attacked, she consults with a social worker about how best to change the bully's behavior. Together they identify the source of the problem in an abusive home. On another occasion she takes risks in trying to help a homeless man, communicating empathetically despite his seemingly incoherent babbling. Such episodes almost invite a spiritual interpretation of Poppy as akin to a laughing Buddha who radiates peace, forgiveness, generosity, and joy. Poppy is no Pollyanna, however, and her occasional effusiveness causes problems. In particular, she realizes too slowly that her lighthearted and erotically tinged banter is misconstrued by her bigoted driving instructor as an alarming sexual provocation.

As audience members we do not doubt that Poppy is happy, but her sister Helen does. Poppy lacks a husband, house, and pension fund, all of which Helen considers necessary for happiness.

> HELEN: "I just want you to be happy, that's all."
> POPPY: "I am happy."
> HELEN: "I don't think you are."
> POPPY: "I am. I love my life. Yeah, it can be tough at times. That's part of it, isn't it? I've got a great job, brilliant kids [i.e., wonderful students], lovely flat. I've got her to look at [referring to her friend Zoe]. I've got amazing friends. I love my freedom. I'm a very lucky lady, I know that."

"I love my life" is a natural way to express happiness, and it is a useful starting point for a definition. To love our lives is to love being alive, but much more. After all, we might be miserable and yet glad to be alive, if only because we hope to become happier in the future. To be happy is to love our lives, at least in most of their primary configurations; it is to value our lives in ways manifested in ample enjoyments and a robust sense of meaning. Let us briefly clarify each of these ideas: valuing, enjoyment, and sense of meaning.[3] (Afterward I comment on the idea of "lives.")

Valuing. To value our lives, in the way relevant to happiness, is to affirm them in their present configurations, which include our primary hopes for the future as well as our current activities and relationships, possessions and accomplishments, and values and ideals. The affirmation is manifested in predominant patterns of enjoyment and sense of meaning.

Valuing our lives should not be conflated with *evaluating* them.[4] In general, to evaluate is to make a judgment of appraisal, rating, or ranking in a hierarchy of quality. Some evaluations are impersonal assessments according to social standards, for example when a government inspector assesses the quality of foods or a judge ranks perfor-mances in an ice skating competition. Other evaluations are based on more personal standards, as when we rate a song or movie according to our personal tastes. Yet not even personal, positive evaluations fully capture what it is to value our lives in ways mani-fested by enjoyment and meaning. Valuing is an affirmative psychological stance that permeates how we experience our lives; it is not a judgment or ranking. If we say that happiness is an attitude toward our lives, we should immediately add that it is an um-brella attitude that encompasses myriad positive attitudes toward people, relationships, activities, and other components of our lives.

Although happiness is not an evaluation, we do sometimes evaluate how happy we are. We evaluate informally when we rank our present happiness as higher or lower than at other times, or higher or lower than someone else's happiness. We evaluate more formally when we fill out a psychologist's questionnaire, ranking our present happiness on a scale of 1 to 7 or 1 to 10. What we rate and rank on these occasions, our happiness itself, is the extent to which we love our lives; it is the extent to which we value them as shown in patterns of enjoyment and meaning.

Loving our lives is comparable to loving persons.[5] To love persons implies cherishing them for themselves, with all their flaws. To be sure, we also evaluate persons and their features such as physique, personality, intelligence, social skills, achievements, and wealth. But love is at risk when evaluations overshadow valuing, especially when eval-uations are accompanied by a longing or readiness to "trade up" to a better spouse.[6] There is a rough analogy here with how happiness is poisoned by envious comparisons between what others have and we lack, as well as by failures to accept irremediable limitations in our lives. Furthermore, we do not love other persons solely *because* they bring us pleasure and meaning. Rather, love is *shown* and expressed in the delight and meaning we derive from the two-way caring relationship with the person. Likewise, love for our life is shown in patterns of enjoyable and meaningful activities, relation-ships, and accomplishments. And just as loving a person has its ups and downs, with episodes of pain, anger, terror, and doubt, so does a happy life.

Enjoyment. I use "enjoyment" in a wide sense to include pleasurable emotions and moods, pleasant sensations and thoughts, enjoyable activities and relationships, and attitudes of being pleased about things. The enjoyments contributing to happiness take innumerable forms. To take an alphabetical sampling, there are enjoyments of art, boating, cooking, drawing, eating, fishing, gardening, helping, ice skating, jokes, kay-aking, laughing, money, novels, opera, philanthropy, quilting, reading, sex, travel, un-derstanding, video games, work, xylophones, yachting, and Zen. More useful than alphabetical listings, enjoyments can be catalogued with different interests in mind. Thus, enjoyments can be grouped by categories of activities and relationships that pro-duce them: work, family, and sports, or specific types of work, family, and sports. They can be sorted into broad aspects of persons, such as psychological, physical, moral, and spiritual. They can be differentiated by duration: brief, lingering, recurring, or rare. And they can be distinguished as active or passive, according to the effort and intention involved.

Of special interest, enjoyments might be sorted by general modes of emotion. Daniel Haybron conjectures that positive emotions and moods, all of which I count as enjoyments, cluster into three categories of dispositions that are central in the personalities of happy individuals: (1) endorsement (e.g., joy, cheerfulness, feeling happy), (2) engagement (e.g., exuberance, passion, vitality), and (3) attunement (e.g., tranquility, confidence, expansiveness).[7] Haybron calls these categories the three faces of happiness, understanding happiness as an overall positive emotional state of "psychic affirmation" of one's life as going well.[8] In contrast, unhappy lives are dominated by negative attitudes, emotions, and moods such as anxiety, fear, depression, sadness, despair, meaninglessness, anger, hatred, rage, envy, and boredom. My definition of happiness differs from Haybron's by explicitly mentioning valuing and a sense of meaning, which are implicit in his account, and by using the colloquial "loving one's life" rather than "psychic affirmation." Otherwise, our accounts have much in common.

In another recent discussion, Fred Feldman attempts to understand happiness in terms of one formal category of pleasure, attitudinal pleasure: "This sort of pleasure is a propositional attitude rather than a feeling, or sensation. We attribute this sort of pleasure to a person when we say that he is pleased about something, or when we say that he 'takes pleasure in' some state of affairs."[9] Persons are happy, according to Feldman, insofar as they have pro attitudes toward the various aspects of their lives, valuing them for their own sake. Much that he says connects with my emphasis on valuing, whose core comprises positive attitudes toward specific aspects and the totality of our lives. Yet he disregards other important pleasures that enter into happiness, including the positive emotions Haybron highlights. Sometimes he blurs attitudinal pleasures and enjoying activities, for example when he says that to be pleased by living in Massachusetts is an attitude, whereas surely it also includes enjoyable activities connected with living there. In any case, I see no reason to follow him in restricting enjoyments in happy lives to any one type. It is true, however, that enjoyments can be categorized by how strongly they contribute to happiness, including how different categories of enjoyment are more or less crucial for an individual's happiness—types in terms of propositional attitudes versus sensuous pleasures, as well as types in terms of such things as sports or scientific inquiry, or engagement and attunement (a point I return to later).

Sense of Meaning. A sense of meaning is not an abstract perspective or set of beliefs. Instead, it is a nuanced set of attitudes that are revealed in what we care about and enjoy. A sense of meaning yokes together two things: (1) having values (ideals, principles, tastes) and (2) finding our lives intelligible. More fully, a sense of meaning is the value we find in (and give to) our activities and relationships; it is also the intelligibility and coherence we find in (and give to) our activities and relationships in light of our values and related beliefs. In the intended sense, a sense of meaning is subjective—there is no suggestion that the values are sound and the intelligibility is reasonable. Thus, Hitler had values and a sense of meaning, monstrous ones. It is important to bear this point in mind when, for convenience, I sometimes refer to a sense of meaning as simply meaning. The context will make clear that in other contexts, when I discuss aspects of good lives in addition to happiness, I have in mind meaning in terms of justified values.

Although a sense of meaning centers on our values, it interweaves with enjoyments in various ways. For example, some activities are meaningful (worthwhile) to us largely because they provide streams of enjoyment, such as riding a roller coaster or playing a video game. Other activities are meaningful to us because they yield enjoyments at the end of an unpleasant process, such as having a tooth drilled by a dentist. But most activities are meaningful in part because they connect with enjoyments: we value them, at least in part, because we find them enjoyable or because they bring about things that we find enjoyable. Appreciating these connections leads me to highlight a sense of meaning as integral to happiness, in contrast with the more standard exclusive emphasis on pleasures in defining happiness.

HAPPY LIVES

I am interested in happy lives as well as happy persons. The ideas are not identical, any more than "lives" and "persons" are synonyms. They are, however, interdefined: Persons are happy insofar as their lives are happy, and lives are happy insofar as persons are happy. This logical connection seems trivial, but it reflects an important point. Because happy persons love their *lives*, the concept of happiness in anchored in both mental states and the world beyond mental states. More fully, the concepts of happy persons and happy lives include an outward reference to activities and relationships, struggles and obstacles, accomplishments and failures, and other components of lives as unfolded in the world. Quite appropriately, Poppy defends her claim that she is happy by commenting on the features of her life that provide meaning and enjoyment: her great job, wonderful students, amazing friends, and cherished freedom.

To be sure, other notions of happy persons and happy lives are not interdefinable. For example, "happy persons" might refer to individuals with naturally happy temperaments, that is, dispositions to be upbeat regardless of any features about their present lives. Again, "happy lives" might have a primary outward reference. In its etymological sense, happy lives referred to good fortune (*hap* = good luck), where good fortune was measured objectively in terms such as lineage, wealth, success, and social standing.

Today, however, it sounds odd to say that a person has a happy life but is unhappy. Instead, we say that individuals blessed with every good fortune can be unhappy, perhaps because they are depressed, and individuals with little good fortune can still be happy. Indeed, sometimes we experience the frustration and perplexity in knowing we have everything necessary for happiness and yet we are miserable.

To repeat, today the predominant concept of happiness centers on our subjective responses to our lives. That concept has a double anchor in mental states and the world, regardless of whether we are talking of happy persons or happy lives. This double anchor is obscured when happiness is mistakenly reduced to pleasure and other mental states. Language encourages this mistake, in that "happiness" and "pleasure" are sometimes used as synonyms. Thus, happy *experiences* are pleasurable experiences such as making love or playing golf. Happy *emotions* are pleasurable emotions such as amusement, delight, contentment, and joy. Happy *moods* are somewhat longer-term enjoyable emotional states, including exuberant states like joy and cheerfulness and quiescent states like serenity and peace. Complicating matters, some meanings of "happy" do not refer to states of consciousness. For example, there are happy *events*, which are occurrences favorable in light of our desires, even though we might not be conscious of them; for example, our stock investments doing well. In short, the everyday language of happiness contains a mélange of meanings. I am interested primarily in happy persons and happy lives, each of which refers to both states of mind and to activities and relationships in the world.

For similar reasons, we need to exercise caution in using psychologists' generic definition of happiness as "subjective well-being." The expression aptly reminds us that happiness centers on our subjective responses to the world, in particular to our attitudes, emotions, enjoyments, and sense of meaning. It is misleading, however, if it suggests that happiness is a mental state that makes no reference to the world beyond our minds. When psychologists define happiness as subjective well-being, they primarily intend happy persons rather than happy lives. Thus, it would be odd to say that a life (as distinct from a person) has subjective well-being, at least if we think of lives as narrative histories of persons in the world, which are not reducible to a series of conscious states. Nevertheless, in speaking of subjective well-being and happy persons, psychologists typically do allude to happy lives. For example, Ed Diener, who popularized the expression "subjective well-being," takes for granted that mental states are expressed in lives—that is, in human existences in the world. In a book co-authored with his son Robert Biswas-Diener, Diener writes: "Subjective well-being encompasses people's life satisfaction and their evaluation of important domains of life such as work, health, and relationships. It also includes their emotions such as joy and engagement. . . . In other words, happiness is the name we put on thinking and feeling positively about one's life."[10]

I would replace "evaluating" with "valuing," and I take personal meaning to be as central as enjoyment (and interwoven with it). With those adjustments, the Dieners' definition of subjective well-being is largely congruent with my definition of happiness as loving one's life and valuing it through enjoyments and a sense of personal meaning. In any case, my interest is to explore happiness as an aspect of persons' lives, lives that are not reducible to mental states. More fully, my interest is in exploring the happiness of persons in leading lives that are morally decent and good, authentic, self-fulfilling, healthy, and happy.

VARIETIES OF HAPPINESS

With her unflagging wit and cheerfulness, Poppy illustrates only one paradigm of happiness. There are many others, including persons who are serene and peaceful, or passionately committed to creative projects, or resilient in coping with great difficulties. Moreover, happiness takes vastly many forms according to its ingredients, pathways, emotional styles, degrees, domains, aspects, and segments.

Ingredients. The ingredients of happiness—the things that make us happy—vary enormously, not only among individuals but even for the same person at different times. On the one hand, ingredients depend on our interests, tastes, and values concerning everything from sex to sports to spirituality. To be sure, some contributions to happiness are widely shared, for example a sense of control, self-esteem, economic security, love, and friendship. Psychologists identify the most common ingredients and report them as statistical averages. These statistics have great interest to employers, therapists, public policy makers, and each of us in pursuing happiness. Yet statistics cannot capture the specific factors and configurations that contribute to an individual's happiness, for example their delight in Mozart or skydiving. The detailed sources of our happiness must be discerned through experience and good judgment, a friend's advice or the insights of a therapist, and perhaps serendipity.

It is easy to confuse the ingredients of happiness with the idea of happiness. We are sometimes told, for example, that happiness is indefinable because what makes individuals happy varies so greatly; hence happiness is whatever anyone thinks it is. This *Alice-in-Wonderland* view is the product of conflating the concept of happiness with the content (sources, ingredients) of happiness. A related confusion occurs when the concept of happiness is conflated with a representative ingredient of happiness. In a 1960 *Peanuts* comic strip, Charles Schulz depicts Lucy hugging Snoopy and exclaiming, "Happiness is a warm puppy." The assertion became iconic after Schulz used it as the title of book that sold over a million copies. When critics charged that the statement was simplistic, Schulz challenged them to come up with "a better definition of what happiness is."[11] Of course Schulz's statement is not a definition at all. The problem is not that puppies make some people unhappy, as they might for people with dog allergies and dog phobias. The problem is that puppies are only one possible source of happiness, not a definition of it.[12] To be sure, epigrams that highlight selected sources of happiness can be illuminating and even make for a fun parlor game. Schulz's statement is an endearing reminder that giving and receiving affection is a major source of happiness, a better reminder than an abstraction like "happiness is love." The Beatles, too, convey something significant, this time about darker sources of happiness, when they parody Schulz with their song "Happiness Is a Warm Gun." But highlighting particular ingredients and sources of happiness should not be confused with defining it.

Pathways. Pathways (or paths) are routes for pursuing happiness, whether tailored to individuals or recommended for people in general. Broadly understood, pathways include chosen strategies (for example, be kinder to yourself) and received influences (for example, being born to loving parents). The confusion is tempting because pathways often do overlap with ingredients. For example, if caring for a puppy is a pathway to happiness, then adopting a puppy is a pathway to happiness. Moreover, both pathways and ingredients can both be called "sources of" or "contributors to" happiness. Nevertheless, there is a point in distinguishing ingredients and pathways. Ingredients are the constituents that provide enjoyment and a sense of meaning; pathways are the routes to obtaining those constituents—or at least suggested routes. Thus, relaxation is an important ingredient in all happiness, but it might be found through music, massages, and Merlot. Spirituality is an ingredient of happiness for many people, but it can be pursued by participating in a particular religion, meditation and yoga, communing with nature, or helping others. And a sense of personal control is an ingredient of happiness that can be found by dieting, cleaning the house, simplifying one's life, or being promoted at work.

More generally, causes of and influences on happiness should not be conflated with happiness itself. Doing so is another source of confusion that leads people to say happiness cannot be defined, since the pathways to happiness vary so enormously. Having said this, we can agree that the pathways of happiness are so utterly personal that advice about how to seek happiness must be filtered through individuals' interests and circumstances. As Wladyslaw Tatarkiewicz observes, "Practically every detailed formula for happiness is such that it can be opposed by another, contrary to it, which can be equally, or only slightly less convincing."[13] Here are a few examples: Live in the present (cherish the moment); keep your eye on the future (stop worrying about present difficulties). Stay socially engaged; seek more solitude. Follow your dreams; be realistic. Live with passion; all things in moderation. Be flexible and willing to compromise; be firm in your commitments and don't compromise your integrity. Be yourself; learn from others. Be courageous; be more cautious. Try harder; relax more. Take care of your health; stop obsessing about your health. Don't sweat the small stuff; pay attention to details. With his characteristic good sense, Tatarkiewicz does not conclude we should stop giving and listening to happiness advice. Instead, we should bear in mind that such advice must be contextualized to individual personalities and circumstances.

Emotional Styles. There are vastly many happiness styles, just as there are many different personality types.[14] Poppy's happiness style is outgoing and fun loving, but shy and subdued persons can be just as happy—in their own way. So might individuals who are peaceful, meditative, serene, tranquil, calm and imperturbable. And although happiness is often associated with optimism, pessimists can have their own styles of happiness.

In this connection we might apply Haybron's three modes of positive response. All three enter into most people's happiness, but one of them might be more pronounced so as to create different emotional styles of happiness: attunement style, endorsement style, and engagement style. *Attunement style*, to begin with, consists of a predominant pattern of experiences of tranquility: peace of mind rather than anxiety, contentment and confidence rather than felt insecurity, and "uncompression"—feeling free and expansive rather than confined and emotionally flattened. Haybron offers the examples of the Dalai Lama, Stoic sages, and, of special interest, Santiago in Ernest Hemingway's *The Old Man and the Sea*.[15] Santiago is old, poor, and has terrible luck. After eighty-four days fishing from a skiff in the Gulf Stream without catching a fish, he hooks a record marlin, eighteen feet long and weighing a ton. Following a monumental struggle, he reels in the marlin and heads home. By then the tide has pulled him far from shore, and he must defend his prize against the onslaught of sharks. When he reaches land only a skeleton remains. Santiago perseveres with remarkable discipline throughout his ordeal—the loss of the trophy fish to sharks, the preceding months without catching a fish, and his years of earning a meager existence as a fisherman. He is at peace with the sea and the universe, and remains resolute and confident that there will always be another meaningful goal and good day ahead as long as he is alive. He is sustained by wonderful memories of his youth, where he saw lions playing on the beaches of Africa. And he is sustained by loving and being loved by Manolin, an adolescent to whom he has been a surrogate father and to whom he passed on his skills as a fisherman.

Endorsement style is a primary pattern of upbeat feelings: experiencing joy more than sadness, cheerfulness more than irritability, laughter more than serenity. An example is Julia Child, portrayed by Meryl Streep in the film *Julie and Julia*. Beginning in childhood, she was outgoing and fun loving, with a fondness for practical jokes. Raised in an affluent family and with a mother who encouraged a lighthearted approach to life, she was largely carefree during her years at Smith College. Then, seeking adventure and with a desire to express patriotism, she entered the Office of Strategic Services (the precursor of the Central Intelligence Agency), where her fondness for playing practical jokes was only partly restrained. A happy courtship with and marriage to Charles

Child led her take up French cooking when the couple were living in Paris. Thus began her remarkable career as a chef, writer, and television educator.[16]

Engagement style is a personality dominated by being deeply engaged in life: exuberant and vital rather than listless, and prone to passionate and exuberant engagement in activities rather than feeling alienated from them. An example is Ben Bradley, the distinguished editor of the *Washington Post* from 1968 to 1991, when the newspaper earned eighteen Pulitzer Prizes and, with its revelations about the Watergate scandal, prompted President Nixon's resignation. Bradley was ambitious, passionate about excellence, and exceptionally happy. In an interview he insisted, "I haven't been unhappy a day in my life," and independent studies of his life provide some confirmation that he enjoyed his work and relationships to an unusual degree.[17]

A quite different example is the mystery writer P. D. James, who at seventy-eight writes: "I do know myself to be greatly blessed. I have met with little malice and much encouragement and kindness. I am sustained by the magnificent irrationality of faith. I have two daughters who have been a joy to me."[18] Her litany of gifts continues: good friends, exciting travel, writing she loves, innumerable awards and honorary degrees, and gratitude for a first-rate high school education. Yet her happiness is infused with awareness of the suffering of others and her own misfortunes. Those misfortunes include being raised by parents locked in an unhappy marriage, never having the money to attend college, coping with her husband's incurable mental illness caused by his military service. Her happiness has a spiritual tone, marked by faith in the world's goodness and by daily cherishing the memory of her husband.[19] She also writes: "There is much that I remember but which is painful to dwell upon. I see no need to write about these things. They are over and must be accepted, made sense of and forgiven, afforded no more than their proper place in a long life in which I have always known that happiness is a gift, not a right."[20]

These styles are only rough, and they can be blended in various ways. There can also be tensions among the three emotional dimensions. For example, the passions of engagement tend to disrupt the calm of attunement, and conversely too much serenity can dampen creative striving. More controversially, Haybron ranks attunement as most important for happiness in general, although I see no need for such ranking: There are just different styles of happiness that might emphasize particular facets of happiness. In any case, we can agree on the importance of not stereotyping happy people as having any one type of personality. Likewise, unhappiness takes many different forms, sometimes dominated by fear, anger, envy, depression, and so forth.

Degrees. Perhaps the most obvious difference among happy persons is quantitative: Some people are happier than others. Colloquially, we use rough adjectives to express how happy we are and to describe others' happiness: completely, very, mostly, somewhat, not so much. Psychologists seek more fine-tuned assessments by using questionnaires asking people to report satisfaction with their lives on scales such as 1 to 10. They also measure patterns of enjoyment by asking people to carry beepers that randomly go off, at which time experimental subjects record their happiness levels. Such techniques are tested for reliability (consistency) and validity (accuracy). These techniques might measure somewhat different things: overall life satisfaction versus levels of episodic enjoyment and meaning. Nevertheless, these things overlap considerably, and both provide important data about happiness levels.

In addition, psychologists extensively study how degrees of happiness connect with various life events, such as having children, falling in love, going through a divorce, helping others, or winning the lottery. Many of their studies confirm or refine common sense, but others yield surprising results. For example, most of us are convinced that winning the lottery would permanently raise our happiness level, but studies show that within a year happiness returns to its earlier level.[21] Furthermore, psychologists provide illuminating explanations of such findings, in this case highlighting the extent of our ability to adapt to change and our tendency to take things for granted. Psychologists also study temperaments and the role of nature (genetics) and nurture (upbringing) in shaping degrees of happiness. They estimate that about 50 percent of our personality, including our normal happiness range, is determined or strongly influenced by genetics, and another 10 percent by our current socioeconomic circumstances.[22] This leaves 40 percent in which we can influence happiness levels through personal choices—for example by changing our attitudes (e.g., developing more positive attitudes) and modifying our activities (e.g., exercising more and watching less television).[23]

Degrees of happiness are important in thinking about happiness in good lives. They have special interest when we are persistently unhappy in ways that threaten other important values, for example when unhappiness threatens a good marriage or a worthwhile job. Again, on occasion we might need to choose between sacrificing some degree of happiness in order to pursue other values that give our lives meaning.[24]

Domains. Whereas *overall* or *global happiness* takes into account all areas of our lives (over relatively long periods of time), *domain happiness* refers to particular areas such as work, family, and recreation. Few people are uniformly happy in all areas of their lives. Like virtue, happiness is typically speckled and mixed with areas of unhappiness.[25] The question arises, then, how overall happiness relates to domain happiness. The answer is complicated and highly personal. It is possible to be unhappy in one domain, even an important area such as work, and yet be to be happy overall—owing perhaps to an exceptionally happy family or spiritual life. It is also possible for miserable work to destroy happiness overall. I discuss domain happiness in chapters 9 and 10.

Aspects. Aspects are generic features that might center on one domain or cut across domains, for example happiness in how we cope with money, stress, people in general, or particular individuals. To illustrate, consider Jill Ker Conway's struggle with her domineering mother. Conway, who later became the first woman to be president of Smith College, reports that while writing her doctoral dissertation she often experienced wide swings of mood, from joy to depression, and even at a given moment she felt happy and unhappy in different respects and with regard to different aspects of her life. Her turmoil centered on a love-hate relationship with her mother, who was punishing her emotionally and economically for pursuing her education in America rather than returning to Australia to become her full-time caretaker. Conway was also newly married to a man she deeply loved. She was happy and unhappy in different respects: "My inner rage at my mother's conduct seethed below the surface, while at another level of consciousness, I was happier than I had ever been."[26]

Segments. Lives might be more or less happy during different segments or time slices—whether years, seasons, days, or hours. Individuals who have naturally happy temperaments, like Poppy, might be happy throughout their lives, but probably most of us have major ups and downs. For example, some people have miserable childhoods that they try to forget as much as possible during adulthood, unless they are writing a memoir. Other people have exceptionally happy childhoods and use them as a basis for pleasant nostalgia. And of course, memory is an imaginative filter that might highlight the good or exaggerate the bad.

In sum, happiness can be viewed from many directions and with many nuances, which might be more or less relevant to the topic at hand. Martha Nussbaum complains that when psychologists ask their subjects to report on their happiness there is a kind of conceptual bullying involved. The authority of the researchers pushes them to "aggregate experiences of many different kinds into a single whole" without the opportunity for them to answer something plausible, such as, "Well, my health is good, and my work is going well, but I am very upset about the Iraq war, and one of my friends is very ill."[27] To be fair, researchers also conduct studies of happiness in selected domains and about particular topics, as I illustrate in my chapters on work, love, and philanthropy. Nevertheless, Nussbaum has a point. Where relevant in discussing happy lives and happy persons, we should take care to mark distinctions about ingredients, domains, aspects, and so forth.

ALTERNATIVE DEFINITIONS OF HAPPINESS

I am proposing that global happiness has three interwoven elements: (1) loving our lives overall, taking into account their present configurations and aspirations for the future, and manifesting that love in (2) ample enjoyments in our activities, accomplishments, relationships, and possessions, and in (3) a robust sense of meaning. To further clarify why I include all three aspects I comment briefly on a few competing definitions, several of which reappear in later chapters.

Desire Satisfaction Definitions. Economists sometimes define happiness as getting what we want (desire satisfaction) or what we most want (preference satisfaction). On the surface the definition seems appealing. Surely happiness does have something to do with satisfying our desires, and desire satisfaction definitions provide an "objective" way to identify happy persons that is useful in conducting economic studies. Nevertheless, there is an obvious problem with desire satisfaction definitions. Getting what we want might not make us happy, in any ordinary sense of happiness. Indeed, satisfying (fulfilling) a desire might bring little satisfaction (pleasure). Or it might bring intense short-lived pleasure but lead to depression, as with the pleasures of drug addicts and shopaholics. Hence the caution: Be careful what you wish for, lest you get it. Hence too the proverb that happiness consists not in getting what we want but rather in wanting what we get. Or, as another proverb would have it, happiness is more about the journey than the destination; more about how we pursue goals than success in reaching them. In fact, maxims about getting what we want, wanting what we get, pursuing what we want in the right way even if we don't get it all concern pathways to happiness more than its definition. Their applicability, and in general how desire satisfaction enters into happiness, depend on individual psychology and circumstances, not on defining what happiness is.

Hedonistic Definitions. Hedonistic definitions reduce happiness to pleasure and the absence of pain. These definitions often accompany philosophical hedonism, the view that pleasure is the only inherently good thing. Hedonism was defended by Epicurus, Jeremy Bentham, and recently the British economist Richard Layard: "by happiness I mean feeling good—enjoying life and wanting the feeling to be maintained" throughout our waking life.[28] Like body temperature, pleasure levels fluctuate considerably, and Layard defines lives as happier insofar as average levels are high.

Happiness does have an essential connection with pleasure, but it is not the simplistic one stated by hedonism. No matter how intense or recurring, pleasure might not add up to happiness. This "adding up" is not a purely quantitative summation, for it involves the meaning we find in life—including the meaning connected with various pleasures. It makes sense to speak of meaningless pleasures. It also makes sense to speak of a pleasurable life that fails to make us happy. Whereas hedonists value only pleasure (as intrinsically good), most of us value things in addition to pleasure, for example friendship, love, community, understanding, excellence, and more decency.[29] These additional things define our engagement in the world, whereas pleasures are entirely subjective states of consciousness. By focusing exclusively on states of consciousness, hedonistic definitions lose the crucial dual reference to mental states and to our lives in the world.

Life Satisfaction Definitions. Some definitions of happiness focus on overall satisfaction with one's life. They have many different versions; indeed my own definition might be regarded as one variation.[30] Here I criticize only those versions that reduce life satisfaction to a positive evaluation of one's life overall, whether that evaluation is episodic or reflects a stable disposition over time.[31] Many psychologists use life satisfaction definitions when they rely solely on questionnaires that ask people how satisfied they are with their lives.[32] For example, the Satisfaction with Life Scale asks people to assign numbers to how happy they are, how successfully they are acquiring what they consider important, how much they would change in their lives, and so forth.[33]

Contrary to life satisfaction definitions, it is intelligible to say that an individual is satisfied with an unhappy life, whether that life refers to external things like relative poverty or internal states like too little enjoyment. Indeed, masochists and guilt-ridden penitents might be satisfied with what they agree are miserable lives. We can say they love a life that has little enjoyment for them, and the meaning they find is in denying enjoyment in order to punish themselves. (If we say they are happy being unhappy, we mean they are satisfied being miserable.)

Again, self-sacrificing idealists might report satisfaction in deliberately sacrificing their personal happiness for some cause or ideal. To elaborate, some life satisfaction definitions emphasize a sense of meaning and downplay enjoyment, including some versions of life satisfaction definitions. Thus, Elizabeth Telfer suggests that lives can be happy without much pleasure: "one can imagine some austere scientist who was pleased with his life because he was achieving great increases in human knowledge and who wanted nothing else from life; and who refused to describe himself as enjoying practicing science, or enjoying doing anything else in his life either. Could this not be a kind of happiness?"[34]

In reply, the scientist is surely not a paradigm we would use in explaining what happiness is. Indeed, we might invoke the case to explain how a life could be meaningful but not very happy. Thus, the scientists might cogently say he sacrificed his happiness to pursue something he valued more highly, namely creativity and service to humanity. Other examples include guerilla fighters, heroic crusaders, creative artists, and thinkers who lead meaningful but not especially happy lives.[35]

Consider Ludwig Wittgenstein, who on his deathbed asks his caregiver to "Tell them [i.e., his friends] I've had a wonderful life." His friend and former student Norman Malcolm found this "a mysterious and strangely moving utterance": "When I think of his profound pessimism, the intensity of his mental and moral suffering, the relentless way in which he drove his intellect, his need for love together with the harshness that repelled love, I am inclined to believe that his life was fiercely unhappy."[36] In saying he had a wonderful life, Wittgenstein might have meant he had a deeply meaningful life, interspersed with moments of great joy. It seems doubtful, however, that he was claiming to have had an especially happy life, and such a remark would be problematic given his tortured, depressed, and irritable personality.[37] Admittedly things are complicated in interpreting deathbed assessments of our lives. Wittgenstein might have intended that he had been happy, in his own strange way, and that his life did in fact have ample joy as well as great meaning for him.

Finally, consider Sisyphus, as portrayed by Albert Camus. For infractions that are unclear and minor, the gods condemn Sisyphus to roll a huge rock to the top of a mountain, at which time the rock rolls back down. He must then walk down the mountain and repeat the process, eternally and without any hope of change. So far, the image is of an utterly meaningless and miserable life of futile, pointless, absurd, unhappy labor. Camus next has us imagine, however, how Sisyphus might be happy even in his extreme misfortune. Imagine Sisyphus as he walks down the mountain, in a calm moment achieving lucidity about his fate. He has a keen grasp of the absurd aspects of his existence, but his dignity and self-respect lead him to scorn the gods for the unjustness of their punishment, and he affirms his courage and self-control over his mental life. Such experiences transform meaninglessness into a sense that his life is intelligible and worthwhile—meaningful despite, and in response to, the absurdity of his situation. Yet a sense of meaning does not suffice for happiness, and Camus next adds two key elements: enjoyment and overall satisfaction. He imagines Sisyphus experiencing joy mixed with his sorrow, and also a Stoic acceptance of his fate that grows into a broader sense that "all is well." "The struggle itself toward the heights is enough to fill a man's heart. One must imagine Sisyphus happy."[38] Sisyphus is happy because of this nexus of joy, meaning, and the overall valuing of his life conveyed by "all is well." What Camus says parallels my definition of happiness in terms of loving our lives, valuing them in ways manifested by ample enjoyments and a robust sense of meaning.

Normative Definitions. Finally, some thinkers reject definitions of happiness as subjective and instead build additional values into their definition of happiness. Normative (value-laden, prescriptive) definitions might refer to (1) happiness that a person or group claimed to be desirable for everyone, or (2) happiness that actually is desirable, as established by justified values. The values embedded in normative concepts of happiness might be virtues—either many virtues or selected ones such as authenticity, honesty, self-respect, and gratitude. Or the values might be mental health values such as the absence of mental disorders and the presence of normal functioning. Frequently the values are religious or spiritual values such as living in accord with God's will, or mindfulness of both the good and the suffering in the world. In any case, normative definitions regard the three elements of valuing, enjoyment, and a sense of meaning as insufficient to define "true," "genuine," "real" happiness. Even more dramatically, some thinkers equate happiness with good lives, with what the Greeks called *eudaimonia*.

Julia Annas writes, "Is happiness really something subjective? . . . We can at least hope that it is not."[39] Happiness concerns "what kind of people we are to aspire to be."[40] A unified and valuable life cannot be reduced to subjective states or to mere satisfaction of desires. Unity requires grasping how our endeavors are "nested" within wider purposes that we most value. Unity matters, both for maintaining personal integrity and for happiness. We have only one life and our activities and relationships need to be integrated in light of our most important values and aspirations. Our happiness depends on how effectively we integrate our desires and values, avoiding disruptive conflicts and disappointments, and achieving what we most value.

So far, what Annas says might be made compatible with subjective definitions of happiness, understanding values as a subjective sense of meaning. She quickly stipulates, however, that not just any values will do; the values must be sound, valid, warranted. In fact, she accepts a version of Aristotle's idea of happy lives as achievements in living virtuous lives. She also applies her normative definition of happiness as good lives to attack the shallowness of a culture obsessed with subjective happiness. I believe that her insights are best rethought as ways to integrate (subjective) happiness into good lives. They do not provide a sound reason to abandon today's predominant concept of happiness as subjective. Granted, in thinking about the life that will make us happy we cast a wide net over all our activities and relationships. But happiness is not unique in this regard. We also make other types of assessments of our lives in their unity—for example, as being meaningful, moral, and fulfilling. More to the point, even though our assessment of our lives as happy takes into account our values, purposes, and priorities, happiness can still be a sense of well-being about those things. That is, we can use a subjective concept of happiness while appreciating (and exploring) how happiness is linked to other aspects of good lives, including morality.

There is nothing wrong with adopting normative concepts of happiness as long as we are clear that we are doing so and remain clear about the specific values we build into the concept. Normative definitions of happiness can be inspiring, and they have a long and distinguished history that leaves us with a rich legacy.[41] Socrates, Plato, and the Stoics equate happiness with living a virtuous life. Aristotle says the exercise of virtue is the core of a happy life, the life of "living well and doing well," although he adds that we need some additional goods such as some wealth, power, friends, and longevity.[42] Augustine and Anselm develop concepts of happiness as living good Christian lives, with ultimate happiness coming in the next life. Each major world religion generates treatises on happiness based on such definitions, including books in the tradition of Catholicism, Islam, Hinduism, Confucianism, Buddhism, Mormonism, etc.[43] A thinker might also define true happiness around values such as creative striving (Friedrich Nietzsche) or confidently and successfully pursuing a rational life plan (John Rawls).[44]

Earlier I drew an analogy between loving persons and loving our lives. We might extend the analogy in comparing the ideas of "true love" and "true happiness." Thus, we might define true love—the real thing—in terms of virtues such as honesty, fairness, mutual caring, and respect. Such normative definitions can be useful, and possibly inspirational, as long as we are clear that we are building in ideals about desirable forms of happiness. In my view, however, normative definitions are better postponed to the end of a study of subjective well-being in good lives and, in part, allowed to emerge as part of that study.[45] Doing so ensures that value assumptions are scrutinized rather than smuggled in via definitions. Doing so also ensures that due attention is paid to a very important core of happiness—namely, loving our lives as manifested in ample enjoyments and a sense of meaning.

To conclude, I understand happiness as loving one's life, valuing it through ample enjoyments and a robust sense of meaning. As such, happiness is understood in terms of subjective states of persons although it also makes reference to their lives. I avoid normative definitions that restrict happiness to good lives, in part because those definitions build in controversial value assumptions that are best examined on their own, and in part to maintain contact with today's predominant concept of subjective happiness. As such, happiness is one important aspect of good lives that deserves attention in its own right, but especially in how it interweaves with other aspects of good lives. The next chapter outlines some connections between happiness and morality.

2

VALUING HAPPINESS

Happiness can be precious, perhaps even preeminent, yet still be one important thing among others.[1]

—Robert Nozick

Happiness and morality connect at four main junctures: the right to pursue happiness, happiness as a good, the duty to pursue happiness, and the virtues that promote and are promoted by happiness. These connections employ concepts emphasized, respectively, in four ethical traditions: rights ethics, utilitarianism, duty ethics, and virtue ethics. The connections can be appreciated, however, without commitments to any particular ethical theory. In this chapter I emphasize the first three connections, postponing the fourth one until later chapters. I also respond to happiness skeptics who regard happiness as overrated.

THE RIGHT TO PURSUE HAPPINESS

The right to pursue happiness seems uncontroversial—until we ask about the nature and extent of the right, as well as the relevant definition of happiness. Regarding the right, is it a fundamental human right, as the Declaration of Independence proclaims: "We hold these truths to be self-evident; that all men are created equal, that they are endowed by their Creator with certain unalienable Rights, that among these are Life, Liberty, and the pursuit of Happiness." Or is the right to pursue happiness merely a legal right, created by the legal and political system in the United States and other countries? For that matter, do human rights even exist, or are all moral rights simply rules about areas of freedom that should be protected because of their important consequences, as rule utilitarians believe? Morally or legally, is the right to pursue happiness implied by and subsumed under the right to liberty, so that there is a redundancy in Jefferson's sampling of rights? And is the right to pursue happiness merely a negative right that prohibits interference from other people or also a positive right to receive happiness-promoting benefits from the community?

Human rights are an important part of my moral perspective, but the following points can be rephrased in terms of other ethical traditions. In my view, the right to pursue happiness is a human right implied by the more fundamental right to liberty. Nevertheless, the right to pursue happiness deserves the emphasis it receives in the Declaration of Independence, for happiness is a great good, and certainly among the basic dimensions of fully desirable lives. The right to pursue happiness is not an absolute right, in the sense of having no justified exceptions. There are few, if any, absolute human rights, for all rights are restricted by the rights of other people and by our responsibilities. Obviously, a right to pursue happiness does not give us a right to violate other people's rights. The right is also limited by a host of additional moral values, including many of the virtues discussed in chapter 3: For example, we have a right to ignore much of the suffering of others, but to do so consistently is to show a lack of compassion.

In my view, liberty rights imply limited positive rights that enable individuals to pursue liberty and happiness. That includes the right to pursue happiness. The extent of positive rights is much contested. Libertarians generally deny that welfare human rights exist, instead limiting positive support for liberty rights to the minimum government needed for national defense and for maintaining a legal system. In contrast, I share the view of most rights ethicists that there are positive rights to a welfare safety net aimed to protect the most vulnerable members of society. What is the point of liberty rights if we lack any resources to exercise them? For example, what is the point of saying an unwanted and abandoned baby has a right to life when no one is willing to pay for its care? Regardless of our general view of positive rights, however, one thing is clear. We are discussing a right *to pursue* happiness, not a right *to be* happy or *to be made* happy. The distinction is marked in an epigram ascribed to Benjamin Franklin: "The constitution only gives people the right to pursue happiness. You have to catch it yourself." The epigram is apocryphal, as Darrin McMahon points out, for Franklin knew that the right to pursue happiness appears only in the Declaration of Independence, not the Constitution.[2] Yet the point remains: There is no right to be happy, any more than there are rights to be healthy and intelligent—as distinct from rights to health care and education. Hence the debate over positive rights concerns the extent to which governments should support opportunities to pursue happiness; it is not about whether governments should make us happy. (The distinction is relevant to the chapter 13 discussion of a "politics of happiness.")

Turning to the definition of happiness, how did Jefferson and his contemporaries understand happiness? Did they understand it as subjective well-being, perhaps as some combination of pleasure and life satisfaction? Or did they use a normative definition of happiness as virtuous living? Historians disagree. Their disagreement is not surprising given that the eighteenth century was a time of transition on many fronts, including predominant definitions of happiness. Normative definitions of happiness dominated from the fifth century B.C.E. to the early eighteenth century, whereas definitions of happiness as subjective became dominant with Romanticism in the nineteenth century. McMahon concludes that most likely Jefferson (and other founding figures) did not understand happiness in the thoroughly subjective way common today. Certainly Jefferson regarded the virtues as vital sources of happiness, including the civic virtues of public participation: "Happiness is the aim of life, but virtue is the foundation of happiness."[3] McMahon argues that ideas of happiness as pleasure and virtue "most likely coexisted in his mind and even overlapped."[4] America's other founding figures also held a hybrid and ambiguous concept of happiness, so that "the 'pursuit of happiness' . . . was launched in different, and potentially conflicting, directions from the start, with private pleasure and public welfare coexisting in the same phrase."[5]

In any case, Americans' conceptions of happiness quickly veered toward the subjective.[6] The right to pursue happiness became the right to pursue personal plans and pleasures. Today we construe the right to pursue happiness as essentially the right to pursue whatever an individual regards as happiness. In my terms, the right to pursue happiness is the right to pursue a life we love, valuing it in ways manifested by enjoyments and a sense of meaning. As such, happiness comprises much of the substance of the right to liberty.

HAPPINESS AS A SELF-INTERESTED GOOD

The right to pursue happiness is important because happiness is important. It is one of the basic goods that characterize fully desirable lives. Certainly it is a self-interested good, that is, a good for us—a good worth having because it contributes to and partly defines our well-being. Indeed, positive psychologists define happiness as subjective well-being, suggesting (implausibly, in my view) that it is the entirety of the desirable subjective aspects of a person, as distinct from "objective" features such as wealth, status, and virtue. Quite possibly, happiness is the greatest subjective good, for it encompasses both enjoyments and a sense of meaning in such a manner that makes us love our lives overall.

Happiness is also highly desired by almost everyone. William James speculates that it is the fundamental desire of most of us in that it underlies our more specific desires: "How to gain, how to keep, how to recover happiness, is in fact for most men at all times the secret motive of all they do, and of all they are willing to endure."[7] James is making an empirical claim that is open to scientific inquiry. He might be correct, but there are good reasons to think he is not. Most of us have myriad desires, including desires for food, shelter, self-preservation, sex, learning, using language, control, be-longing to groups, aggression, helping, self-esteem, recognition, meaningful life, etc.[8] In addition, some of us have masochistic and self-destructive desires that might be perverse ways of pursuing happiness but might also be understood as desires to be unhappy. It would be surprising if all these desires have one "secret" common root, whether that root is happiness, self-preservation, sex, or power. In general, I will as-sume that we are predominantly self-interested creatures who are greatly concerned with our happiness and with many other things that we believe are good for us. We also are capable of caring about a wide range of moral values that we see as good for us and for other people (and perhaps other creatures).

Although I doubt that happiness underlies all other desires, I agree that happiness is one of our basic desires. Most of us, most of the time, do seek lives we love, lives we value through enjoyment and a sense of meaning. The desire for happiness, however, is built on our desires for other things that provide enjoyment and meaning, and many of these things we desire at least partly for them. We care about our friends and love our family members, and we desire their well-being for their sake, as well as for the happi-ness they bring us. The desire for happiness helps to regulate those other desires, not as a secret underlying motive or rationale for them, but as part of our desire to pursue a good life.

More fully, happiness is a self-interested good for at least six reasons. First, the desire for happiness is natural and ubiquitous. Darwin observed that "all sentient beings have been formed so as to enjoy, as a general rule, happiness," for otherwise "they would neglect to propagate their kind," if not kill themselves when their situation turns bleak.[9] By happiness he probably intends pleasure, rather than overall love for our lives (since most nonhuman animals lack a conception of their lives). Contemporary evolutionary psychologists, however, defend his observation with regard to humans' subjective well-being. It seems likely that the capacity to love our lives evolved simultaneously with capacities to envision them as meaningful unities.[10] An evolutionary perspective also explains why most people are not completely happy, for total contentment might foster complacency and thereby threaten ambition and innovation in the struggle for survival.[11] To be sure, naturalness does not entail goodness. We have evolved with bad tendencies, such as cruelty and violence, as well as with good tendencies. Nevertheless, there is a presumption that satisfying strong and enduring desires is desirable insofar as it does not directly harm others. That is as true of happiness as it is of sex, health, love, and friendship.

Second, happiness feels good. To be clear, happiness as loving our lives is not a feeling per se, although there are of course episodic feelings of satisfaction with our lives. Nevertheless, loving our lives involves predominant experiences of enjoyment and a sense of meaning, both of which feel good, and both of which we desire and value for themselves. This is true of all three of Daniel Haybron's emotional faces of happiness: attunement (peace, confidence), endorsement (joy, cheer), and engagement (exuberance, flow).

Third, the desire for happiness plays a key role in unifying our lives. As one of our overarching goals—and as one of the basic aspects of good lives—happiness is essential in evaluating, selecting, and integrating the multitude of other goods we pursue. Our desires frequently push us in conflicting directions. The overarching desire for a happy life, just like the overarching desire to lead a moral life, forces us to decide which of our more particular desires are most important to us, and to discipline or renounce less important desires.[12] Some of these decisions are strategic and based on our overall goals. We might be attracted to several different careers, for example, or several potential spouses, and our envisioned happiness enters as at least one major decision-making criterion. Other decisions are tactical, everyday contextual rankings involved in prioritizing, postponing some gratifications in order to acquire more important ones. Either way, the passion for happiness motivates unity and coherence, as well as seeking variety to prevent boredom. In many ways, then, the pursuit of happiness reflects our nature as self-aware beings who seek lives we love.

Fourth, pursuing and finding happiness serves myriad practical goals. It motivates us to cope with difficulties, to compete and cooperate, to help others, and to solve problems creatively.[13] Of course, episodic unhappiness can also motivate in these ways, provoking us to improve our situation. Yet chronic unhappiness is a handicap, especially when it takes the form of depression and despair. James asks rhetorically, "What can be more base and unworthy than the pining, puling, mumping mood, no matter by what outward ills it may have been engendered? What is more injurious to others? What less helpful as a way out of the difficulty?"[14]

Fifth, happiness promotes mental health, and even partly defines it. To be sure, the happiness–health connection is complicated, if only because there are as many definitions of mental health as of happiness. When mental health is defined negatively, as the absence of mental disorders, its connection to happiness is clear: unhappiness is often the hallmark of depression, anxiety, and difficulties in functioning. When mental health is defined positively as psychological well-being rather than merely the absence of mental disorders, the capacity for happiness becomes part of the definition of mental health.[15] Health psychologist Shelley E. Taylor writes, "Most experts agree that the ability to be happy, or at least relatively contented, is one hallmark of mental health and well-being."[16] Notice that Taylor is careful to specify the ability to be happy rather than actually being happy. Sadness and grief are healthy responses to tragedy, at least for a time.[17]

Sixth, happiness promotes and overlaps with self-fulfillment. Once again, this connection is complicated because self-fulfillment can be characterized in different ways.

Alan Gewirth distinguishes two types of self-fulfillment. Aspiration fulfillment consists of satisfying our strongest desires—strongest in terms of their intensity, motivational force, and centrality in our self-conception. I would add that satisfying these desires must bring satisfaction in the sense of loving our lives. Capacity fulfillment, in contrast, consists of satisfying our best capacities—best in terms of the full range of values rather than just moral values. These two aspects of fulfillment can diverge, and in most lives there is some tension between them. For example, "a person who by intense concentration and practice becomes a superb violinist may come to feel very discontented with his life."[18]

Both modes of self-fulfillment are valuable, and they are intertwined so that desire and value largely mesh. Gewirth says the two modes of self-fulfillment parallel two conceptions of happiness: fulfillment of one's strongest and deepest desires (aspiration happiness) versus development of one's best capacities (capacity happiness).[19] Yet his own example of the violinist suggests we do better to think of aspiration fulfillment (when it yields satisfaction and meaning) as nearest to our ordinary concept of happiness, and think of capacity self-fulfillment as a further important aspect of fully good lives that tends to yield enjoyment and meaning, although not always. Either way, happiness and self-fulfillment are closely linked. (Another close link is between happiness and authenticity, as I argue in chapter 4.)

Finally, counting happiness as a great good and as a vital dimension of fully desirable lives, does not imply it is the highest good for us, much less the sole good. Certainly it is not the sole good when it is understood as wholly *subjective* and defined entirely in terms of mental states, with no reference to our full lives that involve activities and relationships. Robert Nozick powerfully makes this point with his thought experiment about an "experience machine." Imagine that we can program a virtual reality machine to give us any series of imaginary experiences we desire—including falling in love, writing a novel, or earning a Nobel Prize—and feeling happy all the while.[20] Once we enter the machine we feel certain we are having experiences in the real world. Few of us would permanently enter the machine. That is because we (reasonably) value actually doing things, having real relationships, striving for genuine accomplishments, and in general being certain kinds of persons: "We [do and should] care about more than just how our lives *feel* to us from the inside; there is more to life than feeling happy."[21]

In this passage Nozick thinks of happiness as defined entirely in terms of states of consciousness. Admittedly, once inside the experience machine it is not altogether obvious we are even dealing with a person who pursues a life—a life that could be loved in the manner relevant to my definition of happiness. A life, after all, involves activities and relationships in the real world, rather than a mere stream of consciousness based on wholesale illusion. I postpone questions about illusion-based happiness to chapter 5. But Nozick's point remains. We value—and should value—aspects of lives that reach beyond happiness as understood entirely or primarily in terms of subjective states that have no connection with real activities, accomplishments, and relationships.

HAPPINESS AS A MORAL GOOD

I have been discussing happiness as a self-interested good, or what is often called a "prudential good": a good for the individual who is happy. I would go further: Happiness is also a moral good, assuming it is not directly rooted in immorality. This is because it contributes so fundamentally to good lives and because it is so extensively interwoven with the virtues and other moral values. Happiness is both a moral good and a good for us, as are many other fundamental goods such as love, friendship, mental health, and a passion for excellence.

In general, as James Griffin observes, "our understanding of 'a good life' cannot be parceled into 'good prudentially' and 'good morally.'"[22] Griffin echoes John Dewey: "Goodness without happiness, valor and virtue without satisfaction, ends without conscious enjoyment—these things are as intolerable practically as they are self-contradictory in conception."[23] Dewey does not deny that a virtuous person might be unhappy, or a happy person immoral. There can be no dichotomy between morality and happiness because happiness tends to interweave with other moral values—in my terms, through enjoyment, a sense of meaning, and love of our lives. Happiness, he adds, is "a condition of the self," "a matter of the disposition we actively bring with us to meet situations, the qualities of mind and heart with which we greet and interpret situations," and characterized by "harmony and readiness to expand into union with other values."[24]

Especially noteworthy, morality carries with it what Gregory Kavka calls "satisfactions of morality" that contribute to happiness.[25] Assuming we have a conscience, we will find at least some satisfaction in doing what we believe is right and good. We will do so because we value moral decency, and also because believing we are morally decent increases our self-esteem (both directly and via social approval). In addition, we have evolved with some natural altruistic desires, whether weak or strong, to help others, contribute to solving social problems, contribute to a sustainable environment, and so on. And there are the enjoyments of struggling for excellence as we develop and exercise our capacities in ways beneficial to ourselves and others. John Rawls calls this the Aristotelian principle: "Other things equal, human beings enjoy the exercise of their realized capacities (their innate or trained abilities), and this enjoyment increases the more the capacity is realized, or the greater its complexity."[26] There are also negative incentives for basically decent persons to connect their happiness with their moral convictions. Certainly it is difficult to be happy, to love our lives, when we extensively violate our moral convictions in ways that cause chronic guilt and shame.

To be sure, happiness is not a moral good when its direct source is immorality, as, for example, with contented crooks, satisfied sociopaths, and a happy Hitler and Osama bin Laden. In complicated cases, happiness has dual aspects: it is both morally good and bad in different aspects. These complexities, however, are true of most good things, including the virtues. For example, courage is a moral good, and its paradigm instances consist in confronting dangers in morally admirable ways. Yet courage can also be used for immoral ends, and even elicited by immoral ideals—witness the courage of the terrorist or Nazi soldier. In such situations we say that a good is being used for evil. Likewise, when happiness has multiple sources, some good and some bad, we say it is good in some respects but not others.

Of course, we are free to restrict our conception of moral goods to those having morally desirable motivations and intentions. Thus, we can say that courage and self-control are morally good only when they aim at or serve morally desirable goals. That is Kant's approach: "Courage, resolution, and perseverance in one's plans, as qualities of temperament, are undoubtedly good and desirable for many purposes, but they can also be extremely evil and harmful" when used to pursue immoral ends.[27] Usually we understand that courage, resolution, and perseverance are genuine virtues, even though they are easily distorted when unaccompanied by other virtues, such as decency and justice. Again, love and friendship are moral values even though some loves and friendships are more bad than good. Similarly, happiness is in general a moral good, even though it sometimes reflects and serves evil ends.

In regarding happiness as a moral good, when it is not directly based on immorality, should we also regard it as a virtue, that is, a moral excellence of character? According to the French philosopher Alain, "happiness . . . is itself a virtue . . . since virtue means strength."[28] It is clear, however, that Alain employs a normative definition of happiness—"happiness in the true sense of the word," which for him is happiness grounded in proper self-respect. In effect, then, he merely asserts the tautology that virtue-based happiness is virtuous. In general, when happiness is called a virtue we should expect that only desirable forms of happiness are being considered. My interest, however, is in subjective well-being, understood as loving our lives and valuing them through myriad enjoyments and a sense of meaning. In my view, happiness is not a moral virtue, yet it frequently manifests virtues, and unhappiness sometimes signals the lack of those virtues. For example, happiness often manifests self-respect, gratitude, courage, and hope; unhappiness sometimes manifests the vices of ingratitude, envy, greed, and despair when hope is warranted. Thus, if we learn that a person's happiness was achieved with great difficulty during a tragic life, we might admire them in part for how their toughness and courage enabled them to sustain their happiness.

RESPONSIBILITY TO PURSUE HAPPINESS

Self-help books often proclaim a responsibility to pursue happiness—a responsibility in the sense of a duty or obligation, not merely in the sense of the pursuit being under our discretion and purview. Dennis Prager writes, for example, that "we owe it to ourselves [and others] to be as happy as we can be."[29] Taken in isolation, such claims could be dangerous invitations to immorality, especially in our highly individualistic and self-oriented culture. It is easy to slide from a duty to be as happy as we can be to making happiness our *primary* duty.[30] It is also easy to slide from *one* responsibility (among many others) to the *only* responsibility, thereby sliding toward ethical egoism—the view that our responsibilities are exclusively to promote our own good. But if we remain clear that we are discussing only one responsibility among many others, I agree there is a *prima facie* (limited) responsibility to pay due attention to our happiness, not in isolation but as an aspect of good lives.

Self-respect is the foundation of the responsibility to appropriately heed our happiness. Morality requires properly valuing persons, including ourselves. To value ourselves properly is to respect ourselves, and a mark of self-respect is to pursue a good life. Happiness is one of the basic aspects of good lives, interwoven with moral decency, self-fulfillment, health, etc.

Elizabeth Telfer develops an argument along this line: "People have not merely a moral right to pursue their own happiness, but also a duty to do so"; and "anyone who makes respect for the individual his guiding moral principle will be committed thereby to regarding *himself* as one of these valuable individuals who ought to be cherished."[31] Yet Telfer adds a qualification: "We have a moral duty to pursue our own happiness, not regarded as such, but regarded as an essential part of our personal integrity."[32] In my terms, we owe it to ourselves to pursue good lives that require ongoing integration and congruence among desirable activities and relationships. And in my view, good lives, as well as the relevant sort of inner unity, include happiness.

Telfer rightly hesitates to say we have an unqualified duty to pursue happiness, in abstraction from the duty to pursue a good life as required by self-respect. She also rightly emphasizes that the duty is prima facie; it is limited and must be reasonably balanced with other duties. Indeed, some individuals might reasonably sacrifice some of their happiness for a higher ideal, to which they link their self-respect—perhaps an ideal of justice in pursuing civil rights, perhaps warning the public of grave dangers as when a professional blows the whistle on her organization, or perhaps the pursuit of high excellence in valuable activities. Nevertheless, concern for our happiness is part of caring about ourselves and about leading a good life—a life worthy of being loved.

Ironically, the ethicist who most emphasizes duties of self-respect, Immanuel Kant, denies there is a direct responsibility to pursue happiness. Kant highlights duties of self-respect to take care of our health, to maintain our rational capacities, and to develop our talents. He insists, however, there is only an indirect duty to pursue our happiness: "It can even in certain respects be a duty to attend to one's happiness, partly because happiness (to which belong skill, health, wealth) contains means for the fulfillment of one's duty and partly because lack of it (e.g., poverty) contains temptations to transgress one's duty."[33]

Kant has two reasons for denying there is a direct duty to pursue happiness, neither of which is convincing. First, he suggests that such a duty is pointless because everyone already has a strong natural desire to pursue happiness. Yet surely the naturalness of a desire does not preclude a duty. It is natural to want to help an injured family member, and we also have a duty to do so. Furthermore, sometimes we do not pay sufficient attention to our happiness, thereby causing needless suffering to ourselves and others.[34] Many of us have self-destructive tendencies, such as harmful addictions, that undermine our healthy desire for happiness. The desire for happiness is like any other basic human desire, such as for food or sex, which needs to be both morally affirmed and have limits set to it in terms of integrating it into our set of responsibilities.

Kant's second reason emerges from his ethics of absolute (exceptionless) duties, which affirms only one thing as inherently morally good: the good will, that is, the tendency to do our duty because it is our duty. All other goods, including happiness, are at most conditional or dependent goods. Moreover, some happiness is abhorrent, for example happiness based on sadism. In the absence of a morally good will happiness can "produce boldness and thereby often arrogance" and wrongdoing, and hence a good will is "the indispensable condition even of worthiness to be happy."[35] Moreover in determining our duties we should "abstract altogether" from our happiness.[36] And although he allows that happiness as an aspect of fully good lives, in "union and harmony" with morality,[37] he leaves us with a dichotomy between morality and prudence, with happiness placed only in the latter category.[38] That dichotomy should be dissolved.

Having emphasized self-respect, I agree with Kant that additional considerations provide indirect foundations for a duty to have due regard for our happiness. As Kant notes, happiness often contributes to our motivation to meet all our other moral duties. Especially important, the responsibility to heed our happiness supports our responsibilities to people we care about and who are directly influenced by us, for our happiness greatly contributes to their happiness and our unhappiness adversely affects their well-being. But in addition, the responsibility to attend to our happiness is implied by virtues that include morally mandatory minimums. One virtue is self-respect and another is gratitude: A person who is always unhappy despite receiving much good fortune is ungrateful. Wladyslaw Tatarkiewicz seems to have this in mind when he writes: "Primarily for his own sake and because it is a correct attitude to life—correct at least in the case of those who have received a good deal from life—it seems to us that every-one ought to be happy if he can."[39] The caveat, "if he can," is important, since happiness is not completely under our control. We should also be wary of blaming the victim, which is blaming people for unhappiness that is due to things beyond their control. But an individual who receives every good fortune, including mental health, and yet is constantly irritable and angry might fail to meet the minimal responsibility to appre-ciate their good fortune.

HAPPINESS SKEPTICS

Happiness skeptics insist happiness is overrated. They inveigh against the ubiquitous tendency to exaggerate our own happiness, and also against the cultural exaggeration of happiness as a value. They trace these exaggerations to deep and tangled roots that include evolution-generated tendencies of self-seeking, society's celebration of indi-vidualism and consumerism, the therapeutic culture that tends to warp all values in the direction of self-interest, and academic disciplines like economics, political sci-ence, and psychology that historically assumed psychological egoism as their view of human nature (and largely still do). Even positive psychologists, who try to bring more balanced attention to the claims of community, often end up treating happiness (sub-jective well-being) as the new Holy Grail—the ultimate purpose of life and the entirety of good lives.[40] In debunking such exaggerations, at both the individual and social levels, happiness skeptics provide a useful service.

Nevertheless, the skeptics I have in mind go too far. They denigrate our strong in-terest in happiness as cheap, shallow, and ignoble. Indeed, some deny that happiness is even a major good. Happiness, they say, is a value for buffoons, bubbleheads, and ordi-nary people who fail to engage reality deeply. Noble spirits center their lives on deeper values. For example, in *Against Happiness* Erik Wilson contends that honesty and sen-sitivity go with a somewhat melancholy outlook. In a world of tragedy and horror happiness is usually a mark of inauthenticity.[41] Our very happiness implies a lack of truthful awareness of the suffering and horror in the world. A closer look, however, reveals that Wilson is engaged in misleading hyperbole. He actually targets only the most superficial forms of happiness that, by definition, are based on disregarding other important values: "happiness as immediate gratification, happiness as superficial com-fort, happiness as static contentment."[42] He does so because he wants to debunk our culture's preoccupation with these superficial forms. In any case, we should hesitate to dismiss even superficial forms of happiness as worthless, and certainly happiness takes many additional forms worthy of pursuing, forms linked to honesty and authenticity.

Deal Hudson contends that appealing to the right to pursue happiness functions as a persistent rationale for selfishness, as well as a rationale for "uncritical tolerance" of infidelity, drug abuse, and even violence.[43] In his view, even parents' wish for their children, "I only want you to be happy," indulges irresponsible behavior. Hudson concludes that we should renounce concepts of subjective happiness as "well-feeling" and return to classical concepts of normative happiness as "well-being."[44] Yet surely that conclusion does not follow. The problem is not that concepts of happiness center on subjective well-being; instead, it is that our tendency to elevate the right to pursue happiness has become more important than justice and decency. Like any other right, the right to pursue happiness needs to be balanced with the rights of others. The right to pursue subjective happiness is often selfishly abused, but it is not the root cause of selfishness.

Furthermore, I disagree with Hudson that most Americans think of happiness as trumping all other values. Of course selfishness is rampant, but most people link their happiness to additional values that include moral and spiritual ideals, love, friendship, sports, socializing, and striving for excellence at work.[45] And when parents (or friends) tell their children, "I only want you to be happy," perhaps when advising them about career plans or personal relationships, they do so against a background of these additional values. They are not endorsing thievery and murder if that happens to make their children happy.

Raymond Belliotti is the most astute of the happiness skeptics. In *Happiness Is Overrated*, he contends that happiness stands low on the scale of prudential values, and whatever moral value it has derives from its attachment to virtues and duties. Happiness is a relatively superficial value, lacking the gravitas of major moral, aesthetic, intellectual, and even other self-interested values: "Living a valuable, significant, robustly meaningful life is of greater personal value than attaining happiness."[46] We should pursue meaning and major moral values like justice and compassion, not happiness, and if we are "reasonably successful in that quest, happiness may follow. If so, all the better. If not, we can still take pride and derive satisfaction from living well."[47] At most our happiness is "the feather in the fedora," a nice extra.[48]

Belliotti's main argument consists in citing examples of happiness that have lesser worth and contrasting them with examples of unhappiness that have exceptional worth. The happy but less worthwhile lives mostly involve radical ignorance or illusions, for example the psychotic who believes he is Napoleon and living in the nineteenth century, the person utterly lost in the haze of a major drug addiction, the person plugged into Nozick's experience machine, and the brain-damaged individual who is reduced to the state of a happy child.[49] The exceptionally valuable but unhappy lives include those of Abraham Lincoln, Ludwig von Beethoven, and Ludwig Wittgenstein.

I agree with Belliotti that stellar creative achievements have greater value than merely being happy. If we had to choose between extraordinary creative achievements and happiness, we should choose the achievements. In doing so, however, we would be sacrificing something precious. I also agree that the full value of happiness needs to be understood in connection with all aspects of good lives, especially the full range of moral values. In my terms, loving our lives takes on greater value insofar as our lives are worthy of being loved. But rather than developing that insight, Belliotti repeatedly draws back, insisting that happiness is a matter of little importance and that its value is largely reducible to other values with which it is sometimes linked. That is, instead of exploring how the pursuit of happiness is appropriately part of the pursuit of good lives, he devotes himself to moving happiness toward the bottom of a hierarchy of abstract values, eclipsing its connections with meaning, morality, and self-fulfillment. In doing so, he eclipses happiness as a major value. Far more than a feather in the fedora, happiness is more like the feathers that enable the falcon to soar.

Finally, the most radical happiness skeptics argue that happiness would be a great good if we could achieve it, but they contend it is too rare, fleeting, and uncertain to be worth counting as a significant good. Arthur Schopenhauer tells us that happiness is elusive and fleeting: satisfying (fulfilling) a desire does not entail finding satisfaction (pleasure); satisfactions do not last long; satisfying one desire generates a bevy of new ones; the grass is always greener on the other side. The ambitions on which most of us pin our hopes are fragile, riddled with illusion, and the source of as much tragedy as joy. "The present is always inadequate, but the future is uncertain, and the past irrecoverable," so much so that "life bears so clearly the stamp of something which ought to disgust us."[50] In the words of Ecclesiastes, "all is vanity."[51]

This cannot be right. "The present is always inadequate"—but what about the real joy and contentment we sometimes find? "The future is uncertain"—but there is also pleasurable excitement about creative possibilities. "The past is irrecoverable"—but we can also celebrate accomplishments and find peace in accepting our failings. Schopenhauer sets the bar unrealistically high by requiring that happiness be ecstatic, permanent, and unmixed with suffering; he then debunks it as unattainable. In any case, thoroughgoing despair is not something we can live by, for hope is integral to caring. As Bertrand Russell reminds us, "If your child is ill, you may be unhappy, but you will not feel that all is vanity; you will feel that the restoring of the child to health is a matter to be attended to regardless of the question whether there is ultimate value in human life or not."[52] The same is true when one's child is healthy but utterly miserable. Even if happiness is uncertain, most of us manage to find a considerable amount of it, as well as sometimes contribute to the happiness of others.

Remarkably, given the extent of hardship in the world, most people do find considerable happiness.[53] For example, nearly 80 percent of Americans are largely satisfied with their lives, with studies reporting an average life satisfaction of 7.2 to 7.71 on a scale of 10.[54] People are even happier in Denmark, Sweden, and Switzerland. And even people living in desperately poor countries report happiness levels in the middle rather than lower ranges of happiness scales. These cross-cultural uniformities point to human evolution, not society, as the origin of our desire for happiness. Studies of identical twins also suggest a strong genetic foundation of our desires and capacities for happiness.[55]

To conclude, a defense of the moral significance of happiness will not focus on happiness in isolation. Instead we should explore how happiness connects with other aspects of good lives, all of which bear on self-respect, integrity and psychological integration, and the worth of persons. In addition to a right to pursue happiness, there is a prima facie responsibility to pursue happiness as an important prudential and moral good, interwoven with the virtues in ways that positive psychologists are helping us to understand. Because of these connections, happiness enters into justifying and guiding choices, as well as in motivating them. This justifying role—both its importance and its limits—will be of interest in several later chapters.

3

BETTING ON VIRTUE

The claim is not that possession of the virtues guarantees that one will flourish. The claim is that they are the only reliable bet—even though, it is agreed, I might be unlucky and, precisely because of my virtue, wind up dying early or with my life marred or ruined.[1]
—Rosalind Hursthouse

The claim that the virtues are a reliable bet in pursuing good lives is partly true by definition, for good lives are partly defined by the virtues. Yet fully desirable lives are also happy, and the contribution of the virtues to happiness is an empirical matter that cannot be settled with a definition. Proverbial wisdom affirms strong linkages between virtue and happiness, but cynics are quick to point out that vice can yield its own rewards. Fortunately positive psychologists are finding strong experimental support for what Jonathan Haidt calls the virtue hypothesis: "Cultivating virtue will make you happy."[2] Later I discuss the psychologists' methodology, but here I emphasize that their empirical support for the virtue hypothesis comes in the form of statistical tendencies, not universal causation. To some extent, applying the virtue hypothesis to our own lives requires moral faith, that is, faith in morality.

There are dozens of virtues and they can be grouped in different ways for different purposes. I sample nine virtues from three categories: (1) virtues of the heart, centered on valuing what is good (gratitude, self-respect, love); (2) virtues of the will, centered on strength in pursuing good (courage, self-control, hope); and (3) virtues of reason, centered on wisdom in discerning and pursuing the good (moral understanding, humility, mindfulness). These categories are rough and overlap, but they suffice to illustrate linkages between good character and happiness, linkages I provide an overview of here and then selectively return to in later chapters.

VALUING WHAT IS GOOD

Virtues of the heart embody ideals of caring and commitment. They comprise ways of appreciating what should be appreciated, respecting what deserves respect, and loving what is worthy of being loved. They also connect us to the world by providing motivation through enjoyment and meaning, thereby promoting happiness. Certainly that is true of gratitude, self-respect, and love.

Gratitude: Valuing What We Have

Count your blessings. Thank your lucky stars for your health (family, friends, education, talents, opportunities). Stop taking everything for granted. Each day is a gift.

As a virtue (rather than an emotion), gratitude is the character trait manifested in a morally appropriate sense of appreciation, which in turn is manifested in emotions and attitudes of appreciation on appropriate occasions. Gratitude has a wide and narrow sense. In its wide sense, it is appreciation of the good in our lives, regardless of the source of that good. In a narrow sense, it is directed toward particular individuals or groups whom we believe have given us (or persons we care about) gifts, especially the gift of caring about us. Even when we dislike a gift, we are thankful for the giver's good will; it's the thought that counts. Their caring affirms our worth in a highly personal way, as someone worthy of their caring. In return, the moral norm of reciprocity makes it appropriate for us to respond with good will, either with a simple thank you or with a reciprocal gift. Sometimes neither is possible, as when we appreciate a teacher's contribution to our lives only after her death. Gratitude might then motivate reciprocal giving to third parties in the memory and spirit of the teacher.

Gratitude is celebrated as the key to happiness, for good reason. A strong sense of gratitude makes us mindful of what is valuable in our lives, highlighting our good fortune and downplaying misfortune. It can also help us cope with problems by placing them within a perspective of our overall good fortune. Insofar as we are thankful for our good fortune, we experience more joy, self-esteem, meaningful connection to others, and a sense of well-being. In these ways, gratitude counteracts the misery caused by poisonous envy, nagging regrets, entrenched resentment, and self-pity.[3] In addition, the causal connection between gratitude and happiness goes both ways: Gratitude tends to enhance happiness, and happiness tends to foster gratitude.

More fully, Philip Watkins distinguishes seven psychological pathways by which gratitude promotes happiness.[4] First, it increases joy and delight, from appreciating what we have and from knowing we are beneficiaries of others' good will. Second, by heightening our awareness of the good in our lives, it counteracts our tendency to take things for granted. Third, it deflects attention from what we lack in comparison to others, and thereby serves as an antidote to envy. Fourth, by highlighting the goods we already have, it limits or delays indulgence in material goods we cannot afford. Fifth, it fosters perspective on what is important and thereby helps us cope with stress in pursuing vital goals, as well as reduce irritableness over trivia. Sixth, it counteracts painful regrets about our failures, anger about past injustices to us, and depression about losses. Finally, it has social benefits: It motivates expressions of gratitude to others, which in turn elicits their esteem toward us.

In its wide sense, gratitude naturally broadens into global and spiritual forms. Paul Camenisch celebrates how gratitude becomes "an entire outlook on life" in which individuals "live with a joyful sense of the interrelatedness of things whereby life is enriched by the generosity of persons or powers outside themselves. . . . [They] see much of life's goodness grounded outside themselves in the uncoerced, undeserved bounty of other agencies well-disposed toward them."[5] In most religions, God is preeminent among the agencies of cosmic gift giving, but secular spirituality also emphasizes gratitude. Henry David Thoreau moves in that direction in *Walden*, where he records his "simple and irrepressible satisfaction with the gift of life."[6] So does Robert Solomon who advocates gratefulness "to life itself, to the universe as a whole": "We are the beneficiaries of a (more or less) benign universe, or even the lucky beneficiaries of good fortune in a cruel universe. This should dictate gratitude, even if there is no one or nothing in particular to whom that gratitude is directed."[7]

Albert Schweitzer, who is agnostic about a supernatural deity, calls gratitude "a mysterious law of existence" through which we "fulfill our destiny" through caring relationships and service to others, motivated in part by a sense of gratitude and reciprocity for our good fortune.[8] His ethics of "reverence for life" expands morality to include valuing all living things and appreciating our interdependence with them. At the same time, he emphasizes gratitude toward people whose good will benefits us, including parents who intentionally promote our good, strangers who seek to benefit humanity in general, and professionals such as teachers and physicians who provide their services with a strong mixture of self-interest and service. Daniel Dennett reports such an experience of gratitude toward everyone involved in saving his life during a nine-hour heart surgery, including the cardiologist, surgeons, physician assistants, nurses, physical therapists, x-ray technicians, and hospital food workers.[9]

Not all emotions and attitudes of gratitude manifest the virtue of gratitude or are desirable, all things considered. This is especially true when gratitude functions within exploitative relationships that mix love with dominance and fear. For example, the gratitude of the battered child toward abusive parents, who nevertheless provide food and shelter and contribute to whatever happiness the child finds, might prevent the child from seeking help. Even when gratitude is clearly a virtue, it might have bad consequences and need to be balanced by other virtues such as self-respect.

Self-Respect: Valuing Ourselves

Stop beating yourself up. Give yourself a break. Show some kindness to yourself. Take pride in your accomplishments. Believe in yourself. Love yourself.

Self-respect is valuing ourselves in morally desirable ways. It has two dimensions, recognition and appraisal.[10] *Recognition self-respect* is valuing ourselves as having moral worth equal to others. *Appraisal self-respect* is valuing our particular character, achievements, abilities, and other good qualities. The connection with happiness is clear. People who hate themselves are not likely to love their lives. More positively, insofar as we have a strong sense of self-worth we are likely to have greater confidence and enthusiasm in pursuing all our endeavors.

Recognition self-respect can be understood using concepts from different ethical theories. Kant understands it as appreciating our dignity and worth as rational moral agents who have duties to ourselves, such as to preserve our lives and develop our talents. Locke understands it as appreciating our human rights that express equal dignity and worth. Mill highlights the importance of individualism in identifying and developing creative abilities. And Aristotle highlights connections between self-respect and a proper sense of pride and shame.

Self-respect overlaps with self-esteem, a cornerstone of mental health and happiness alike.[11] The relevant forms of self-respect and healthy self-esteem are global—valuing ourselves overall, as distinct from valuing specific achievements or traits. Officially, health psychologists understand self-esteem in subjective terms, as having positive attitudes toward ourselves. They implicitly invoke the virtue of self-respect in understanding self-esteem as the appropriate middle ground between narcissism and self-degradation. Healthy self-esteem is manifested in a stable sense of self-worth, as well as episodic emotions of pride and joy in our accomplishments. Low self-esteem correlates strongly with a disposition to depression, and depression with unhappiness.[12] To be sure, occasional and minor depression is normal in happy lives, and it is desirable when it enables us to see where meaning is threatened.[13] Severe chronic depression, however, kills happiness.[14]

By embodying the conviction that we are worthy of happiness, self-respect reinforces our natural desire for happiness. It provides an additional motive for seeking pleasurable activities, and it provides a second-order desire to satisfy first-order desires connected with the values that make life worth living. To be sure, self-respecting individuals, including saints and heroes, might sacrifice their happiness on behalf a noble cause (though they typically experience happiness if their plans succeed).[15] Nevertheless, valuing ourselves implies taking our happiness seriously (as discussed in chapter 2).

Love: Valuing Others

Get outside yourself. Nurture relationships. Cultivate friendships. Perform random acts of kindness. In giving we receive. Love makes the world go 'round.

As an attitude, love is deep caring that implies emotional engagement and often commitment. As a virtue, love is deep caring that is *desirable*, both in terms of its object and consequences. Although myriad types of love contribute to happiness, here I have in mind love for people. Even it takes innumerable forms, including love in friendships, filial and parental love, humanitarian love, and erotic love.

Love defines who we are and largely creates the meaning we find in life. That explains why unwanted divorces and deaths traumatize us, and why new loves enliven us. As an attitude, love creates meaning by attaching our lives and our identities to other creatures.[16] Typically it also brings enjoyment and joy, mixed with vulnerability to suffering. Insofar as love structures personal relationships, it bestows value on the beloved and makes us feel valued in return, thereby increasing self-esteem and happiness. Love often involves evaluating as well as valuing, but valuing is primary.

As a virtue, love is directed to what is worthy of being valued, and it creates justified meaning. In good lives, persons manifest love for persons and relationships whose value we appreciate rather than invent.[17] In this way, love reveals value, as well as bestows it. Love is an umbrella virtue that connects and overlaps with many additional virtues. For example, it includes compassion, which is a caring response to suffering, and kindness, which is sensitive responsiveness to the needs of others. It also includes generosity, which is admirable giving beyond what is required by duty. Generosity takes different forms. *Economic* generosity is giving money or items having monetary worth, in amounts beyond what is routinely expected. *Evaluative* generosity is good will in judging others, a readiness to accent their strengths and forgive their errors. *Emotional* generosity is manifested in habits of kindness, helping, and encouragement. All these forms of generosity are illustrated by Dorothea Brooke, the heroine in George Eliot's *Middlemarch*, who never wins nor seeks worldly fame but who "lived faithfully a hidden life" of benevolence toward people around her and on whom she had an incalculable effect for good.[18]

In studying correlations between love and happiness, psychologists ask about reverse causation: Does love contribute to happiness or does happiness contribute to love? The answer is both.[19] Just as loving relationships produce enjoyment, a sense of meaning, and happiness, happiness augments capacities for finding and sustaining love relationships.

STRENGTH IN PURSUING GOOD

Virtues of the will are defined by ideals of effective agency. Many of them cluster under "fortitude," which includes courage in confronting danger, self-control in summoning effort and resisting temptation, and hope in sustaining a positive outlook about the good we can achieve.

Courage

Face your fears. Be brave. Be bold. Don't be a wimp. No guts, no glory. Have the courage of your convictions.

As a virtue, courage is confronting danger in morally desirable ways, without panic or paralysis. As such it manifests caring for goods worth caring about, including happiness. Courage contributes to the pursuit of a wide array of goods, and forms of courage are distinguished by types of dangers that put those goods at risk. Thus, physical courage responds to threats to our lives and bodies. Intellectual courage responds to ridicule and self-doubt in pursuing our convictions. Social courage responds to actual or perceived threats from others. Courage of integrity, which overlaps with all these, responds to threats to moral integrity.

In addition, Daniel Putnam highlights psychological courage: "the courage it takes to face our irrational fears and anxiety, those passions which, in Spinoza's terms, hold us in bondage," such as destructive addictions and phobias.[20] Here the dangers include social stigma when we openly acknowledge psychological problems, pain and suffering in trying to resolve problems, and more generally destabilized psyches. Putnam's concept is illuminating because neurotic anxieties are such potent threats to happiness. J. Alfred Prufrock, in T. S. Eliot's poem, is unhappy or less happy than he could be because he is paralyzed by fears, not only the terror of asking a woman for a date but even the worry about eating a peach in public (the mess of it!), let alone the fear of initiating a creative undertaking that might "disturb the universe."[21]

Like most virtues, courage depends for its full worth on how it interacts with other virtues.[22] It is debatable whether brave-in-battle Nazis are courageous: Should we ascribe misguided courage to them or instead deny there is anything virtuous in their evil? Either way, the case is not a paradigm used in teaching courage. Paradigms of courage imply confronting dangers to genuine goods with wisdom and control. Thus, courage is often best understood as a special case of self-control.

Self-Control

Get a grip. Get organized. Get on with it. Get some exercise. No pain, no gain. Be patient. All (good) things in moderation.

Self-control is often defined negatively, as self-denial and resisting temptations. It is better conceived positively, as self-mastery shown in habits of action, emotion, attitude, reasoning, and belief. The virtue of self-control is self-mastery in pursuing desirable (not just desired) goods and habits. In this way, self-control is linked to prudence and wisdom.

Epictetus begins his *Handbook* with an arresting commonplace: "Some things are up to us and some are not up to us."[23] The pursuit of happiness turns on marking the distinction in particular situations, exercising self-control by accepting what we cannot change and by pursuing the good we have a reasonable hope of attaining. Our capacity for self-control turns as much on a clear vision of what we can control as on sheer willpower. It also depends on the skillful use of tactics in pursuing the good, together with skilled resistance against temptations in which we gradually modify our motivational habits, rather than relying on the *oomph* of brute willpower.[24] Like contemporary cognitive-behavioral therapists, Epictetus emphasizes control over our patterns of thinking and feeling.[25] This control is achieved by confronting and blocking irrational ways of thinking that cause depression, despair, and anger. It is also achieved by cultivating positive perspectives and ways of attending to the good in our lives. Epictetus anticipates the Serenity Prayer: "God grant me the serenity to accept the things I cannot change; courage to change the things I can [and should]; and wisdom to know the difference."[26]

Despite their insights, Epictetus and other Stoics understand self-control in an unduly self-protective way. They seek a degree of emotional security and serenity that would undermine pursuits of love, creative excellence, and other risky goods.[27] They move too far in the direction of fatalism: "Do not seek to have events happen as you want them to, but instead want them to happen as they do happen, and your life will go well."[28] They are also too optimistic about the possibility of gaining complete control over our inner lives. In fact, aspects of our character and personality are sometimes as intractable as the external world. Scientists estimate that half of a human personality is genetically given, and this bears on the range of degrees of happiness possible for us.[29] Few of us have full control over all our desires, and only within limits can we reshape our attitudes within the standards of rationality.

In pursuing happiness, then, there should be no dichotomy between turning inward to what we can control and simply accepting the external world as it is. Happiness depends in part on turning inward—identifying, understanding, and modifying our ways of thinking, feeling, valuing, and desiring. It depends equally on turning outward to goals and relationships that excite us, even though they might add to our vulnerability.

Hope: Faith, Optimism, Trust

Look on the bright side. Find the silver lining. See the glass as half full.
"Accentuate the positive, eliminate the negative." (Johnny Mercer).[30]
Faith is self-fulfilling. The best is yet to come.

Compared to courage and self-control, hope seems a soft virtue. It is not. As a virtue (rather than an emotion), hope is not sentimental wishing, and neither are its close cousins, faith and optimism. Hope requires toughness in combating the ubiquitous threats of doubt, despair, desperation, and cynicism. As an attitude and emotion, hope combines desire with the expectation of a chance of satisfying the desire. As a virtue, hope is the attitude that desirable events (not just desired ones) have a reasonable chance of occurring plus the active disposition to promote their occurrence. Hope is premised on uncertainty, on an appreciation of the risks in life combined with a fervent desire that things will go well rather than badly. Hence the saying "The two enemies of hope are presumption and despair."[31]

Hope might be for our own pursuits, for the pursuits of others, or for pursuits we share with others. Usually it implies desiring valuable future events, although we can also have hopes about outcomes that have already occurred but we await knowledge of. Hope contributes to happiness precisely because happiness depends as much on our sense of the future as on the present. Happiness requires an overall positive affirmation of our lives as meeting our expectations, and to that end hope makes a vital contribution. It sustains our commitments through good and bad times, buoying spirits and preventing despair. Attitudes of hope tend to generate pleasurable emotions of hope as well as enrich our sense of meaning.

Hope is often a foundation for optimism. Martin Seligman documents that pessimists are "catastrophizers." They "tend to believe bad events will last a long time, will undermine everything they do, and are their own fault. The optimists . . . tend to believe defeat is just a temporary setback, that its causes are confined to this one case . . . [and that] defeat is not their fault."[32] As a desirable trait, optimism remains rooted in realism, occasionally drifting in the direction of positive spin and even positive illusion, but constrained by a basic truthfulness. It is a style of thinking that searches truthfully for evidence that negative thoughts are unwarranted or exaggerated. Cognitive therapists help their clients increase optimism by developing cognitive strategies to counter excessively negative habits of thought. As a virtue, optimism differs from the shallow boosterism of the positive thinking movement that artificially and at times dishonestly bolsters optimism by disregarding hard facts.[33]

WISDOM IN PURSUING GOOD

Practical wisdom consists in *knowing how* to live a good life and, with some regularity, putting this know-how to work in our circumstances. It is not theoretical understanding in the form of *knowing that* some philosophical, scientific, or religious outlook on the world is true. Wisdom implies practical moral understanding, humility, and mindfulness.

Moral Understanding

Know thyself.[34] *Keep things in perspective. Stay balanced. Establish priorities. Don't sweat the small stuff. Turn problems into opportunities, lemons into lemonade.*

Practical moral understanding implies insight into what is worth caring about, and then embedding that insight into strategies for achieving worthy goals—including happiness. As such, it enters into defining and exercising all the virtues. Here I highlight moral insight and imagination, along with practical skills of maintaining balance, perspective, flexibility, and self-understanding.

Moral insight cannot be encapsulated in a set of simple rules ranked in priority. Instead, moral values are many and varied, and their claims need to be understood contextually. This understanding requires sensitivity based on experience, and it requires imaginative understanding about how best to apply and integrate moral ideals. John Dewey calls for "creative intelligence" in resolving ethical dilemmas by finding a practical solution that "coordinates, organizes and functions each factor of the situation which gave rise to conflict, suspense and deliberation."[35]

Balance refers to reasonable allocations of time and energy, and to desirable integrations of activities and relationships. It also includes congruence between our desires and ideals, our needs and those of others, short-term and long-term plans, adaptation and transformation of our social environment, and so on. Achieving, maintaining, and restoring balance is often straightforward, given a modicum of insight and self-discipline. But sometimes it requires major realignments of commitments. It might require imaginative and even creative insight into how to carry on under difficult circumstances.[36]

Perspective, as an aspect of wisdom, implies clarity about what is most important in practical situations. We are pulled in many directions, and perspective consists in seeing where attention and effort should be focused. This "should" is partly understood in terms of personal priorities that give our lives meaning but also in part by reference to moral values. Bernard Madoff was clever but not wise when he bilked investors out of tens of billions of dollars, and that would be true even if he had managed to avoid getting caught. Maintaining perspective requires that our values be reasonably expressed in everyday emotions and patterns of attention. For example, it implies avoiding habits of irrational anxiety, depression, anger, and hate.

Flexibility, as an aspect of wisdom, includes skill in adjusting perspectives in appropriate ways, or as Valerie Tiberius elaborates, "shifting perspectives at the right time, in the right way, and for the right reasons."[37] In addition to keeping a clear grasp on the core commitments that are most important to us, wisdom (and perspective) involves knowing when one cluster of values and priorities should move to the foreground, as when we go to work and should leave our love problems at home, and when we come home from work and should focus on family priorities. As Tiberius also emphasizes, flexibility includes knowing when to pause to reflect on our lives in order to restore a healthy perspective, while avoiding excessive rumination about ourselves that undermines immersion in meaningful activities. It involves knowing when to maintain professional distance in order to avoid inappropriate emotional involvement in the lives of clients and colleagues. And it implies knowing when to become passionately immersed in creative and other activities that require concentration.

Self-understanding implies knowing our strongest desires, those that most strongly motivate and define us in terms of our self-conceptions. It requires knowing our values and ideals, and our strengths and weaknesses. And it requires knowing how to organize our days in order to combine immediate enjoyment with the meaningful pursuit of long-term plans and relationships. Self-understanding does not require complete self-awareness and avoiding all illusions, for mild positive illusions sometimes support hope. But it does mean knowing what we value most highly and desire most strongly, and where are primary strengths and weakness lie.

Humility

Stop living in the past. What's done is done. Enough already with the guilt and shame. Forgive yourself, make amends, and move on. Have reasonable expectations.

Humility implies proper valuing of our abilities and accomplishments—neither unreasonably low nor high—and as such it is closely linked to self-respect.[38] Nevertheless, by setting proper limits on how to value the self, and by identifying reasonable expectations for the self, humility contrasts with an array of vices of excess: "arrogance, vanity, conceit, egotism, grandiosity, pretentiousness, snobbishness, impertinence (presumption), haughtiness, self-righteousness, domination, selfish ambition, and self-complacency."[39] Humility is also linked to the Stoic ideal of creative resignation, which is accepting the limits on our lives and having reasonable rather than insatiable expectations. In that way, humility overlaps with self-control.

Humility pertains to the past and future, in addition to our present self-image. Regarding the past, it implies accepting what cannot be changed rather than becoming paralyzed by painful regrets and anger. To be sure, the goal of living without any regrets is implausible. Some regrets about the past are natural and healthy reminders of how to avoid similar mistakes in the future.[40] The problem is with regrets accompanied by depression and disruptive anger, whether aimed at ourselves or others. If we let it, the past has enormous power to paralyze, cripple, and distort present enjoyment. Resigning ourselves to what is irreversible is a creative resignation that frees us to move on.

Willingness to forgive is a vital way to release resentment about offenses against us. It connects with humility in that it typically requires attunement to our own failings and wrongdoing. To fail to forgive might indicate a lack of proper humility, but the appropriateness of forgiveness depends on the context. Therapists sometimes call for blanket forgiving as healthy, especially when anger, hatred, and resentment make our lives miserable.[41] In doing so, they go too far. At least sometimes, unrepentant evil should not be forgiven; the ethics of forgiveness are complex.[42]

Regarding the future, humility implies having goals that we have a reasonable chance of meeting. Self-esteem is one of many psychological mechanisms at work here. As William James summarizes, happiness-promoting self-esteem is shaped by the ratio of our success divided by our pretensions (aspirations, expectations). If we want to increase self-esteem we can try harder to achieve our goals, but alternatively we can try modifying our goals, abandoning the unrealistic ones: "To give up pretensions is as blessed a relief as to get them gratified. . . . There is the strangest lightness about the heart when one's nothingness in a particular line is once accepted in good faith. . . . How pleasant is the day when we give up striving to be young,—or slender!"[43]

Mindfulness

Live in the present. Savor the moment. Take time to smell the roses.
Go with the flow. Stay focused. Carpe diem. Happiness lies in the journey, not the destination.

We are most alive when we are attuned to the good in our immediate situation (which includes our present hopes for the future). This appreciation also falls under the first category of virtues (valuing what is good), but its cognitive dimensions are conveyed by the Buddhists' term "mindfulness." Mindfulness in pursuing happiness includes bearing in mind the large values that structure our lives. It also includes appreciation of little things, as Benjamin Franklin reminds us: "Human Felicity is produc'd not so much by great Pieces of good Fortune that seldom happen, as by little Advantages that occur every Day."[44]

Mindfulness takes different forms, however, that might be in tension. For example, it might consist in peacefully concentrating on the moment by serenely going with the flow, or it might mean energized engagement as we passionately pursue goals. Saying that we should be mindful tells us little until we are told what we should be mindful of. If we are mindful in the sense of riveted on our goals, we might miss out on many of the smaller joys that come to us along the way. If, on the contrary, we are open to the enjoyment and meaning available to us at any moment, we might fritter away our lives and put our most important goals at risk.

Traditional lists of virtues lack a unifying term for desirable forms of enthusiasm. The Romantics use the term "passion" normatively, as well as health-oriented terms such as "vitality" and "vigor." Nietzsche spoke of the will to power—the healthy and creative expression of strong desires, powerfully mastered.[45] Contemporary positive psychologists count vitality as a virtue insofar as it contributes to desirable pursuits. All these terms can refer to bad things, for example destructive passions and enthusiasms, and "someone who is tense, angry, or jittery is energized but not necessarily vital."[46] I invoke these terms with honorific connotations as desirable forms of loving valuable activities.

Vitality takes many forms. It might mean zest, which Bertrand Russell calls "the most universal and distinctive mark" of happiness, just as sustained boredom is a common mark of unhappiness.[47] Zest has both emotional and cognitive aspects in appreciating what is genuinely good. We live with zest when we take deep pleasure in a wide array of things. We experience recurring wonder, joy, passion, fun, and delight. We are open to the vast goodness that presents itself in everyday life. We are fully alive and love life. At the same time, our diverse activities and enjoyments are held together and balanced within a framework set by commitments and relationships of love.

Flow, as Mihaly Csikszentmihalyi defines it, is an activity or state in which attention is fully immersed and concentrated and where we are motivated intrinsically (rather than solely by external rewards such as money or prestige), exercise our skills and control, have clear goals, and receive provide immediate feedback about how well we are meeting those goals.[48] In flow experiences we typically focus outwardly on features of the world without self-consciousness. Typically, although not always, flow experiences are enjoyable, but the enjoyment is not a continuous pleasure.

Savoring is attending to a pleasurable activity, or to the pleasure itself, in ways that augment the pleasure's intensity, vividness, or duration. We relish a delicious meal and a fine wine. We bask in the sun and luxuriate in the sauna. We are thrilled by a soprano's overture and comforted by a cat's purring. We marvel at sunsets and are overwhelmed by sexual pleasures. Hedonic absorption easily slides into self-indulgence, but without many and varied pleasures, however fleeting, life loses its charm.

Zest, flow, and savoring are not the only ways to add vitality to each day. Another way is to periodically take stock of lives in order to keep things in (reasonable) perspective. Taking stock can involve linking the day's plan and results in terms of gratitude for what we have received as opportunities and gifts, and linking them to progress toward a valued future.

I have sampled nine virtues (from three categories) that contribute to happiness, but there are many others. The next chapter focuses on authenticity, a virtue that falls into all three categories. Later chapters explore virtues such as simplicity and balance, as well as expand on some of the virtues introduced in this chapter.

POSITIVE PSYCHOLOGY

Because I have drawn on the work of positive psychologists and will continue to do so, it is time to comment on their aims and methodologies in studying happiness and the virtues.[49] Positive psychology is a new branch of psychology, named by Martin Seligman in 1998 to highlight its study of "positive"—desired and desirable—character traits, emotions, attitudes, lives, institutions, and communities. Of special interest, positive psychologists are studying and have already substantiated the virtue hypothesis that "cultivating virtue will make you happy." Or as Seligman states, "Authentic happiness comes from identifying and cultivating your most fundamental [moral] strengths and using them every day in work, love, play, and parenting."[50]

How do positive psychologists study the virtues? Roughly, they identify a large spectrum of what society considers virtues. Next they develop operational definitions of each virtue by giving specific indicators or empirical criteria for each of them. Using these indicators, they ask individuals to self-report their virtues. This is not done crassly by merely asking questions like "Are you courageous?" Instead, people are asked to give numerical responses to nuanced questions such as "I have taken frequent stands in the face of strong opposition."[51] The questionnaires employed are checked for their reliability (consistency) and validity (accuracy), for example by correlating results from the questionnaires with additional criteria such as what family and peers say about us. Next, individuals are asked to report their happiness (subjective well-being), again using quantitative-oriented questionnaires that are checked for reliability. Another popular test is more "experiential." It uses beepers that go off throughout the day, at which time experimental subjects report how happy they feel at the time; the results are then tabulated. The results of questionnaires and experiential tests are not identical, but usually they are closely correlated.

Analyzing all this information, psychologists identify statistical correlations between self-reported virtues and self-reported happiness. Often these correlations allow for two interpretations: the virtues promote happiness, and happiness motivates virtuous activities. Further tests are needed to identify the direction of causality, but frequently causality goes in both directions, at least somewhat. Using this procedure, information accumulates to support, refute, or revise the virtue hypothesis. Thus, tacitly the virtue hypothesis is understood as: "Virtues, understood as what most societies consider virtues and what individuals self-report as such, tend to promote happiness, under-stood as subjective well-being and measured by self-reports."

This procedure yields valuable information about statistical tendencies among tar-geted populations, although it carries five risks that need to be borne in mind. First, there is the danger of falling into ethical relativism that simply endorses social conven-tions.[52] Seligman and his colleagues believe they can avoid relativism by uncovering universal virtues affirmed by all societies.[53] The core universal virtues or (what others call cardinal virtues) are wisdom, courage, humanity, justice, temperance, and tran-scendence. Each of these virtues can be manifested in a cluster of ubiquitous moral traits, which they call "strengths," listed parenthetically as follows: wisdom/knowledge (creativity, curiosity, open-mindedness, love of learning, perspective), courage (bravery, persistence, integrity, vitality), humanity (love, kindness, social intelligence), justice (citizenship, fairness, leadership), temperance (forgiveness and mercy, humility, prudence, self-regulation), transcendence (appreciation of beauty and excellence, grat-itude, hope, humor, and spirituality). In addition, moral strengths might be expressed in more specific traits; for example, kindness might be manifested in generosity, nurturance, care, compassion, altruistic love, and niceness; and integrity might be expressed through honesty and authenticity.

In avoiding ethical relativism, there are new dangers of overgeneralization and abstraction in depicting "universal" virtues. There are also dangers of omission. For example, the virtue of self-respect is surprisingly absent from their classification. Nev-ertheless, because the classification is open to revision, we can expect improvements, including in making adjustments to how different cultures accent different virtues and understand them in different ways. Yet at various points moral debates arise about what counts as virtues and what should count.

Second, there is the danger that positive psychologists will make controversial moral assumptions and pronouncements disguised as science. Seligman rightly denies he is preaching morality, but certainly he seems to make moral assumptions.[54] He affirms "good character as a core assumption of Positive Psychology,"[55] and he claims to seek "a fresh and scientifically grounded answer" to Aristotle's question, "What is the good life?"[56] He also slides between what people desire (a matter of fact) and what is desir-able (a matter of value), as in his discussions of "gratifications" and "flow activities."[57] Now, Aristotle engaged in normative ethics by making moral judgments about desir-able forms of character, conduct, and ways of living, and he did not reduce those judg-ments to summations of society's beliefs. He also used a normative definition of happiness, whose core was living virtuously. Seligman's claim to complete moral neu-trality is not compatible with his frequent invocation of Aristotle.

Seligman's definition of happiness gives rise to a related difficulty. In order to avoid smuggling in moral assumptions, happiness needs to be defined as subjective well-being, without shifting to normative definitions. For example, in studying the virtue hypothesis the goal is to learn how one thing, happiness, contributes to another thing, virtue. If happiness were defined normatively as virtuous activity, empirical studies would be transformed into tautologies: virtues promote virtuous living. Seligman largely proceeds as if happiness is subjective, for example by relying on self-reports about levels of overall satisfaction.[58] Yet sometimes he generates confusion by tacitly embedding moral values in the "authentic happiness" he studies: "The positive feeling that arises from the exercise of strengths and virtues, rather than from the shortcuts, is authentic."[59] And in an appendix he writes: "I use *happiness* and *well-being* interchangeably as overarching terms to describe the goals of the whole Positive Psychology enterprise,"[60] an enterprise he sometimes portrays as value-laden.

Third, positive psychologists usually study one virtue at a time. For example, studies of philanthropists tend to focus on the virtues in giving, such as generosity and civic-mindedness. Moreover, Seligman and his colleagues urge us to seek happiness by exercising our personal ("signature") virtues and strengths, and add that "we are comfortable saying that someone is of good character if he or she displays but 1 or 2 strengths within a virtue group."[61] It is important to avoid sliding from the claim that (a) an individual has one virtue being studied, to the claim that (b) the individual is a virtuous person overall, or even to the claim that (c) the individual is a virtuous person in a particular situation by integrating all relevant moral values. Moreover, it is quite possible for some individuals to find happiness by exercising their "personal strengths" in largely selfish and immoral ways. For example, they might achieve happiness by exercising bravery and self-control in pursuing their self-interest with little concern for others. In general, classifying and clarifying the virtues is only a first step in understanding good character. An equally important step is exploring how the virtues interact, in myriad ways, in shaping right action and morally admirable conduct, and also how they come in many different forms and degrees.[62] Insofar as positive psychologists take account of these complexities, it is likely they will be drawn further into normative ethics.

Fourth, there is the danger that focusing narrowly on how the virtues contribute to happiness can diminish their inherent value by reducing them to mere tools of self-seeking. We usually have mixed motives in meeting our moral responsiveness, and there is nothing wrong with that. In fact, it is desirable insofar as our motives reinforce each other. But the contribution of the virtues to our personal happiness should not lead us to forget that the virtues make claims in their own right. That is, they make moral claims about desirable ways of being and acting, even when our personal happiness is not maximized. When this is forgotten, and when the virtues are repeatedly celebrated solely because they contribute to happiness, our moral perspectives slide toward subjectivity and mere self-interest.[63]

Finally, positive psychologists sometimes equate happiness with good lives, thereby distorting the implications of their discoveries with regard to aspects of good lives other than subjective well-being.[64] For example, one of their most consistent findings is that increases in absolute amounts of money have only a minor impact on happiness, once we are beyond the poverty level, although our perceptions of relative wealth do affect our happiness significantly. (That is, money tied to status matters.) This is an important discovery, confirming platitudes about money not making us happy. The psychologists fail to add, however, that there might be reasons other than happiness for seeking wealth, for example economic security for ourselves and our families, as well as our ability to help others through philanthropy. (As Woody Allen quipped, "Money is better than poverty, if only for financial reasons."[65]) Good lives have several dimensions that need to be distinguished, even as we study their connections.

With these caveats in mind, we should embrace and learn from the work of positive psychologists as refining commonsense views about the interplay of happiness and the virtues. By happiness they mean "subjective well-being," typically measured by a combination of high levels of enjoyment and overall satisfaction with one's life, although we should scrutinize their use of words like "authentic happiness" which could introduce hidden normative assumptions and definitions. This combination of enjoyment and overall satisfaction coheres with my definition of happiness as loving one's life, valuing it in ways shown by ample enjoyments and a robust sense of meaning, allowing me to draw directly on their studies of happiness. By virtues, the psychologists are trying to stay close to wide understandings of character traits valued by most of us, while providing helpful operational definitions. To that extent, positive psychology enriches and complements moral understanding, although it does not replace moral inquiry. From its inception, positive psychologists have drawn upon work of theoretical and applied moral philosophers, sometimes directly collaborating with them. This interdisciplinary spirit promises to enrich moral understanding and scientific understanding alike.

A final note, by way of an addendum. As this book goes to press, Seligman published a new book titled *Flourish: A Visionary New Understanding of Happiness and Well-Being*, in which he sharply reverses much of what he said about happiness. He now says that he "dislikes" the word *authentic*, "detests" the word *happiness* (although he continues to use it in the new subtitle!), and had grudgingly used the title *Authentic Happiness* because his publisher thought it would sell more books. He now says that "happiness" "is an unworkable term for science, or for any practical goal such as education, therapy, public policy, or just changing your personal life."[66] These reversals remind us that positive psychology is still very much in flux as a new area of inquiry. They are also inconsistent with his continued sympathetic study of happiness in the new book (and even its use in its subtitle).

Briefly, I find Seligman's denigration of happiness misguided, but I applaud his re-thinking of positive psychology to have the broader goal of studying and promoting well-being, conceptualized as having five elements: positive emotion (under which he now subsumes happiness, thereby conflating episodic emotions with life satisfaction), engagement (active interest in the world), positive (caring) relationships, a sense of meaning, and achievement (success). The criticisms I raise above remain relevant, however, to what he says about well-being. In particular, he continues to blur (1) subjectively defined values, for example used in characterizing a subjective sense of meaning and (2) justified (defensible) values, used to characterize meaningful lives and positive relationships. He also conflates (3) what individuals and groups desire for its own sake and (4) what is desirable (worthy of being desired) for its own sake. Religious terrorists or tyrannical spouses might meet Seligman's criteria for well-being, but they do not live good lives of the sort positive psychologists study in connection with the virtues. To his credit, in some passages Seligman moves toward marking these distinctions, for example when he writes: "meaning is not solely a subjective state," implying that individuals can be mistaken in their value judgments.[67] The basis he gives for the distinction, however, combines appeals to "the dispassionate and more objective judgment of history, logic, and coherence" and majority views and false generalizations: "today it is accepted without dissent that connections to other people and relationships are what give meaning and purpose to life." To avoid disguising moral assumptions in the mantle of scientific neutrality—both in conducting their studies and in conveying their results to the public—positive psychologists will need to be more explicit about when and how they distinguish sound and unsound moral judgments in depicting well-being, human flourishing, and the virtues. Given the interdisciplinary spirit of their studies, I am confident they will.

4

AUTHENTICITY

"Just get out there and be yourself," which sounded pretty fine to me.
Then I began to ponder it a bit. "Be myself," indeed; but which self?[1]
—James Dickey

Authenticity is a virtue of such importance that it qualifies as one of the basic aspects of good lives. It also illuminates the path to happiness with shimmering aphorisms: "Know thyself" (Socrates),[2] "Be yourself" (Nietzsche),[3] "Become who you are" (Nietzsche),[4] "Choose oneself" (Kierkegaard),[5] "Trust thyself"[6] (Emerson), "To thine own self be true" (Shakespeare),[7] "Do your own thing" (1960s slogan), "I did it my way" (Frank Sinatra).[8] The idea is that by developing our true selves we tap into wellsprings of enjoyment and meaning that increase happiness. This is a profound truth and a compelling illustration of how the virtues are a good bet in pursuing happiness. Nonetheless, authenticity is not a simple guide to happiness for three reasons. First, authenticity is a complex virtue with multiple aspects that can be understood in different ways and that pull in different directions bearing on happiness. Second, authenticity is partly identified by what makes us happy, and hence it is not an entirely independent guide to happiness. Third, unlike happiness, which is defined solely in terms of subjective responses, authenticity combines subjective responses with a reference to justified values, thereby creating potential tensions between happiness and some aspects of authenticity. All these themes could be illustrated with examples about love, work, philanthropy, and other topics in later chapters, but at the end of this chapter I illustrate them with examples about biomedical enhancements.

ASPECTS OF AUTHENTICITY

Adjectives like "authentic," "genuine," "real," "true," and "valid" are understood in light of both the nouns they modify and their intended contrasts.[9] Thus authentic (valid) passports are not forged or expired, authentic (genuine) porcelain is not an imitation, and authentic (real) money is not counterfeit or Monopoly money. What, then, is the relevant contrast between authentic and inauthentic versions of ourselves? It is not a contrast between our current selves and look-alike robots, avatars, or figures in wax museums. Instead, at least six sets of contrasts are at play: (1) wholehearted versus shallow caring; (2) self-honesty versus self-deception; self-knowledge and self-understanding versus self-ignorance; (3) self-acceptance versus self-denigration; self-affirmation and self-esteem versus self-denigration; self-love versus self-hate; (4) self-creation versus passive conventionality; (5) self-realization and self-fidelity versus self-betrayal; self-fulfillment versus lack of fulfillment; and (6) self-expression with integrity versus hypocrisy.

1. **Wholehearted Caring**. Authentic identity presupposes an identity, and identity centers on what we care about. Wholehearted caring is especially important as a basis for the sense of meaning integral to happiness. Within limits, such commitments are open to modification, and sometimes to radical change, but they must have sufficient stability and depth to provide unity over time. The importance of such caring explains why seventeen-year-old Holden Caulfield, in *The Catcher in the Rye*, is a flawed icon of authenticity.[10] To be sure, Holden is on his way to developing a core of caring. He already has commitments to his writing, reading, and immediate family, and he has vague fantasies about protecting innocent children. Yet his caring has yet to develop into a set of stable commitments based on wholehearted caring. Even his vision of ubiquitous phoniness reflects his lack of mature commitments that, if present, might make him more tolerant of others' imperfections.

Harry Frankfurt draws attention to several features of wholehearted caring: affirming something as having value; guiding our actions in light of it; identifying ourselves with it, both in our own minds and publicly (where appropriate); being devoted and committed to it; accepting responsibility for its well-being; and vulnerability to harm or loss of it.[11] Wholehearted caring generates "volitional necessity," such that we cannot easily abandon it without doing violence to who we are. Frankfurt understands wholehearted caring in terms of second-order desires, that is, in terms of desiring to have the desires we have. Alternatively, we might understand it in terms of the presence of strong and stable desires and the absence of shame, guilt, alienation, and other forms of self-conflicts about what we care about and care for.

2. **Self-Honesty**. Honesty with ourselves facilitates and partly defines authenticity. We cannot be our true selves if we are utterly scatterbrained, addled by drugs, psychotic, or otherwise unable or unwilling to honestly understand ourselves. Self-honesty is the source of self-knowledge and self-understanding. This includes understanding our desires, especially what we desire most strongly; our values and basic beliefs, not in the abstract but as they are expressed in patterns of emotion and conduct; and our abilities and limitations, in relation to our circumstances. The link with happiness is clear: Our

desires and values, combined with abilities to act on them, generate meaningful enjoyments. In addition, happiness as loving our lives requires knowing how to integrate our desires and values within our particular circumstances.

The exact requirements of self-honesty are contested. For one thing, there are disagreements about how self-honesty interacts with other virtues in good lives, including other aspects of authenticity. In adjudicating these disagreements, some thinkers rank honesty as paramount, but others warn that any one-sided demand to abandon all self-deception threatens hope, faith, caring, love, and happiness, all of which are at times promoted by positive illusions (as discussed in chapter 5). For another thing, some thinkers claim that self-understanding requires a commitment to their cherished worldviews. For example, they might insist that everyone should share their belief in God or, like Jean-Paul Sartre, insist that belief in God signals self-deception. We do better to think of self-honesty as a procedural value defined by standards of rationality rather than by any particular worldview. As a procedural value, however, it requires grappling with important matters, where importance is defined in terms of values that make a legitimate claim on us, including self-respect and self-acceptance.

3. **Self-Acceptance**. Authenticity implies accepting and affirming ourselves as we are. The relevant form of acceptance implies self-respect, self-love, and reasonably stable self-esteem—attitudes that foster enjoyment and meaning. We need not be proud of everything about us, and self-acceptance is compatible with pockets of shame (e.g., about having unsightly teeth), guilt (e.g., about betraying a friend), and regret (e.g., about lacking a college education). Complicating matters further, who we are includes our aspirations to change. Yet we need to make peace with ourselves regarding our human nature (e.g., our sexuality) and our individual nature (e.g., our sexual orientation).[12] But whether through humility or humor, we need to find a way to be comfortable in our own skins—physically, psychologically, and morally.

Self-acceptance might require painful resignation in abandoning unrealistic ambitions and hopes, which in the past contributed to happiness. Nevertheless, happiness tends to increase as we accept what cannot be changed, thereby making peace with ourselves and reducing inner conflicts. Accepting intransigent aspects of our personalities frees us to develop other aspects. Even Nietzsche, who unreservedly honored excellence, appreciated the need to accept our flaws: "To 'give style' to one's character—a great and rare art! It is practiced by those who survey all the strengths and weaknesses that their nature has to offer and then fit them into an artistic plan until each appears as art and reason and even weaknesses delight the eye. . . . For one thing is needful: that a human being should *attain* satisfaction with himself."[13]

4. **Self-Creation**. Authenticity implies making something of ourselves, developing our interests and talents in directions of our choosing. As Charles Taylor writes, "There is a certain way of being human that is *my* way. I am called upon to live my life in this

way, and not in imitation of anyone else's. But this gives a new importance to being true to myself. If I am not, I miss the point of my life, I miss what being human is for *me*."[14] The connection with happiness is clear: Happiness lies in creating a life we can love, manifesting that love in enjoyment and meaning.

The ideal of self-creation is exhilarating—and dangerous. Sartre understands it as "inventing" a self—any self we choose, so long as we are honest with ourselves about our freedom and circumstances.[15] Yet, to the contrary, creativity suggests bringing about something that is both new and valuable, where the standards of value are not arbitrary in the way Sartre suggests. In my view, authenticity is a virtue and ideal that implies creating a self that lies within the realm of moral responsibility. In this regard, it is linked to self-realization.

5. **Self-Realization**. Authenticity suggests fidelity to a higher or better self that we have the capacity to develop into, and to that extent it implies striving for self-realization and self-fulfillment. The fidelity consists in creating a desirable self and expressing it in good lives. Self-realization is connected with normative happiness, understood as living a virtuous life. But even subjective happiness, via self-esteem, is linked to a sense of achievement and fulfillment.

Controversy arises the moment we ask whose values provide the standards for self-realization and for good lives. If we stipulate that the values are whatever an individual chooses, then self-realization is reduced to a thoroughly subjective ideal. In extreme versions, this subjectivity is absurd: Alcoholics who deliberately choose self-destructive lives are not fulfilling themselves. At the same time, narrow visions of canonical values can be oppressive in their own ways. We need a pluralistic value perspective that is rooted in a distinction between sound and unsound values and yet celebrates myriad desirable ways in which the virtues can be manifested.

6. **Self-Expression with Integrity**. Finally, authenticity requires that the self we discover, accept, and create is expressed in our social circumstances, with a high degree of integrity.[16] It implies standing on our values and trying to avoid hypocrisy, phoniness, artificiality, and superficiality. What this means in practice is open to dispute. Happiness enters in being at ease in the world rather than paralyzed or troubled by insecurities. Of course, rarely can we express all aspects of the self, and respect for others forbids many types of self-expression. The acceptable and desirable realm of self-expression is often unclear and contested. Where is the line between discretion and cowardice, prudence and lack of conviction?

To sum up, authenticity has six major dimensions. Each dimension can be understood in different ways, and despite extensively overlapping they are sometimes in tension with each other. For example, there is a tension between self-acceptance and self-realization. Self-acceptance enjoins making peace with who we are now; self-realization enjoins making the very best of us. I illustrate these tensions later with examples concerning biomedical enhancements, but let us turn at once to the second theme.

HAPPINESS AS A GUIDE TO AUTHENTICITY

The second reason why authenticity is not a simple guide to happiness is that happiness is also a guide to authenticity. Authenticity is partly identified by what makes us happy, and hence it is not an entirely independent pathway to happiness. To be sure, happiness is not the only guide to authenticity, for authenticity also involves self-honesty and pursuits of excellence characterized by an array of additional values. Nevertheless, what makes us happy often indicates our authentic self. To be authentic, in Joseph Campbell's words, "Follow your bliss."[17]

At its core, authenticity implies discovering and pursuing what we care about most deeply. How do we tell what that is? Immediate feelings provide some help—an activity or personal relationship just feels right; it feels like it fits us and we fit it. Yet such feelings are frequently unstable and otherwise unreliable guides to what we most care about. We learn more about our authentic selves by understanding recurring patterns in what brings us happiness—in recurring and sustained sources of interest, meaning, enjoyment, and joy. As much as authenticity contributes to the pursuit of happiness, then, happiness in turn contributes to identifying our authentic selves. The upshot is that authenticity and happiness need to be pursued together in good lives.

Rousseau was one of the first thinkers to identify happiness as a guide to authenticity, an ideal he helped articulate and popularize. His starting point still resonates: "Always asking others what we are and never daring to question ourselves on this matter, in the midst of so much philosophy, humanity, politeness, and sublime maxims, we have merely a deceitful and frivolous exterior; honor without virtue, reason without wisdom, and pleasure without happiness."[18] He urges us to recover and to "re-become" the unique self we are meant to be.[19] To do so, he advises, we should reflect on the times when we are most happy. These times are probably not the fleeting moments when we feel the most intense pleasure. Instead, they are times when we esteem ourselves, feel at peace with ourselves, are at home in the world, and love our lives.

The happiest time in Rousseau's life was his sojourn on the sparsely populated Swiss Island of Saint-Pierre. Removed from the pressures and superficial pleasures of society, he was attuned to nature emotionally and as an amateur botanist. Although nature was a stimulus for his happiness, the primary pathway was direct communion with himself: "What do we enjoy in such a situation? Nothing external to ourselves, nothing if not ourselves and our own existence."[20] This receptiveness is the "sentiment of existence" through which contentment and peace permeate our activities. The natural state in which it flourishes cannot endure, for we must live in societies and undergo "the earthly passions the tumult of social life engenders."[21] In this way, healthy self-love (*amour de soi*) based on affirming our natural desires continually degrades into an unhealthy self-love (*amour proper*) based on our perceived social status.[22]

The idea that happiness is a touchstone for authenticity permeates our therapy-oriented culture. It is reflected, for example, in the definition of authenticity offered by Philip McGraw, television's Dr. Phil: "The authentic self . . . is the you that flourished, unself-consciously, in those times in your life when you felt happiest and most fulfilled."[23] But can happiness anchor authenticity if happiness is itself wrapped in perplexity? The times we are most happy do not always form a coherent unity, and brief feelings of happiness are an elusive guide. For example, sometimes we feel happy when our social status increases, and other times when we experience solitude that eclipses social status. Even Rousseau's happy moments included social recognition as a renowned thinker and writer as well as his solitary bliss. Clearly, the happiness that anchors authenticity cannot be fleeting feelings (episodic happiness). Instead it is a relatively stable state of loving our lives overall.

Rousseau believes that satisfying our natural desires is the path to happiness and authenticity. In part he believes this because he assumes our natural desires are inherently good, and that is dubious as a generalization. We have evolved as a species, and developed as individuals, with tendencies toward goodness, but we also have natural tendencies toward destruction and domination, and they too might contribute to or detract from happiness. We are social creatures whose individuality unfolds by participating in communities, as much as by solitary reverie, and whose self-expression needs to take society into account. Rousseau takes account of the positive aspects of society by affirming that our natural impulses include sociability. Yet he goes too far in praising self-oriented desires over society-oriented ones.

Authenticity is much celebrated by rebels who renounce all interest in social prestige. Yet, given our social nature, most of us acknowledge some legitimacy to social status. Alain de Botton illuminates the "status anxiety" we must deal with, defining it as "a worry, so pernicious as to be capable of ruining extended stretches of our lives, that we are in danger of failing to conform to the ideals of success endorsed by our society and that we may as a result be stripped of dignity and respect; a worry that we are currently occupying too modest a rung or are about to fall to a lower one."[24] The particular ideals of success vary considerably by social settings, but typically they involve meeting social standards in everything from body build and clothing to cars and houses, and from tastes in music and movies to parentage and university pedigrees. Botton observes that there is now a global respect for people who attain wealth, material goods, power, and fame through their own efforts.[25] This new standard embodies elements of individual initiative, intelligence, creativity, and courage. The concept of authenticity emerged largely as a contrast for narrow social conformism, and yet we know that both our identities and our happiness are substantially connected with society. Status anxiety indicates our confusion: Where is our authentic self amidst our obsessions with social status?

Botton concludes that some status anxiety is inevitable and tolerable so long as we avoid certain forms of it: "Status anxiety may be defined as problematic only insofar as it is inspired by values that we uphold because we are terrified and preternaturally obedient; because we have been anaesthetized into believing that they are natural, perhaps even God-given; because those around us are in thrall to them; or because we have grown too imaginatively timid to conceive of alternatives."[26] In effect, Botton suggests that status anxiety is appropriate so long as it is emerges from values and communities of our choosing. It is irrational only when we play to audiences that do not warrant our attention in light of authentically chosen and justified values.

SUBJECTIVE-NORMATIVE TENSIONS

The third reason why authenticity is not a simple guide to happiness is that authenticity combines subjective responses (including happiness) with reference to justified values, thereby creating potential tensions between happiness and other aspects of authenticity. Like self-fulfillment, authenticity combines (a) what we care about most deeply—our strongest passions and interests—with (b) what is best in us. These two dimensions are not entirely congruent. The first is defined in subjective terms, whereas the second alludes to justified values that define what is best or at least good among our capacities. Whereas happiness is entirely defined as subjective well-being, authenticity is a normative ideal and virtue that needs to be understood in terms of justified values. Those values include honesty with oneself, integrity, and also the defensible values that enter into self-realization, responsible self-creation, and self-expression with integrity. This objective dimension, and our best judgment about the values defining our better self, generates possible tensions with happiness, and occasionally outright conflicts.

An individual's authentic self might require sacrificing some enjoyments and some happiness. For example, freedom fighters might deliberately sacrifice their personal happiness in order to pursue their authentic commitments to justice. They might do so knowing they are likely to die prematurely and without having the opportunity to realize many of their important goals. Again, generous parents make considerable sacrifices of wealth and opportunities that otherwise could be directed toward their other interests, including interests that might maximize their happiness. They might derive great happiness from making such sacrifices for their children, but they might also knowingly cut into their overall happiness to some degree out of love for their children.

To be sure, instances of willing self-sacrifice are always open to the alternative interpretation that the individuals believe they are happier dying for their cause. But the element of selflessness is still present, and only a cynic could believe that humans are incapable of foregoing some personal happiness in order to serve causes and help people they care about. Indeed, conceptions of our authentic selves are intimately tied to our belief in defensible values: for example, caring for worthwhile things, being honest about important things, creating a worthy self, and aspiring to fulfill desirable aspects of ourselves—all of which require asking what we should and should not care about.[27]

In addition, as with other virtues, authenticity is only a good bet for happiness, not a guarantee. What we care about most deeply tends to promote happiness but it also renders us vulnerable to sorrow and disappointment. Suppose that two people are deeply and authentically in love with each other, in all honesty, with genuine passion and with full conviction that they belong with (and to) each other. They also make each other happy, and hence their happiness and authenticity are in unison, indeed their happiness is a key indicator of their authenticity. Tragedy occurs. Perhaps one of them contracts a terrible illness and dies young, leaving the survivor emotionally devastated. Or perhaps the love itself contributes to the death of the partner by inadvertently placing them in a situation where an accident occurs. Or both partners might die tragically, like Romeo and Juliet, from an unsupportive and cruel society. In each case, it is possible that the partners could have had happier lives—both in terms of degree and duration—by not pursuing their authentic loves and selves. Of course, in these cases bad luck thwarts the possibility of happiness, rather than some inherent conflict between authenticity and happiness. Nevertheless, the general point remains. In pursuing our authentic selves we might be drawn into paths that lessen or undermine happiness. The deep caring that defines our authentic self—whether in love, friendship, work, social causes, or striving for excellence in the arts or sports—might not maximize our happiness.

Charles Taylor highlights the subjective and normative aspects of authenticity and warns of the danger in losing sight of either aspect. As a virtue and ideal, authenticity implies authoring our lives by discovering what we care most deeply about and creatively nurturing what is unique and special in us, even in rebellion against social forces that threaten doing so. It also requires, however, that we develop what is genuinely valuable in us, as defined by a "horizon of values" that are justified rather than arbitrary.[28] Although Taylor says little about happiness, it should certainly be counted as one of the values that genuinely matter—that have objectively defensible worth. The point is that happiness is by no means the only value that makes legitimate claims on us. Responsible self-shaping also requires responsiveness to honesty, love, justice, gratitude, and a host of other virtues. Exactly how these values are applied in achieving self-fulfillment is as complicated as life itself. In part it is a personal expression, but it is just as much a search for truth through dialogue with other responsible agents to whom we are morally accountable.

To repeat, insofar as authenticity is a coherent value, it implies responsiveness to defensible values: "I can define my identity only against the background of things that matter. . . . Authenticity is not the enemy of demands that emanate from beyond the self; it supposes such demands."[29] This connection is especially important in understanding self-aspiration toward some version of our better self. The ideas of self-creation, self-realization, self-aspiration, growth, self-honesty, and self-acceptance all need to be understood in terms of seeking things worthy of being cared about. For example, self-honesty implies honesty about significant aspects of ourselves and the world, not just a blanket acknowledgment of every trivial fact. Furthermore, the values defining things worth caring about can be in tension with happiness. Our authentic self might demand self-honesty and striving for excellence in ways that generate stress and require sacrificing some degree of happiness.

The two sides of authenticity—satisfactions and defensible values—together with the possible tensions between them are easily eclipsed from two directions. On the one hand, we might lose belief in defensible values, thereby reducing authenticity to mere subjective preferences. Taylor aptly dubs this the "slide to subjectivism," and he warns that it is ubiquitous in our relativist and mass consumer society, as well as in a variety of intellectual currents such as postmodernism. This postmodernist slide can be seen in Ziyad Marar's reduction of values to the concern for social status and "applause." He writes, "In searching for justification, we are searching for applause. This is an extremely painful claim to accept. To crave applause is humiliating. Who wants to admit that without feeling accepted by an intimidating audience we cannot feel completely happy with ourselves?"[30]

Earlier, Jean-Paul Sartre renounced the possibility of objectively defensible values in understanding authenticity as the freedom to "invent" our values. In his view, authentic individuals live in the conviction that "freedom is the unique foundation of values and that nothing, absolutely nothing, justifies me in adopting this or that particular value, this or that particular scale of values."[31] And when he adds that authentic individuals accept responsibility for their choices, he means primarily they are aware of authoring them. They are not responsible in the sense of being accountable in light of objectively defensible values, for there are no such values in his view—with the possible exception of honesty about the facts surrounding choices and freedom itself. As Charles Taylor argues, this "slide to subjectivism" in thinkers like Sartre and Marar makes nonsense of authenticity itself as a value seriously concerned with self-realization, understood in terms of an array of defensible values.

A second way to mask the tensions between authenticity and happiness is to introduce normative concepts of happiness that build in authenticity. Often this occurs indirectly and with confusion, as it did when John Stuart Mill slides between subjective and normative concepts of happiness. In *Utilitarianism* Mill introduces the idea of "higher pleasures" as constituents of happiness.[32] Implausibly, he says that one pleasure is higher than another if a majority of persons who have experienced both decidedly favor the one over the other. In fact, he seems to assume that some forms of happiness have greater worth in terms of defensible values, as when he says the happiness of Socrates is of higher quality than a pig's happiness. Later, in *On Liberty*, he develops an inspiring conception of authenticity, or what he calls individuality: "He who chooses his plan for himself employs all his faculties. He must use observation to see, reasoning and judgment to foresee, activity to gather materials for decision, discrimination to decide, and when he has decided, firmness and self-control to hold to his deliberate decision."[33] Mill then builds individuality into happiness as "one of the principal ingredients of human happiness."[34] In addition, it leads to "different experiments of living" that enrich the lives of all of us and counters the "tyranny of majorities" in mass democracies. Masses are nothing more than "collective mediocrity," and "if a person possesses any tolerable amount of common sense and experience, his own mode of laying out his existence is the best, not because it is the best in itself, but because it is his own mode."[35]

Mill, then, has two strains in his thinking, as many of us do: authenticity promotes happiness, but happiness is more desirable insofar as it embodies defensible values. These higher pleasures and more valuable happiness, of the sort Socrates exemplifies, can warrant sacrificing some lower pleasures and happiness. A clearer statement is possible by saying that authenticity (Mill's individuality) tends to promote happiness—in the sense of loving our lives, valuing them through enjoyment and meaning—but occasionally authenticity is expressed by sacrificing some happiness for other important values that add depth to our lives.[36]

BIOMEDICAL ENHANCEMENTS

To sum up, authenticity is not a simple guide to happiness for three reasons: (1) authenticity has multiple aspects, and these aspects sometimes pull in different directions; (2) happiness plays an important role in guiding authenticity, and hence authenticity is not an altogether independent guide to happiness; and (3) in addition to subjective responses, authenticity alludes to defensible values that might on occasion be in tension with happiness. I now illustrate these themes using decisions about biomedical enhancements, that is, biomedical technologies intended to increase positive well-being (including happiness) beyond treating disease, disorder, and disability. Dramatic advances in biomedical technology render such decisions increasingly commonplace, including choices about using performance-enhancing drugs, cosmetic surgery, and mood-brightening drugs. Not surprising, philosophical exploration of these decisions has advanced beyond simple concerns for safety to concerns about authenticity and happiness.[37]

To begin with the multiple-aspects theme, consider decisions about cosmetic surgery. Debra Dunn is an attractive forty-year-old who was bothered for years by a hardly noticeable bump on her nose caused by a childhood injury. Cosmetic surgery resulted in what doctors and friends saw as an improvement but which left her feeling distraught because "she no longer bore any resemblance to herself."[38] Her malaise grew to the point where she avoided mirrors and cut back on social activities. Additional surgeries, costing three times the original amount, left her somewhat more pleased with her appearance but deeply regretting her initial decision to seek the first surgery. We might approach this example in terms of mental health (low self-esteem), but we can also say that Dunn experienced difficulties centered on authenticity.

We can say that Dunn is torn between self-acceptance and self-aspiration. Perhaps she also has difficulties being honest with herself about this conflict, as well as about what is most important to her. In terms of the happiness-guide theme, the case illustrates that identifying our authentic selves turns in part on what makes us happy, in some stable and enduring way. The case illustrates how difficult it can be to discover where our "true self" lies, and hence why authenticity cannot be a simple guide to happiness. Even when cosmetic surgeries increase happiness, as most of them do, the increase is often only temporary, given our tendency to psychologically adjust and take such changes for granted.[39]

The case is linked to issues about social status and narrow standards of beauty in our society that place pressure on both sexes but especially on women. These issues were extensively debated with regard to cosmetic surgery for breast enhancement. Feminists initially condemned society's sexist pressures on women to conform to male preferences. The issue became complicated when it was discovered that a large majority of women were happy with the surgeries they chose.[40] This returns us to the happiness-as-guide theme, but there remain concerns about stereotypes of beauty that, once internalized, place unfair pressures on women to constantly refashion their bodies, not to mention that make some Jews unhappy with their noses and some Asians want to change the slant of their eyes.[41]

Erik Parens suggests that two opposing ethical frameworks lead us to favor self-acceptance or instead self-development in thinking about biotechnology: "One side emphasizes our obligation to remember that life is a gift and that we need to learn to let things be, the other emphasizes our obligation to transform that gift and to exhibit our creativity."[42] Parens notes that these two frameworks should not be equated with the differences between secular libertarians who celebrate personal choice versus religious thinkers who object to biomedical enhancements as playing God and failing to appreciate God's gifts. Religion can enter into the first framework as well, in the form of a spirituality of using God's gifts in creative ways to improve ourselves and our world. Parens believes that each ethical framework highlights an important moral dimension of enhancement technologies, and that considerations of gratitude (and self-acceptance) and on creative expression (and self-realization) need to be balanced. In any case, the issue illustrates how different aspects of authenticity might be interpreted and selectively emphasized within different value perspectives. Authenticity is not a simple guide to happiness because authenticity itself is a complex and even elusive virtue.

Turning to the second theme—that happiness is a guide to authenticity as much as vice versa—consider decisions about mood-brightening drugs like Prozac. Psychiatrist Peter Kramer gives us the example of Tess, a pseudonym for the first patient he treated with Prozac.[43] Her depression was dramatically cured, and she became more cheerful and optimistic, with greater confidence and courage in pursuing her endeavors—she took on a new identity. Eventually Kramer weaned her off Prozac, but eight months later she returned, asking to go back on Prozac because she didn't feel like herself without it. After agonizing about the ethics of prescribing drugs for basically "cosmetic" purposes in healthy persons who want to feel "better than well," Kramer wrote a prescription for enhancement—for "positive health" in the sense of positive well-being beyond the mere absence of mental disorder. That positive well-being centers on her happiness, although of course her happiness affects her positive health as well. It also centers on her authenticity, insofar as happiness is an indicator of where her true self lies.

Finally, to illustrate the tension between subjective and normative aspects of authenticity, consider the controversy over steroids in sports. Does authenticity consist in accepting and being content with my current abilities, as shaped by my genetic inheritance and past efforts? Or does authenticity permit or even require pursuing self-realization by employing bodybuilding steroids in the pursuit of greater athletic excellence? Are steroid-using athletes phonies who betray their talents, as well as cheaters who violate regulations? Or are they more authentic because they seek to be the best they can be?

They are inauthentic, according to the President's Council Report, commissioned by President George W. Bush: "Some performance-enhancing agents, from stimulants to blood doping to genetic engineering of muscles, call into question the dignity of the performance of those who use them. The performance seems less real, less one's own, less worthy of our admiration."[44] More strongly, by using these enhancements "we mock the very excellence of our own individual embodiment that superior performance is meant to display."[45] I disagree with the President's Council on this point. Athletes use steroids in striving for excellence, thereby paying homage to both their commitment to excellence and to ideals of excellence in competitive sports. (That does not mean they are justified in cheating and risking their health.) Nevertheless, whether or not we agree with the President's Council, it is clear the controversy turns in part on the potentially conflicting aspects of authenticity centered on values of excellence, and on different criteria for understanding the defensible values characterizing authenticity.

As noted earlier, the subjective-normative tensions surrounding authenticity are easily eclipsed by invoking normative definitions of happiness, which tend to define authenticity and happiness as fully congruent. Smuggling additional values into happiness without clear acknowledgment of what those values entail has proven tempting in discussions of biomedical enhancements. That occurs in the President's Council Report, which contends that mood-brightening pharmaceuticals like Prozac should be used "sparingly, medically" rather than as enhancements.[46] Again, according to the Council, cosmetic uses of psychopharmacology are inauthentic and do not produce "true happiness"—plainly, an appeal to a normative concept of happiness reflecting the Council's conservative value perspective.[47] The Council works with a false dichotomy between "superficial" concepts of happiness as pleasure and a largely unarticulated normative concept. This dichotomy eclipses the concept of happiness as loving our lives and manifesting that love in a sense of meaning as well as ample enjoyments. Furthermore, in renouncing subjective happiness, the Council engages in a priori psychology—that is, bad, nonempirical psychologizing—to reach the conclusion that biomedical enhancements foster self-alienation: "I am no longer the agent of self-transformation, but a passive patient of transforming [enhancement] powers."[48] In sharp contrast, liberals regard voluntary choices to use mood enhancements as an expansion of our powers, and experienced as such after a normal period of adjustment to change.

To conclude, authenticity is not a simple guide to happiness; instead, authenticity and happiness are best pursued in tandem. Authenticity has different aspects that are sometimes in tension, creating conflicts whose resolution is guided by both the concern for happiness and commitments to additional moral ideals. At times happiness is as much a clue to authenticity as authenticity is a key to happiness. Authenticity is a virtue connected to a horizon of other values that make a claim on us in their own right, even when they do not directly advance our happiness, so that authenticity and happiness are at times in tension with regard to self-honesty, self-acceptance, self-creation, and self-realization.

5

HAPPILY SELF-DECEIVED

The life-lie, don't you see—that's the animating principle of life.[1]
—Henrik Ibsen

Classical philosophers were preoccupied with self-deception about wrongdoing and sin, and as a result they tended to condemn all self-deception as dishonesty, cowardice, and hypocrisy. In contrast, contemporary philosophers highlight permissible and even desirable instances of self-deception, such as self-deceiving hopes that bolster meaning and abilities to cope with life-threatening diseases.[2] A parallel contrast is present in psychologists' discussion of self-deception as harming or benefiting the self. Thus, traditional psychoanalysts emphasized how self-deception (understood as psychological defense[3]) tends to harm the self, whereas today's cognitive and evolutionary psychologists highlight how self-deception promotes happiness and adaptation. Witness Roy Baumeister's recipe for happiness: "You form and maintain some positive social bonds or human relationships; you satisfy your basic needs for meaning; you maintain goals and aspirations that are low enough to be within reach; you manage to do reasonably well in objective terms; and you cultivate self-flattering, optimistic illusions."[4]

Compared to wrongdoing and sin, happiness seems a lightweight topic in thinking about illusions and self-deception, more the proper domain of comic writers like Jonathan Swift, who describes it as the "perpetual possession of being well deceived."[5] Indeed, philosophers in discussing self-deception still tend to regard happiness as a shallow motive that deflects attention from more serious concerns about authenticity and duty. That is a mistake. Not only is happiness among our most basic motives, but it is a dimension of good lives that interweaves with meaning, morality, authenticity, and self-fulfillment. I explore three questions about how happiness and self-deception are connected. First, can we deceive ourselves about whether we are happy? I argue we can. Second, is self-deception a friend of happiness, as Swift suggests, or is it just as often a foe? It can be either, depending on the context. Third, how does being happily self-deceived interact with other aspects of good lives? As we might expect, the interactions are complex.

SELF-DECEPTION ABOUT WHETHER WE ARE HAPPY

I understand *self-deception* broadly to include (1) motivated irrationality in the form of biased beliefs and attitudes that clash with available evidence, and (2) purposeful evasion in the form of willful ignorance, self-pretense, selectively highlighting and downplaying evidence according to what we want to believe, and relying on others to support our hopes and favored self-image.[6] Mere ignorance and false belief do not suffice, for in addition there must be some inner dynamic at work whereby we avoid distressing topics, evidence, or inferences.

Psychologists generally assume that "people know when they are happy and when they are not."[7] If so, there is little possibility of self-deception about whether we are happy. To the contrary, I want to show this possibility exists. As always, my focus is on happy *lives*, rather than episodic happiness in the form of emotions (pleasure, joy), moods (cheerful, tranquil), and attitudes ("I'm happy to have a job").

Consider Peter Weir's movie *The Truman Show*. The protagonist Truman Burbank (played by Jim Carrey) is a thirty-year-old insurance salesman who seems exceptionally happy. He is cheerful and smiling, energetic and exuberant, friendly and well liked. We soon learn, however, that his life is not completely idyllic. His marriage has grown stale and he is fantasizing about a college girlfriend from a decade earlier, making inquiries into her whereabouts, and planning a trip to the Fiji Islands where he thinks she might reside. Nevertheless, these romantic yearnings are compatible with his overall happiness. Perhaps they contribute to it, and certainly he is far from being miserable due to anxiety, depression, despair, anger, envy, regret, guilt, or shame.

His life, however, is based on wholesale illusion. Since birth, he has been skillfully manipulated by Christof (played by Ed Harris), a God-like television director who orchestrates most events in his life and broadcasts it to a large and loyal worldwide audience as a kind of ultimate reality show funded by myriad product placement ads. The island town where he resides is actually an elaborate television set constructed as a biosphere. Everyone in the town, including his wife and friends, is a talented actor playing a scripted role. Thousands of hidden cameras allow Christof to sustain the deception by modifying the plot in response to chance events and Truman's choices. For example, when a stage light used to simulate a star breaks loose and falls near Truman, Christof has his writers broadcast a radio story about debris dropped from a plane.

For many years Truman avoids pursuing clues that might have led to escaping the "island," despite an intense phobia of open water that Christof instilled in him. Fighting his phobia, he eventually does escape. Yet we can easily imagine an alternative plot in which self-deception prolongs the illusion. Thus we might imagine that his general contentment and fear of change lead him to disregard his doubts and silence his suspicions. Indeed, most likely he engages in some self-deception during his years of complacency, as Christof hints at one point. In this way self-deception supports his happiness, but he is not deceived about whether he is happy (to some extent).

Or is he? Once we discern Truman's illusions, do we continue to think of him as happy? The answer depends on which concept of happiness we apply, and several concepts might be of interest in thinking about self-deception. I show how we can be self-deceived about happiness using several types of definitions of happiness, discussed in chapter 1, that figure prominently in the literature on self-deception, before applying my own definition of happiness.

Most normative definitions require that happiness be based on rationality and basic honesty, thereby ruling out the possibility of a happy Hitler or Osama bin Laden. In this normative sense, Truman is not truly happy, for he has not attained the kind of happiness he values and that is genuinely valuable. Invoking a normative definition, Wladyslaw Tatarkiewicz assumes that "a condition which we find repugnant cannot constitute happiness. . . . This is the situation of the man whose happiness springs from his family life but whose wife is unfaithful. If he is unaware of this [because of deception or self-deception] he may be satisfied, but we would not call him happy."[8] Tatarkiewicz would not consider Truman happy.

Today, as I have emphasized, the predominant concepts of happiness are subjective rather than normative; they center on a given individual's actual mental states (emotions, beliefs, desires) without accompanying claims about justified values. Even so, the subjectivity can be more or less extreme. Some concepts require at least contact with basic truths about our situation rather than radical self-deception about them. In particular, preference-satisfaction happiness consists in satisfaction (fulfillment) of what we regard as our important desires. An enriched preference-satisfaction concept adds that we must also derive satisfaction (pleasure) from satisfying our desires. In defending a modified preference-satisfaction concept, Richard Kraut considers a man whose happiness is based entirely on "being loved, admired, or at least respected by my friends," but whose so-called friends do not care a whit for him and are merely manipulating him for their own purposes.[9] Let us add that the man is partly self-deceived about this, that he has occasional doubts about the truthfulness of his friends but silences his doubts by turning his attention elsewhere. We then have a case much like Truman.

Kraut says the man *feels happy* while under his illusion but he is not living a *happy life* for his important desires are not being satisfied, and no doubt Kraut would say the same about Truman. Clearly, then, we can deceive ourselves, as well as be deceived, about whether our important desires are actually being fulfilled and just how much enjoyment we are deriving from their fulfillment. Hence, we can be self-deceived about whether we are happy in the preference-satisfaction sense as well as the normative sense.

Turn now to definitions that understand happy lives exclusively in terms of mental states without requiring real-world fulfillment of desires. Here the possibility of self-deception about happiness might seem less obvious, although much depends on the details. A hedonistic definition, of the sort used by Jeremy Bentham, equates psychological happiness with high levels of pleasure and low quantities of pain.[10] Usually we can authoritatively report whether we are in a state of pleasure or pain. (Not always: Sometimes our emotions are confused, ambivalent, and products of self-deception.) Hence, most self-deception about episodic pleasure levels is relatively minor. But assessments and reports of our happiness remain quite vulnerable to self-deception, for they constitute fallible generalizations about our overall levels of pleasure and pain. One type of self-deceiving bias is situational: For example, if our present mood is euphoric, we might be inclined to exaggerate our average enjoyment level, and if we are depressed we might underestimate it. There are many additional biases that can lead to self-deception about our overall pleasure levels that emerge from attempts to protect self-images, for example as being a happy person or an unfortunate person.

A more complex definition of happiness, the one I favor, understands happiness as loving (liking, being satisfied with) our lives overall and manifesting that love in ample pleasures and a robust sense of meaning. Loving our lives is not reducible to levels of pleasure, but instead it involves valuing (affirming, cherishing) our lives—in their entirety or in large segments. Accordingly, happiness has two main aspects: (a) loving, liking, or being satisfied with the main structures of our lives, including our aspirations for growth and change, and (b) as based on and manifested in ample enjoyments and a strong sense of meaning (where "a sense of meaning" is subjective and does not require commitment to defensible values). Why not just (a)? Because, as discussed in chapter 1, we might love our lives as deeply meaningful without being very happy; perhaps this was at least partly true of Nietzsche, Freud, and Wittgenstein.[11] Why not just (b)? Because our life might be richly pleasurable in ways linked to activities and relationships that we find meaningful but that do not "add up" to a life that we can love—perhaps because we also experience too much tragedy, bad luck, depression, anxiety, or self-hatred. Using this concept of happiness, Truman is mostly happy, and knows he is, at the beginning of the movie when he is fully deluded.

Can we, then, deceive ourselves into believing we are happier than we are, using a life-satisfaction concept of psychological happiness? Certainly. Perhaps at some point in his dawning awareness of his situation Truman became uncertain and even self-deceived about just how satisfied he was with his life; the movie leaves this possibility open. But let us add a second example where we can be more certain.

Anna Karenina experiences great joy when she leaves her dull husband to live with the dashing Vronsky. Over several years, however, her happiness erodes as her relationship with Vronsky becomes increasingly superficial and unfulfilling. Worse, she desperately misses her son whom she was forced to leave in her husband's custody. Many days she pretends (to herself and others) to be cheerful, and she bolsters the pretense with the help of nightly doses of morphine. When her sister-in-law Dolly visits, Anna claims several times to be happy, as she has partly succeeded in deceiving herself into believing she is. The visit, however, provokes a crisis in which she abandons her self-pretense and acknowledges to Dolly and to herself, "Yes, I am unhappy. If anyone is unhappy, it is I."[12]

Why does Anna deceive herself into thinking she is happy, or happier than she actually is? One reason is that acknowledging her unhappiness risks intensifying her misery, which is exactly what happens. Prior to her confession to Dolly, she leads a life of quiet desperation. The confession transforms her desperation into despair centered on the conflict between love for Vronsky and her son. Another reason is that she senses that acknowledging her unhappiness would confront her with the painful necessity of making a decision about how to proceed with her life—or how not to proceed, as she moves toward suicide.

Daniel M. Haybron points out that we should not be surprised when chronically anxious (or depressed) individuals deceive themselves into thinking they are happier than they are, regardless of which definition of happiness is being used: "It may be adaptive in many situations to be anxious while believing that one is happy, and more generally presenting oneself as happy. For overt displays of anxiety project weakness and vulnerability, whereas displays of happiness send the opposite message."[13] This is especially true in American society where people are pressured to be upbeat, optimistic, and happy. Relying on interpersonal deception alone might generate inner tensions (cognitive dissonance) that self-deception helps to reduce.

If we can be self-deceived in thinking we are happier than we are, can we also be self-deceived in thinking we are *un*happier than we are? The possibility seems remote if happiness is equated with pleasure, since we usually know when we are not feeling pleasure, but we can be self-deceived in how we sum up the extent of our pleasure overall. Self-deception about unhappiness is more straightforward, however, if we apply our concept of psychological happiness centered on life satisfaction, an idea involving judgments and assessments of our lives overall. Thus we sometimes discover and decide that we were happier than we once thought. Typically this occurs after living through changes that provide wider perspective about what can reasonably be expected from life.

Something like this occurs in Anne Giardini's novel *The Sad Truth About Happiness*. Maggie, the thirty-something protagonist, agrees to take a quiz designed to estimate life expectancy. The last of several dozen questions is, "Are you happy right now?" Bringing to mind the one major frustration in her life, the lack of a lover, and down-playing how much she is happy about, she answers that she is not as happy as she would like to be, an admission that further lowers her happiness level. She then makes a con-certed effort to increase her happiness. The effort fails and she concludes that pursuing happiness directly and single-mindedly is self-defeating—the truth in the paradox of happiness. Following a zany sequence of events, she further concludes there is no com-plete and permanent happiness, and hence her initial state reflected the way life usually is: happy in some respects, not happy in others. Happiness requires ongoing innova-tion, adjusting, balancing, and accepting the possibilities for happiness we currently have available to us.[14]

Just as there are pressures to appear happier than we are (to ourselves and others), occasionally there are pressures not to acknowledge our happiness to ourselves. Mr. Ramsay, in Virginia Woolf's *To the Lighthouse*, is "for the most part happy," although he refuses to admit as much to himself and others, "as if to be caught happy in a world of misery was for an honest man the most despicable of crimes."[15] For example, rather than acknowledge his happiness when he is asked to give an important talk, he depre-cates the invitation by muttering that he has to talk some nonsense to the audience. His evasions arise in part from seeking reassuring praise from his wife and students, and in part from fear: "It was a disguise; it was the refuge of a man afraid to own his own feelings, who could not say, This is what I like—this is what I am."[16]

SELF-DECEPTION ABOUT WHAT MAKES US HAPPY

It is possible, then, to be self-deceived about whether we are happy and about how happy we are, using my definition of happiness and several others. This result should make us cautious in applying the results of psychological studies of happiness to spe-cific individuals. Most psychological studies rely on self-reported levels of happiness, and self-reports can involve self-deception. No doubt often the self-deceptions move in different directions and hence tend to cancel each other out, but not always. In ad-dition, psychological studies report statistical data that might not apply to a given in-dividual. Still, these studies are valuable in understanding general tendencies to deceive ourselves in pursuing happiness, and also what those tendencies imply concerning mental health and well-being.

As noted in chapter 3, psychologists have developed tools to ensure reliability (self-consistency) in self-reports over time.[17] They do more than merely ask individ-uals whether they are happy (although that is one question they ask). Instead, they ask a series of questions, such as: Taking everything into account, how satisfied are you with your life, on a scale of 1 to 10? Again, what is the balance of enjoyment and nonenjoyment in your life? Answers to such questions can be distorted by passing moods, confusion, intoxication, and other temporary aberrations, so psychologists take steps to guard against these distortions. For example, they test the validity (truth) of self-report questionnaires by checking self-reports against what close friends and relatives say about individuals. They also check claims about average levels of enjoyment by using a beeper technique: Subjects in experiments carry beepers that go off randomly throughout the day, at which time they record their present level of happiness. Moreover, I suspect that the resulting overall averages in studies tend to cancel out the effects of self-deception, which sometimes inflate and other times deflate reported happiness.

Using these techniques, much valuable data is being accumulated about what tends to make us happy, that is, about the sources and conditions for happiness, to which I now turn. Psychologists have amply documented that we are under myriad specific illusions about what makes us happy, and it is plausible to assume that self-deception is frequently involved. This widespread presence of illusions in pursuing happiness comes as no surprise; it reflects common sense. Yet psychological studies often have more nuanced results that do surprise. It comes as a surprise, for example, that such things as beauty (as judged by objective observers) and money (in absolute amounts) do not in general increase happiness, although the illusions that we are beautiful and that we are relatively rich do increase happiness.[18]

Furthermore, psychologists suggest that self-deception is frequently healthy because it helps us cope. An anthology of psychology essays, for example, accepts as its unifying theme that "self-deception is a normal and generally positive force in human behavior," promoting survival, mental health, and happiness.[19] Again, in her influential book *Positive Illusions*, Shelley Taylor argues that "normal human thought and perception is marked not by accuracy but by positive self-enhancing illusions about the self, the world, and the future."[20] It is human nature to bolster self-esteem with self-flattering illusions, exaggerate the extent to which we have control over our lives, and hold unrealistically optimistic views about the future.

I take these claims seriously, although I think Taylor overstates them.[21] For example, after defining illusions as false beliefs, she quickly shifts to a much broader notion of illusions as "beliefs that have no factual basis or that require looking at the facts in an optimistic way."[22] This notion conflates upbeat beliefs of two very different sorts: (1) false and biased beliefs contrary to the available evidence (which includes self-deception) and (2) unproven beliefs, including faith and hope, that go beyond the evidence but that might turn out to be true. The latter are not illusions in any usual sense—true beliefs are not illusions!

I suspect that Taylor uncritically borrows Freud's use of "illusion" in his attack on religion in *The Future of an Illusion*. Freud writes, "What is characteristic of illusions is that they are derived from human wishes. . . . Illusions need not necessarily be false—that is to say, unrealizable or in contradiction with reality."[23] This unorthodox usage conflates self-deception with reasonable hope and faith. Of course hope and faith, which go beyond the evidence, are vital to the happiness of most of us, but they are not always rooted in illusion or self-deception.

Furthermore, in response to the objection that illusions can cause great harm and signal mental disorder, Taylor says that "positive illusions" are only mild illusions. In effect, she stipulates they are not pathological, in contrast with the "extreme" illusions of paranoids and megalomaniacs.[24] There is some circularity, then, in her argument that positive illusions are a mark of health and well-being: "mild" implies mental healthiness. Moreover, perhaps most concepts of mental health and disorders often embed or presuppose moral values; for example, healthy self-esteem is defined partly in terms of virtuous self-respect, which lies between the excesses of narcissism and self-deprecation in depression.[25]

In *Stumbling on Happiness*, Daniel Gilbert reaches a more cautious and plausible conclusion about how self-deception contributes to happiness.[26] He draws together many studies, including his own, that demonstrate how self-deception both promotes and thwarts happiness. Happiness requires a fluid combination of illusion and realism that our brains have evolved to provide: "The mind may be gullible, but it ain't no patsy. The world is this way, we wish the world were that way, and our experience of the world—how we see it, remember it, and imagine it—is a mixture of stark reality and comforting illusion. We can't spare either."[27] We need to be in touch with reality in order to achieve our goals. That implies, I would add, some degree of intellectual and moral honesty. Equally, we need illusions to motivate us by bolstering confidence and hope. To that end we have a "psychological immune system that defends the mind against unhappiness," akin to Freud's psychological defense mechanisms against anxiety.[28]

Gilbert shows that we constantly fill in or leave out considerable detail about topics of interest to us, selectively attend to and disregard evidence, and emphasize or downplay facts. We do so self-deceivingly by "unconsciously cooking the facts and then consciously consuming them" in ways that render us strangers to ourselves.[29] This process occurs with regard to the future, past, or present.

In anticipating the future, we overestimate the positive emotional impact of favorable events. For example, we think that winning the lottery will permanently elevate our happiness, yet for most of us it does so only for a short time, typically for less than a year. We also overestimate the negative emotional impact of misfortunes such as serious injuries and diseases. The illusions are created by focusing on the immediate event and our likely reactions at the moment, thereby neglecting emotional adjustments ("habituation") that occur during subsequent months and serve to modulate both delight and discomfort. We also project our present attitudes into the future, thereby failing to appreciate how new social contexts can alter our attitudes. Again, our tendency to be over-optimistic about controlling events arises from our need for self-confidence in grappling with life's uncertainties. And in assessing the evidence about future events, we engage in biased reasoning (rationalization) by accenting evidence for what we want to believe and disregarding or downplaying evidence against it.

In recalling the past, many of these same tendencies shape our memories of happiness. We remember selectively and symbolically, recalling major episodes and omitting much detail. The memory that "I was very happy in high school" might be based on highlighting my athletic prowess or academic promise while disregarding adolescent turmoil and anxiety. We also project aspects of the present into the past. For example, middle-age memories of college years concerning political views, sexual activities, and consumption of alcohol are influenced by our present attitudes.

In viewing the present, "we look around *selectively*" with an eye to nurturing and nursing our self-esteem.[30] We appraise our skills and achievements favorably by comparing them against people who do worse than us. For example, almost all of us think we are better-than-average drivers. We think we are making steadier progress toward our goals than the evidence supports. And our desire for control leads us to exaggerate the degree to which we can direct events. For example, when gambling we think we increase our chances of winning by rolling the dice in a certain way, or simply by rolling the dice ourselves rather than allowing others to do so.

Gilbert, then, offers a balanced understanding of how self-deception can promote or prevent happiness. Even so, I would add two caveats. First, Gilbert implausibly equates happiness with pleasure, or what he calls "emotional happiness": "Emotional happiness . . . is the feeling common to the feelings we have when we see our new granddaughter smile for the first time, receive word of a promotion, . . . cure cancer, or get a really good snootful of cocaine."[31] He sets aside "judgmental happiness," which refers to favorable attitudes toward events, as well as "moral happiness," which is happiness considered morally desirable. Missing from his threefold distinction is happiness in the sense I am using—life satisfaction in the form of loving our lives and manifesting that love in ample pleasures and a robust sense of meaning. Technically, then, his book is about pleasure rather than life satisfaction, although he often conflates them.

For example, when he says that happiness is the primary or even exclusive motive for what most of us seek in life, he conflates desires for pleasures with desires for happiness centered on loving our lives overall.[32] Again, he reports that most of us are influenced by cultural prescriptions to think that having children will make us happier, and we continue to believe this after having children. In doing so, we overlook the gritty realities of changing diapers, losing sleep, fighting with teenagers, and paying staggering college bills. The "actual satisfaction" of parents, as monitored by episodic studies, reveals that the joys of parenting are greatly overrated. Yet, happiness as pleasure is one thing, happiness as overall satisfaction with our lives is quite another, and estimates of the joys of parenting pertain more to the latter. No doubt there are many days when parents would rather be relaxing at the beach than dealing with the stresses of parenting, but it might be equally true that parenting brought them greater overall joy and meaning than a more relaxed life could.

Second, what does Gilbert mean by self-deception and illusions?[33] Officially, he restricts them to biased false beliefs. It is plausible, however, to interpret his "psychological immune system" against unhappiness as encompassing both self-deceptive illusions and non-self-deceiving hope and optimism and illusion (a conflation we saw in Taylor as well). Moreover, to the extent that unconscious processes amount to routine brain processing, they constitute self-deception only using a very broad sense that includes all false beliefs our brains play a role in generating.

SELF-DECEPTION AND HAPPINESS IN GOOD LIVES

Fully good lives combine subjective and objective well-being.[34] Subjective well-being is happiness, which I understand as loving our lives and manifesting that love in ample enjoyment and a robust sense of meaning. Objective well-being includes necessities for life, such as a reasonable amount of money and power. It also includes what I emphasize here: a desirable life as judged by moral and other justified values that identify what is worth loving and living for, what is genuinely fulfilling, and what provides a justified sense of meaning. Subjective and objective well-being interweave, and they are bridged by the sense of meaning that is so important to happy lives. Thus, although our sense of meaning is subjective, it puts pressure in the direction of justified values and truthfulness about them, for most of us attempt to ground our sense of meaning in such values.

It remains true, as psychologists and common sense agree, that self-deception is the friend of happiness within wide limits, insofar as it promotes enjoyment, a sense of meaning, and an overall love of our lives. Nevertheless, self-deception can also undermine our sense of meaning and thereby dilute happiness as well as undermine aspiration to lead a good life. I discuss four ways this might occur in addition to the specific disruptions of (meaning-full) emotions discussed by Gilbert.

First, most of us seek a happiness rooted in values that provide depth of meaning in terms of justified values. We know there is the danger that we might lead superficial lives severed from values worth living for. This danger is illustrated in Tolstoy's *Death of Ivan Ilych*. Ilych concludes that what he once considered a happy and good life was not genuinely so. His life had been pleasant, comfortable, conventional, centered on social recognition as a judge, and containing little compassion for others. During his final weeks, as his pain increases and cannot be controlled, he appreciates the simple kindness shown to him by good-natured servant Gerasim. In his last hours he undergoes a spiritual awakening: "All that had then seemed joys now melted before his sight and turned into something trivial and often nasty."[35] Worse, he saw his life as "not real at all, but a terrible and huge deception which had hidden both life and death."[36] Ilych had been a self-deceiver because he systematically indulged his self-centered biases and turned away from what he knew or should have known was morally important: "It occurred to him that his scarcely perceptible attempts to struggle against what was considered good by the most highly placed people, those scarcely noticeable impulses which he had immediately suppressed, might have been the real thing, and all the rest false."[37]

The deathbed test for assessing which values are worth living for can be applied in imagination at any time. That test provides helpful perspective precisely because it encourages stripping away the distortions of shortsightedness and social pressure. But it is easy to exaggerate the importance of this test, for deathbed perspectives are limited in their own way, neglecting as they must our need for grappling with long-term plans.[38] Indeed, closeness to death can undermine our interest in many valuable things, and that happens with Ilych. Even if we share his final vision of honesty and love as the highest values, there is no reason to belittle the conventional but morally valid values in his life: friendship, responsible support of his family, and contribution to the community through meaningful work. Nor should we dismiss values such as comfort, power, wealth, and social esteem, which Ilych also enjoyed. Self-realization usually involves integrating them with what we construe as the higher values of honesty and love—values with which they can be in tension. Deathbed perspectives usually do not help us with this important task, and they cover up the conflicts between equally authentic values for what comes directly out of us and what society has to offer us. We are free, then, to reject Ilych's self-doubts as overblown. Nevertheless, Tolstoy's story engages us because we know that self-deception can erode fully desirable ways of life, including the kind of happiness we wish to have in a life that we both love and consider worthy of being loved because it is deeply meaningful in terms of justified values.

Tolstoy's story reminds us that we value more than psychological happiness, and that we especially value psychological happiness when it connects with justified and important values. Robert Nozick offers the same reminder using his thought experiment of the experience machine (mentioned in chapter 2).[39] Few of us would permanently enter an experience machine by becoming blobs attached to neuron-stimulating electrodes even if we could program the machine to create a convincing but illusory sense of well-being. We would not call such lives good (if they are lives at all), but happiness and goodness are two entirely different things according to extreme subjectivism.

Another way to put the central point is that (subjective psychological) happiness is not by itself a complete and adequate justification for a way of life and for the value perspective on which it is based. For additional values enter in assessing instances of happiness. For example, a particular religious perspective might bring happiness and provide other practical benefits in how individuals live. This "pragmatic justification" of beliefs and lives is relevant, in my view, in assessing participation in religious communities. Although relevant it is not sufficient, however, to justify actions implied by a particular religious belief, much less to establish the truth of the belief.[40] To take an extreme case, when religious views are tied to flagrant immorality, such as terrorist beliefs and acts, no amount of happiness of the believers can justify holding the beliefs, much less establish the beliefs as true.

Second, most of us want our happiness to be connected with authenticity. Authentic happiness, in a relevant sense, expresses an individual's autonomous value perspective without major self-deception and illusions. As discussed in chapter 4, authenticity centers on procedures used in forming our identity, including accepting ourselves and developing areas of wholehearted caring, as well as expressing ourselves with a certain degree of integrity. Another requirement is that we respond to the world rationally and truthfully, rather than self-deceivingly and dishonestly. The opportunity to develop an authentic identity presupposes that we can think and act voluntarily, rather than being completely coerced or manipulated.[41]

L. W. Sumner clarifies authentic happiness in this sense. In a case reminiscent of Kraut's case of the man deceived in thinking he has friends, Sumner describes a woman whose happiness turns on believing she is married to a loyal and loving husband, when in fact he is using her for entirely self-serving purposes. Self-deception is involved, as well as deception by her partner, for "there were sufficient cues for her to pick up, had she not been blinded by love."[42] Sumner grants that the woman lives a happy life while under the illusion. But her happiness is not authentic—in the sense of being tied to a fully authentic identity—because it does not reflect her values and desires in response to roughly accurate information about the world.

Third, most of us seek a durable happiness based on a stable sense of meaning. Contingencies of the world, as well as our desires for change and growth, preclude any fixity. But at least we seek happiness that we can carry forward in cherished memories as part of our sense of meaning; friends and family die, but we cherish the love we had for them and received from them. Illusory and self-deceiving friendships and loves are not like this; they evaporate once we learn about them. Certainly *habits* of self-deception make it less likely we will maintain a grip on the sources of meaning in our lives.

That is the deeper truth in Henrik Ibsen's *The Wild Duck*, a play that is often misinterpreted as a wholesale endorsement of self-deception. Hjalmar Ekdal bases his happiness on illusions that he is the sole provider for his family, when in fact his wife and other family members bring in most of the family's income; that he is creating a revolutionary photographic apparatus, when in fact he is merely tinkering with useless gadgets; and that he is the biological father of his beloved daughter Hedvig, when in fact his former business partner had an affair with his wife and is the biological father of Hedvig. Ekdal's illusions are largely the product of self-deception, which is supported by his wife and by Dr. Relling, who believes that "life lies" constitute "the animating principle of life": "Deprive the average man of his vital lie, and you've robbed him of happiness as well."[43] When his illusions are overthrown by Gregers Werle, the son of his former business partner, Ekdal angrily accuses Hedvig of never having loved him. The emotionally fragile Hedvig kills herself, plunging Ekdal and his wife into despair.

As a cautionary tale about our need for self-deception, Ibsen's play is in tune with what psychologists have discovered about the pursuit of happiness. But it is not a one-sided endorsement of self-deception. Werle, after all, is destructively self-deceived in his call for Ekdal to abandon his self-deception. More important, Ekdal is self-deceived in his misinterpretation of Hedvig as never having loved him. She did love him, and hence Ekdal's earlier happiness is actually rooted in this truth. Ekdal's ability to love is his redeeming feature, otherwise his self-deception makes him just a comic and pathetic man. That is the greatest danger in habits of untruthfulness that generate wholesale illusions. We can reach a point where we lose our ability to distinguish truth from falsehood in matters of moral importance.[44]

Finally, most of us seek happiness based on expressing our values with a certain degree of integrity. Failure to do so is illustrated in Eugene O'Neill's play *The Iceman Cometh*, which is also often misinterpreted as an unqualified endorsement of self-deception. Like Ibsen, O'Neill does portray self-deception as a compromise maneuver that, along with social lies, enables us to maintain self-esteem and a sense of community. Together with ample booze, self-deception sustains the down-and-out denizens of Harry Hope's bar, who look forward to Hickey's periodic visits. Self-deception also enables Hickey and his wife Evelyn to maintain their troubled marriage, although eventually at great cost. Their shared illusion that Hickey will stop his philandering fosters explosive hatred that culminates in Hickey's murdering Evelyn: "I even caught myself hating her for making me hate myself so much. There's a limit to the guilt you can feel and forgiveness and the pity you can take!"[45] Hickey deceives himself into thinking he murders Evelyn from loving motives, to end her suffering, but in a culminating scene he reveals, to himself as well as to his listeners, that hatred was his motive.

Larry, the most compassionate character in the play, articulates these ambiguities of self-deception. Early in the play he exclaims sardonically, "The lie of a pipe dream is what gives life to the whole misbegotten mad lot of us, drunk or sober."[46] Hickey's murder of Evelyn belies that generalization. So does the suicide by Parritt, who regards Larry as a father figure and who may in fact be Larry's son. Parritt is the most tortured character in the play because he had betrayed his mother by turning her in to the police. His suicide is presented as a glimmer of integrity in an otherwise shameful life.

In the end, reflecting on Parritt and Hickey alike, Larry looks with pity and compassion "at the two sides of everything"—especially self-deception.[47] Self-deception, like happiness, is morally complex, and often for the same reasons.

To conclude, happiness is a powerful motive, and what makes us happy reveals what we value and hence who we are. So does what we deceive ourselves about. Moreover, the happiness we seek is interwoven with our desires for meaning, authenticity, stability, and moral decency—at least when happiness is conceived as loving our lives and manifesting that love in ample enjoyments and a rich sense of meaning. Exploring self-deception in the pursuit of happiness, then, can be doubly illuminating—and doubly confusing. For good reason, both self-deception and the pursuit of happiness are discussed in terms of paradoxes.

6

SUFFERING IN HAPPY LIVES

> The crux of the matter is that all values are only factors making for happiness provided that a person feels attached to them and that every attachment holds an element of risk, since it brings not only joy, but also distress.[1]
>
> —Wladyslaw Tatarkiewicz

How is happiness related to suffering? Are they contraries, such that suffering just is episodic unhappiness and directly tends to make lives unhappy overall? Or is suffering compatible with happiness, even integral to it by deepening meaning and joy? If instances of both occur, as in my view they do, what makes the difference in particular instances? Answers to these questions help shape philosophical conceptions of happiness. They also have practical relevance to pursuing happiness, as I illustrate with examples from three health-specified categories of suffering: physical illness, neurotic suffering, and healthy suffering. Suffering, as intended here, includes both emotional distress and physical pain beyond mild discomfort. It is a state of consciousness rather than an event; "suffering a loss" in the stock market might or might not cause suffering as distress. I focus on our own suffering, but of course it can be in response to the suffering of people we care about.

PHYSICAL ILLNESS

Recall that "happiness" has several senses. In particular, it might refer to *episodic happiness*, which is any positive emotion or mood such as enjoyment, joy, cheerfulness, and humor; alternatively, it might refer to *global happiness*, which is a happy life or large segment thereof (that is, longer than brief moods). Suffering is usually experienced as the contrary of episodic happiness, but how does it bear on global happiness? The answer depends on how we understand happy lives. In my view, we are globally happy insofar as we love our lives, valuing them in ways manifested by high levels of enjoyment and a robust sense of meaning. Sometimes we experience suffering as a threat to enjoyment and meaning, and thereby a threat to happy lives. Other times we give suf-fering a meaning that at least opens the possibility of integrating it into a happy life.

In pursuing happiness we respond to suffering in two elemental ways, avoidance and acceptance. To avoid might mean to prevent, escape, or try to ameliorate suffering as undesirable and at odds with enjoyment. To accept might consist of grudging resigna-tion or graceful acquiescence to suffering as necessary and perhaps meaningful in ways potentially integrated into our happiness. We can also shift between avoidance and acceptance, for example by initially avoiding suffering (perhaps by drugging it away) and later accepting it and giving it meaning.

These responses to suffering are illustrated in comedienne Gilda Radner's memoir of struggling with ovarian cancer, *It's Always Something*. Radner experiences terror and depression as well as physical pain. At times her disorientation and loss of control threaten her self-worth and her very sense of who she is.[2] During these times she is deeply unhappy, and her suffering constitutes episodic unhappiness.[3]

Gradually laughter returns, and along with it the strength to continue writing her memoir, despite fear and physical discomfort: "I was laughing again, I was making jokes, I was going to bingo. I was enjoying my glorious life."[4] She still has days domi-nated by depression and anger when suffering just is unhappiness. But she puts those days in perspective as elements in an otherwise happy life. Moreover, her responses to suffering undergo a transformation as she learns to live each day as fully as possible: "I've learned what I can control is whether I am going to live a day in fear and depres-sion and panic, or whether I am going to attack the day and make it as good a day, as wonderful a day, as I can."[5] During these times she accepts suffering as part of a happy life. She comes to love her new life, radically changed as it is by illness, "taking the moment and making the best of it, without knowing what's going to happen next."[6]

Her ability to accept suffering depends in part on the disease itself, which at times overwhelms her body and mind. Movement toward acceptance also depends on her attitudes and effort, bolstered by support from her husband (actor Gene Wilder), close friends, and caring therapists. At times her suffering takes on a meaning that renders it compatible with a happy life. Meaning combines comprehension with value (positive or negative); it is comprehension in terms of values. One type of meaning is the imme-diate assessment of suffering as bad, undesired and undesirable, something to be escaped if possible. Another type is narrative meaning, whereby suffering is placed within a broader story that gives it positive (or negative) significance. In both instances, meaning is a subjective "sense of meaning" that might or might not be justified by true perceptions and sound values. It is always possible to stand back and assess whether an illness narrative is warranted or even coherent.[7]

Illness narratives are stories that place suffering and disease within wider frame-works, nonfiction stories that we tell ourselves and others. Arthur Frank distinguishes three types of narrative: chaos, restitution, and quest. Radner embraces each at different times. Chaos narratives understand illness as radically disruptive, largely senseless, and something to be contained rather than integrated into happy lives. Suffering is perceived as external to meaning—its opposite and obstacle. When her disease is most ravaging and her emotional resources weakest, Radner regards her situation as chaos. The only understanding to be had is that her suffering makes no sense; the only value to be assigned is disvalue. Such is the power of intense suffering to absorb our attention, destroying any sense of well-being.[8]

The other two types of illness narratives integrate suffering into meaningful and happy lives in different ways. Restitution narratives interpret sickness and suffering as challenges to be met in order to restore health. Here there is hope that sickness and suffering are temporary episodes within the broader trajectories of our lives. Radner sees her disease and her suffering in this way during and after her first successful round of chemotherapy. In contrast, quest narratives arise when there is no longer confidence of a return to complete health. The sickness might be accepted as chronic and as manageable rather than curable. Or hope might remain but a cure is perceived as uncertain, generating ambiguity and ambivalence. "Quest stories meet suffering head on; they accept illness and seek to use it" in pursuing meaning and insight.[9] Radner's book culminates in a quest narrative based on accepting the unlikelihood of fully restoring health.

A sense of meaning is necessary but not sufficient for happiness. Ample enjoyments are also necessary, where the standard for "ample" is highly personal. That includes the meaning given to suffering within restitution and quest narratives. Nevertheless, for most of us meaning is as important as enjoyment in happy lives, and sometimes meaning opens the way for enjoyment and joy.[10] To be sure, intense suffering excludes enjoyment and hence tends to eclipse episodic happiness, even though a sense of meaning might still be present. But global happiness is possible even in lives containing serious disease and disability.

As an illustration of disability, consider Reynolds Price's memoir, *A Whole New Life*. In his early fifties, Price is made paraplegic as the result of surgery to remove a twelve-inch malignant tumor inside his spinal cord. He reports, "I've led a mainly happy life. . . . And that claim covers all my years except for the actual eye of the storm . . . from the spring of 1984 till fall '88."[11] During that period suffering decimates his happiness. Gradually, biofeedback and hypnosis enable him to work and cope despite pain: "I'd grown essentially free from pain. Not free from its constant presence in my body—it roars on still, round the clock every day, in my back and legs and across my shoulders—but free from any real notice of it or concern for its presence."[12] Indeed, following his illness he becomes more prolific, publishing over a dozen novels and other books, while continuing his career as a professor.

We generally assume that good health is among the most important conditions for happiness, perhaps *the* most important. Yet, psychologists report that we greatly exaggerate how disease and injuries, even severe ones like paraplegia and quadriplegia, undermine happiness.[13] Although happiness plummets initially when we learn of severe health problems, most of us adjust and learn to cope. We have remarkable capacities to habituate to radically altered circumstances. We also have capacities to give suffering meaning within wider value perspectives linked to happiness, usually in retrospect but sometimes at the time we suffer. In turn, meaning opens possibilities for renewed enjoyment. In these ways, suffering is not merely encapsulated within happy lives but integrated into them.

NEUROTIC SUFFERING

The strongest predictor of unhappiness is neuroticism: the tendency to experience excessive and irrational negative emotions such as anxiety, fear, depression, hate, anger, and pessimism.[14] Neurotic suffering attacks happiness from every direction. It saps enjoyment and replaces it with chronic suffering. It erodes meaning, insofar as neurotic suffering makes no sense to us. It assaults confidence and hope that we can create a life we love. Nevertheless, neurotic suffering does not always eclipse happiness, as I illustrate with examples of depression, phobia, and addiction.

Depression has "overtaken anxiety as our presiding discontent."[15] Depression can be a healthy and rational experience, even a "window to the soul," when it is a normal feeling of dejection.[16] Yet depression easily becomes pathological, whether in the form of episodic crises (major depressive disorder), chronic states (dysthymia), or manic depression (bipolar disorder). Andrew Solomon describes the onset of his depression as follows:

> The first thing that goes is happiness. You cannot gain pleasure from anything. . . .
> But soon other emotions follow happiness into oblivion: sadness as you had known
> it, the sadness that seemed to have led you here; your sense of humor; your belief
> in and capacity for love. Your mind is leached until you seem dim-witted even to
> yourself. . . . Eventually, you are simply absent from yourself.[17]

Untreated, depression can destroy happiness and in extreme cases lead to suicide. Fortunately, most depression is treatable with medication and psychotherapy, and that is true of Solomon's. Although it remains a recurring threat, woven into his identity, he has learned to accept it and give it meaning. He describes his life as "vital, even when sad," a life whose course he does not "regret entirely," and he has even come to love who he is "in the wake of" the depression.[18] His suffering is integral to his happiness. Rather than mere gaps and holes in an otherwise happy life, it is integrated in the patterns of experience and meaning that constitute his happiness.

Pathological phobias provide a second set of examples. Phobias are anxiety disorders that can involve intense and recurrent episodes of terror and doom. Phobic attacks might be narrowly targeted and merely exaggerated versions of normal responses, such as heightened fear of public speaking. Alternatively, they might be wide ranging and less connected with normal responses, such as fear of open spaces.

Allen Shawn, the distinguished composer and pianist, suffers from multiple phobias, including agoraphobias focused on heights, open land, being on water and bridges, and also claustrophobia in response to plane rides, elevators, subways, theaters, and enclosed malls. The phobias are greatly restrictive. When severe panic attacks strike, he is immobilized, for example cowering in terror in the middle of an unfamiliar country field or city block. He turns down many invitations to social gatherings because of anticipatory anxiety over traveling to them, and in general his anxiety erodes pleasure and self-confidence. The title of his book, *Wish I Could Be There*, is inspired by Elfriede Jelinek's explanation of why she could not travel to Stockholm to accept her 2004 Nobel Prize in Literature: "I would like to attend the ceremony if I were able to. But unfortunately I'm ill with agoraphobia. I'm unable to be in crowds and I can't bear to be looked at."[19]

Shawn's life is not altogether unhappy, however. He has rewarding work, children he loves, and deep friendships. Fortunately for his career as a musician, he does not suffer from the most common phobia, performance anxiety and public speaking. Moreover, through reflection and research, he has managed to transform some of his phobias into a source of interest and meaning: "I prefer to believe that certain types of neuroticism are the inevitable accompaniments of characteristics that nourish the human organism as a whole.... Those who particularly notice what is worrisome or anticipate—even to their detriment—what will be painful may be just those who notice nuances of life others might neglect."[20]

A third set of examples are neurotic compulsions involving addictions, specifically substance dependency disorders. Whereas phobias are powerful fears that motivate avoidance, addictions are strong attractions. Often they come in clusters, such that ending one addiction leaves others intact. Caroline Knapp suffered from multiple addictions, including alcoholism, anorexia, bulimia, and smoking, the latter of which probably caused the lung cancer that killed her at age forty-two. Her memoir, *Drinking: A Love Story*, illustrates how an addiction can simultaneously contribute to happiness and undermine it. She began drinking alcohol as a teenager, increased drinking during college, and continued heavy drinking for two decades. She sought help by attending Alcoholics Anonymous after nearly causing a fatal accident while drunk.

As her title suggests, Knapp loved what alcohol did for her—heightening happy times, softening anxious ones, and resisting boredom and depression: "I loved the way drink made me feel, and I loved its special power of deflection, its ability to shift my focus away from my own awareness of self and onto something else, something less painful than my own feelings."[21] She was a "high-functioning alcoholic" who never let drinking detract from her excellence as a journalist; arguably she used drinking to increase her effectiveness at work by helping her relax during leisure. Yet alcoholism took its toll on happiness in other respects. She was deeply frustrated by her lack of control over her drinking and the behavior it produced. Her love life became an alcohol-blurred series of one-night stands and short-term relationships. Even worse, using alcohol to manipulate her emotions was stunting: "You lose your bearings, the ground underneath you begins to feel shaky. After a while you don't know even the most basic things about yourself—what you're afraid of, what feels good and bad, what you need in order to feel comforted and calm—because you've never given yourself a chance, a clear, sober chance, to find out."[22]

These examples of depression, phobia, and addiction illustrate how neuroticism can both erode happiness and yet be compatible with it in some instances and to some degree. Of course, the examples provide no basis for generalization about all mental disorders, which take myriad forms. Psychiatrists employ an expansive definition of mental disorders that includes virtually all psychological syndromes that cause significant distress, disability, or danger, omitting only those judged culturally acceptable. At one extreme, advanced Alzheimer's disease precludes happiness altogether by destroying the person. At another extreme, mild versions of Down syndrome tend to create exceptionally happy temperaments. Other disorders affect happiness depending on circumstances, individual attitudes, and individual brain chemistry. Even within the categories of mood disorders such as depression, anxiety disorders such as phobias, and substance-related disorders such as alcohol dependency, there are many variations in how suffering is external to happiness or can be coped with as part of happy lives.

Although happiness and mental disorders are related in complicated ways, some psychologists propose that the capacity for happiness is one of the defining criteria for positive mental health. Thus Karl Menninger defines "mental health as the adjustment of human beings to the world and to each other with a maximum of effectiveness and happiness."[23] Again, the most famous definition of positive health is promulgated by the World Health Organization: "Health is a state of complete physical, mental and social well-being, not merely the absence of disease or infirmity."[24] On most reckonings, complete mental well-being includes happiness.

Some time ago, however, Marie Jahoda qualified the proposal to make happiness a criterion for mental health. She noted that happiness, whether as episodic states or life satisfaction, can itself be healthy or irrational. A person whose happiness is completely unaffected by misfortune might not be a picture of mental health—although the issue is complicated, for example in the case of Stoics and Buddhists (not to mention the contribution of illusion to happiness, discussed in chapter 5). At the same time, an excessive disposition to unhappiness can be regarded as a mark of unhealthiness: "To regard the unhappy disposition as a criterion of poor mental health is one thing. To regard unhappiness, regardless of the circumstances in which it occurs, as such an indication is a different matter."[25] Nevertheless, as Jahoda granted, it is plausible to include among the criteria for positive mental health the capacity and tendency to experience some happiness under normal circumstances. "Normal" includes a wide range of circumstances containing manageable and meaningful suffering, and more recent studies suggest that each of us has a limited (and probably genetically shaped) range of degrees of happiness.[26]

HEALTHY SUFFERING

Healthy suffering, as intended here, means suffering linked to defensible values rather than physical dysfunction and mental disorder. In particular, it is suffering linked to meaning-giving forms of caring, for example caring about people, pets, work, and ideals. Healthy suffering has a better chance than neurotic suffering of being accepted and given a meaning in happy lives. After all, most meaningful activities and relationships carry risks of suffering, and it is no accident that "caring as commitment" and "cares as worries" are linked linguistically. Tatarkiewicz observes that suffering contributes to happiness in three ways: "firstly because *effort* is necessary to the attainment of anything at all, and effort may be connected with suffering. Secondly, suffering intensifies happiness by way of *contrast*. . . . Thirdly, suffering for many people is a *stimulating*, enlivening factor."[27] He also notes that joy and sadness are frequently inseparable, as the nineteenth-century Romantics emphasized.[28] Melancholy, yearning, anguish, and doubt, when experienced deeply and authentically, deserve the same affirmation as delight in beauty and sensual pleasure. The deepest joys are mixed with the possibility of sorrow and tragedy.

The extent to which meaningful suffering and other adversities contribute to happiness is an empirical matter. Common sense testifies that the contribution is substantial, and psychologists have confirmed this belief. At the same time they caution that "each life course is so unpredictable that we can never know whether a particular setback will be beneficial to a particular person in the long run."[29] A few illustrations will suffice.

Creative writers seem unusually prone to anguish. William Styron, for example, reports that "writing is hell," although he immediately adds, "I find that I'm simply the happiest, the placidest, *when* I'm writing."[30] Apparently, the hell comes when the writing is not going well, which is often, and happiness comes when he is writing in flow. In *The Courage to Write*, Ralph Keyes explores "the curious blend of terror and tedium that writers deal with every day," at every stage of writing, from starting a book, completing it, seeking publication, and dealing with criticism and neglect.[31] Why, then, keep at it? Because suffering is an unavoidable part of an activity they find deeply meaningful and, in many respects, deeply enjoyable. Indeed, writers who keep working learn to cope with fear and use it to their advantage, as a challenge that motivates.

Even more familiar, love can be a source of torment. Romantic love can be bitter-sweet, even when it is returned rather than unrequited. It can generate forms of ago-nized jealousy and self-doubt we didn't know we had in us. Marital love can be hell when partners are mismatched, but the good news from psychologists is that married people tend to be significantly happier on average. Psychologists report less welcome news about happiness in loving and raising children. On average, decreases in levels of happiness begin soon after having children and continue downward (with a slight blip upward when children start school) until about the time children leave home, after which happiness levels begin to rise back to their previous levels.[32] The explanation is that parenting is very hard work and relentless responsibility. Nevertheless, most par-ents report that children are among the greatest joys of their life. Perhaps the reports are due in part to faulty memories, but more likely parenting dramatically enriches the meaning parents derive from their lives, and that sense of meaning increases as the daily worries of parenting are left behind.

Death of loved ones strikes a devastating blow to happiness, although psychologists have discovered some consoling news: "70% to 80% report finding some positive aspect in their experience with loss."[33] Even when the death of a loved one is senseless, and in that regard permits no meaning as comprehensibility, the grieving process can yield meaning as significance. One way this occurs is through growth in character: we learn greater empathy and compassion. Another way is through cognitive shifts: we appreciate how fragile and dear life is. Yet another way is through strengthened rela-tionships with friends and family. In addition, grief itself is a meaningful experience in which we apprehend and appreciate a significant loss in our lives.[34]

For some tragedies, and the suffering accompanying them, neither explanation nor justification is possible—that is the understanding conveyed in spiritual reflection from *The Book of Job* to Harold Kushner's *When Bad Things Happen to Good People*. Yet it remains possible to place the tragedy within a wider circle of value. Job learns how to accept tragedy without having a theodicy to explain why God permits it, and while still loving and affirming the good in his life. Kushner, too, finds a way to accept the death of his son from progeria, the rapid-aging disease with which he was diagnosed when he was three. Kushner rejects conventional theodicy as wishful thinking, if not dis-honest sentimentality, clearing the way to continue loving his son, even in death, and sustaining that love as part of a life he values. In underscoring the possibility of giving suffering meaning, Kushner is not claiming that tragedy itself is a source of happiness. He finds joy not in the tragic death of his son, but in his enduring love for him.

PHILOSOPHICAL CONCEPTIONS

Philosophical conceptions of the relation between suffering and happiness are shaped in part by personal attitudes toward suffering and in part by broader perspectives on morality, happiness, and the world. *External views* emphasize avoidance: suffering is bad and external to happiness; suffering is episodic unhappiness that at most becomes encapsulated pockets within happy lives. *Internal views* emphasize meaning: suffering is integral to happy lives. *Mixed views* seek a balanced understanding of how suffering can be at odds with happiness and yet often be given a meaning that opens the possibility of being integrated into happy lives. Taken together, the preceding examples support a mixed view, or so I will suggest. They also remind us that much suffering is experienced as (episodic) unhappiness, and only subsequently put in perspective and given a meaning within the wider narratives of happy lives.

To begin with my definition, a happy life is one we love, valuing it in ways manifested by ample enjoyments and a robust sense of meaning that might or might not be rooted in justified values. Nevertheless, happiness itself is an important value. It is a self-interested value and, when it is not directly based on immorality, it is a moral value. Certainly it is prized by nearly all of us, and it guides and coordinates the pursuit of many other values. As such, happiness is an important dimension of good lives, in which it is interwoven with other values in generating enjoyment and a sense of meaning.

There are myriad types of good lives, and suffering can be meaningfully integrated into them in different ways. This pluralistic perspective is in tune with the pragmatism of John Dewey and William James. As a social progressive, Dewey is committed to alleviating suffering that undermines happiness and personal growth. At the same time, he underscores our capacities to give meaning to suffering, opening the way to integrating it into happy lives. He writes, "One may find happiness in the midst of annoyances; be contented and cheerful in spite of a succession of disagreeable experiences, if one has braveness and equanimity of soul. . . . Happiness is a matter of the disposition we actively bring with us to meet situations, the qualities of mind and heart with which we greet and interpret situations."[35] Moreover, happiness is promoted by meaningful pleasures that have a "harmonizing and expanding tendency"—a tendency to bring additional sources of enjoyment and meaning.[36]

James discusses meaningful suffering in his sympathetic critique of healthy-mindedness, which he defines as the tendency to see good in all things. He celebrates the optimism and positive thinking in the healthy-minded pursuit of happiness. He rejects one-sided healthy-mindedness, however, because it fails to take suffering seriously: "Systematic healthy-mindedness, failing as it does to accord to sorrow, pain, and death any positive and active attention whatever, is formally less complete than systems that try at least to include these elements in their scope."[37] A justified perspective must include meaningful suffering as a risk in love, commitment to justice, and other dimensions of good lives.[38]

Although my pluralistic views of good lives and happiness are broadly ecumenical, I have staked out a controversial view of how happiness and suffering are related. In concluding, I want to comment on four contrasting ways of relating happiness and suffering: (1) all suffering is intrinsically bad and external to happiness, which is the sole intrinsic good; (2) suffering is intrinsically bad and sufficiently ubiquitous to render happy lives impossible; (3) all suffering is good and ideally becomes integral to happy lives; (4) suffering is indifferent, neither inherently good nor bad.

First, the view that suffering is intrinsically bad is usually associated with philosophical hedonism: pleasure is the sole intrinsic good and suffering is the sole intrinsic bad. For example, Jeremy Bentham equates happiness with pleasure and the absence of pain. More carefully, episodic happiness is pleasure, and global happiness is the degree to which lives contain pleasure and lack suffering.[39] He allows that pain can be an instrumental good, for example when the pain of poverty motivates the pursuit of wealth in order to increase pleasure. Nevertheless, he thinks lives are happy only insofar as they maximize pleasure and minimize pain.

Hedonism is implausible as a general moral perspective. Not all pleasures are good, for example the pleasures of sadism. And pleasure is not the only good: Creative endeavors and loving relationships can be valuable even when they are not a steady source of pleasurable states of consciousness.[40] The present point, however, is that Bentham's value perspective as applied to suffering is implausible because it omits the importance of meaning in happiness. Moreover, his definition of happiness is implausible because it is quite possible for a life to be unhappy even though it contains ample enjoyment and even a predominance of pleasure over pain. It might not contain sufficient meaning to "add up" to a life we can love and value overall. Of course, what provides and promotes happiness is a highly personal matter, and some individuals might find meaning in a life of ample pleasure. Moreover, enjoyment and a sense of meaning are distinct aspects of happiness, and happy lives might emphasize one more than the other. Indeed, enjoyment and meaning are sometimes at odds or in tension, once again as in love and creative endeavors.

Second, happiness skeptics regard suffering as intrinsically bad and so ubiquitous that it renders happy lives impossible. Arthur Schopenhauer contends that lasting happiness is impossible because suffering is ubiquitous and always bad. He portrays the satisfaction of desire as a source of boredom and disillusionment; in fact, it is very often quite satisfying! He even portrays desire itself as suffering; in fact, it is often pleasurable. And he uses an implausible standard for "true" happiness: the "permanent satisfaction of the tormenting desires or cares that constantly breed new ones"—that sounds like a recipe for death, not happiness.[41]

Schopenhauer does acknowledge the possibility of enjoyment-creating meaning through music and the other arts, and occasionally through philosophy and love. Indeed, enjoyment and meaning tend to be mutually supportive, far more than they conflict, with meaning enriching enjoyment and enjoyment enriching meaning. Perhaps we must grant Ecclesiastes that "in much wisdom is much grief: and he that increaseth knowledge increaseth sorrow."[42] But we should immediately add that meaning-giving knowledge is also a source of enjoyment and joy. The complex interactions of suffering, enjoyment, and meaning were reflected in the examples of physical illness, neuroticism, and creative endeavors. Those discussions support a cautious optimism that much suffering can be given a positive meaning, even if some cannot. Likewise, some suffering is a direct threat to happiness, and some is only a challenge to find meaning in suffering. Much depends on the nature of the suffering, and much depends on our attitudes.

A third view is that all suffering is good insofar as it becomes part of happy lives, which ideally it should. This view is usually set forth in connection with normative definitions of "true happiness." For example, Friedrich Nietzsche offers a normative definition of happiness that celebrates the creative will to power: "What is happiness?—The feeling that power is growing, that some resistance has been overcome."[43] A healthy will to power is shown in vitality, self-mastery, and self-love, all of which are compatible with much suffering. Indeed, overcoming resistance to our passions typically requires suffering, and hence suffering is integral to creativity and to the true happiness made possible by creativity: "That the creator may be, suffering is needed."[44] Suffering is the twin of happiness, which grows together with it.[45] We are not happy despite suffering, but in part because of it. "What actually arouses indignation against suffering is not suffering in itself, but rather the senselessness of suffering."[46] The decisive test for whether we are living creatively is the deep love of life (*amor fati*) shown in a willingness to relive our lives just as they are over and over again (eternal recurrence).

As Bernard Reginster clarifies, in valuing suffering for its own sake Nietzsche does not value it "by itself, but only as an ingredient of the good," which for him consists in creative struggle that requires overcoming challenges that include suffering (frustration, pain).[47] Reginster points out that Nietzsche's ideal is extraordinarily demanding. Some suffering is so great that it crushes even the most creative spirits, and for ordinary people (about whom Nietzsche cares little) even universal tragedies such as death and disability can be crushing. Furthermore, Nietzsche's indifference toward if not delight in the suffering of common humanity is misanthropic. Even his attitude toward his disciples is something less than humane: "To those human beings who are of any concern to me I wish suffering, desolation, sickness, ill-treatment, indignities . . .: I have no pity for them, because I wish them the only thing that can prove today whether one is worth anything or not—that one endures."[48]

In contrast with Nietzsche's atheism, although in tune with his attempt to yoke all suffering to "true happiness," religious-oriented definitions of happiness are invariably normative, building in both moral and spiritual attitudes about true happiness. As tailored to particular faiths, these definitions are typically attached to theodicies that find value in all suffering, at least within redemptive frameworks. Such views can be profound, but they also run the risk becoming sentimental and even callous by romanticizing suffering, as Voltaire satirizes in *Candide*. Deal Hudson, a Catholic, reminds us that Christian love has often been abused: "To say 'Blessed are the poor' (Luke 6.20) outside the theological context of grace and repentance is to state a maxim with cruel social implications."[49]

Hudson holds a mixed view of suffering that avoids sentimentality. Much, though not all, suffering can be given a meaning and integrated into happy lives. "While we know from experience that suffering may lead to God, we should also remember that it leads to despair and cynicism: suffering can break and cripple as well as redeem. There is no way to say in advance what will cripple, any more than we can predict what will redeem."[50] With a keen sense of tragedy, Hudson highlights the potential for religion to give meaning and thereby contribute to happiness. I disagree, however, with his insistence that subjective definitions of happiness are illegitimate. He believes that all subjective conceptions of happiness reflect the current cultural debacle in which skepticism about objective moral values abounds, what he calls an ethics of "well-feeling" rather than of genuine "well-being." He claims that "the failure to appreciate the role of pain and suffering in the formation and maintenance of a happy life has led, in part, to the emergence of well-feeling" as the dominant cultural motif.[51] In my view, we do better to begin with the now predominant understanding of happiness as subjective, and then relate it to the other values characterizing good lives.

A fourth view is that pain is indifferent, neither inherently good nor bad, and as such is wholly external to "true happiness." Especially with regard to physical pain, this is the view of the Stoics. Epictetus, for example, emphasizes that the causes and meaning of suffering depend significantly on what we value: "What upsets people is not things themselves but their judgments about the things. For example, death is nothing dreadful . . . but instead the judgment about death that it is dreadful—*that* is what is dreadful."[52] Physical pain is not automatically a source of unhappiness; it just feels a certain way—it hurts. Some people are happy despite great suffering, and others are unhappy in response to minor annoyances. Ultimately, we suffer not because of bad things per se but because of our own attitudes: If we learn to avoid pains that are avoidable, and to be resigned and indifferent to pains that are unavoidable, we will achieve a tranquility that makes us invulnerable to suffering: "Do not seek to have events happen as you want them to, but instead want them to happen as they do happen, and your life will go well."[53]

Just as physical pain is not inherently bad, pleasure is not intrinsically good, for it too is filtered through more complex value judgments. Epictetus understands happiness normatively, as the satisfaction of rational, healthy desires based on the exercise of virtue. In this way, happiness is "objective" in two ways: it involves rational desires that connect with the objective, real, world; it also involves objectively justified moral values—the exercise of genuine virtue. Thus Epictetus begins with the very useful reminder that "some things are up to us and some are not up to us."[54] Virtue implies self-control in matters that are up to us, acceptance and resignation in matters that are not up to us, and practical wisdom in discerning the difference.[55]

So far so good, and many of Epictetus's views have influenced cognitive-behavioral therapies for depression, anxiety disorders, and addictions.[56] But Epictetus adds a particular value judgment that celebrates serenity, especially virtue-linked serenity, as a singular good. In his view, reason and virtue imply a kind of radical self-control aimed at emotional invulnerability. As an exclusive strategy, this self-control would greatly diminish life for most of us. The Stoics enjoin us not to love to the point where we grieve at the loss of the beloved, to avoid creative struggles and contests where the victory is not entirely up to us (unless we accept failure peacefully). This self-control ensures tranquility by barricading the self against catastrophes and the deeply painful losses in love, hopeful striving, and reasonable risk taking.[57] In doing so, it threatens as well the goods made possible through those creative activities.

To conclude, external views emphasize how suffering threatens happiness, and in doing so they highlight the importance of enjoyment in the pursuit of happiness. Nevertheless, they neglect meaning, usually by conceiving of happiness entirely in terms of pleasurable mental states such as pleasure and tranquility. Internal views draw attention to how meaningful suffering can deepen happiness, and how the pursuit of happiness is fused with the quest for meaning. Nevertheless, they run the risk of romanticizing suffering and eclipsing the awareness of tragedy. A more plausible mixed view takes account of how suffering can be a threat to happiness and yet can often be given a meaning that at least opens the possibility of integrating it into happy lives.

7

PARADOXES OF HAPPINESS

Happiness is a reward that comes to those who have not looked for it.[1]
—Alain

To get happiness, forget about it. This adage is known as *the* paradox of happiness, but it contains several paradoxes, depending on which aspects of pursuing happiness are highlighted. Without claiming completeness, I distinguish a dozen aspects, grouped under the headings of aim, success, freedom, and attitude. With one exception, the paradoxes are not logical conundrums, and most of them are not even seeming contradictions. Instead, they identify empirical incongruities and ironies that contradict widely held beliefs about the sources of and pathways to happiness. The paradoxes convey insights into the complexity in pursuing happiness in good lives, but in doing so they often use hyperbole to highlight one-sided truths.

How we define happiness influences how we understand the paradoxes. My interest is happiness as subjective well-being, understood as loving our lives and valuing them in ways shown by high levels of enjoyment and a rich sense of meaning. Accordingly, I set aside normative conceptions of happiness as embodying virtue, for these conceptions tend to make the paradoxes true by definition: for example, "pursue goodness rather than happiness and you will find goodness-defined happiness." At the same time, I am interested in how the paradoxes link happiness as subjective well-being to moral and other justified values in good lives.

AIM: PLEASURE, SELF-INTEREST, GUIDANCE, AND CONSTITUENTS

Paradoxes of aim assert that pursuing happiness directly, deliberately, and devotedly is self-defeating or otherwise problematic. Instead, we should concentrate on other goals, activities, and relationships that (a) we find meaningful or (b) are meaningful in terms of justified values. The difference between (a) and (b)—between a subjective sense of meaning and a justified sense of meaning—indicates a schism in how these and other paradoxes of happiness are understood. In this chapter, however, I will usually set aside the distinction in order to focus on the main thrust of the paradoxes, which is that happiness should be pursued indirectly. Roughly stated, the most effective strategy in pursuing happiness is to avoid preoccupation with it and instead to pursue meaningful activities and relationships; then, with any luck, happiness will come as a by-product. This indirectness suggests that the pursuit of happiness should be rethought as *the happiness of pursuit*—the happiness found in pursuing other goals that indirectly yield happiness.[2] The indirectness seems puzzling because usually we assume that attentive effort is needed in pursuing important goals, and surely happiness is such a goal. Paradoxes of aim have different foci, the most famous of which is pleasure.

1. Paradox of Hedonism

According to the paradox of hedonism, pursuing pleasure directly is self-defeating. It results in less pleasure and meaning than does a strategy of seeking meaningful endeavors and relationships for their sake, letting pleasure and happiness come indirectly. John Stuart Mill states the paradox in reporting on his recovery from a major psychological depression during his early twenties:

> I never, indeed, wavered in the conviction that happiness is the test of all rules of conduct, and the end of life. But I now thought that this end was only to be attained by not making it the direct end. Those only are happy (I thought) who have their minds fixed on some object other than their own happiness; on the happiness of others, on the improvement of mankind, even on some art or pursuit, followed not as a means, but as itself an ideal end. Aiming thus at something else, they find happiness by the way.[3]

Throughout his writings Mill conflates pleasure with happiness as a long-term state of persons and lives. Only a few pages after stipulating that "by happiness is intended pleasure," he defines happiness as a "manner of existence" that is "exempt as far as possible from pain, and as rich as possible in enjoyments, both in point of quantity and quality."[4] Either way, Mill construes the paradox of happiness as the paradox of hedonism. It is self-defeating, he contends, to fixate on our pleasure. That fixation erodes pleasure, either by making it appear less grand than we had hoped for, so that it is "felt to be insufficient," or by distancing ourselves from the full and immediate experience of it, whether by "putting it to flight by fatal questioning" or by "forestalling it in imagination."[5] In general, freeing ourselves from preoccupation with our own pleasures increases the odds of finding happiness.

[P]aradoxical as the assertion may be, the conscious ability to do without happiness gives the best prospect of realizing such happiness as is attainable. For nothing except that consciousness can raise a person above the chances of life by making him feel that, let fate and fortune do their worst, they have not the power to subdue him; which, once felt, frees him from excess of anxiety concerning the evils of life and enables him, like many a Stoic in the worst times of the Roman Empire, to cultivate in tranquility the sources of satisfaction accessible to him.[6]

The paradox of hedonism contains an important truth. The most enriching enjoyments are tied to activities and relationships valued for themselves, that is, for their perceived intrinsic worth. They yield pleasures because we first desire them and find them desirable (worthy of being desired), for reasons beyond their pleasure-producing aspect.[7] Psychologically, this truth was important for Mill in grappling with his depression, a mental state that tends to involve self-preoccupation. Philosophically, it plays a role in his development of utilitarianism, specifically in his conception of the good—the good that is to be maximized, considering everyone affected by our actions impartially.

Mill never works out a fully coherent version of utilitarianism, and this failure bears on his treatment of the paradox of hedonism. Thus he insists that we should pursue love, friendship, and intellectual activities as "ideal ends" for their own sake, rather than simply for the pleasures or further good consequences they produce. Yet his utilitarian theory reduces all values, and hence all "ideal ends," to pleasures. Famously, he stresses higher pleasures, but tacitly he understands them as linked to activities and relationships that are valuable for reasons in addition to the pleasure they produce. The result is something of a muddle that blurs his analysis of the paradox of hedonism. It remains paradoxical indeed to say that pleasures are the only intrinsic goods while denying that we should focus on them as "ideal ends" in pursuing happy lives. Mill would have benefited from more consistently carrying his psychological insights about the paradox of happiness into his ethical theory.

Henry Sidgwick invokes the paradox of hedonism in arguing against egoistic hedonism, that is, the version of ethical egoism that says we ought always and only to maximize our own pleasures. Egoistic hedonism is self-defeating because it enjoins pleasure seeking and yet results in diminished pleasure. Happiness, understood as "the greatest attainable surplus of pleasure over pain," cannot be pursued successfully by concentrating on our pleasures because the fullest and richest pleasures come from being fully stimulated by people, events, and things in the world that "must be temporarily predominant and absorbing."[8] Sidgwick states the paradox more cautiously than Mill, and he understands it as advising us to limit rather than to abandon the direct pursuit of happiness: "Happiness is likely to be better attained if the extent to which we set ourselves consciously to aim at it be carefully restricted."[9] In this way, Sidgwick provides an important corrective to Mill by affirming that it is appropriate to pursue happiness as one of our direct aims so long as we avoid narrow preoccupation with it, limiting reflection on our happiness to periodic reviews of how well our lives are going.

2. Paradox of Self-Interest

A second paradox widens the focus from pleasures to self-interest, that is, to our overall good, which includes happiness and much more (for example, economic security and good health). According to the paradox of self-interest, aiming directly and exclusively at self-interest is self-defeating. It fosters self-absorption, self-indulgence, and selfishness. By doing so, it constricts the range and depth of gratifications available when we pursue interests in other people and endeavors that we regard as valuable in their own right—and that actually are valuable in their own right. The paradox of self-interest is frequently voiced from the pulpit, and Bishop Joseph Butler examined it with psychological acuity in his eighteenth-century sermons: "How much soever a paradox it may appear, it is certainly true, that even from self-love we should endeavour to get over all inordinate regard to, and consideration of ourselves."[10] Secular humanists also make the theme prominent. Thus George Orwell writes that people "can only be happy when they do not assume that the object of life is happiness."[11] Again, Bertrand Russell makes the theme salient in *Conquest of Happiness*. He presents the theme as a momentous discovery in moving away from his anxious self-preoccupation during youth into his richly satisfying adulthood. Self-absorption, including preoccupation with our own happiness, destroys meaningful and happy personal relationships. Equally bad, it causes boredom by blocking the development of deep interests and zestful pursuits. Accordingly, "the secret of happiness is this: let your interests be as wide as possible, and let your reactions to the things and persons that interest you be as far as possible friendly rather than hostile."[12]

For their part, classical economists and psychologists tended to be oblivious to the paradox of self-interest because they assumed psychological egoism, the view that humans are only motivated by (direct concern for) self-interest. Today, renegade economists appreciate personal commitments to the well-being of others that restrict narrow self-interest and even require personal sacrifice. For example, Robert Frank argues that we evolved with capacities for love and loyalty because of "a simple paradox, namely, that in many situations the conscious pursuit of self-interest is incompatible with its attainment."[13] Likewise, positive psychologists explore how other-directed virtues contribute to our enlightened self-interest and our happiness, as discussed in chapter 3. Earlier the humanistic psychologist Abraham Maslow proclaimed that "people who seek self-actualization directly, selfishly, personally, dichotomized away from mission in life, i.e., as a form of private and subjective salvation, don't, in fact, achieve it."[14]

Raymond Belliotti would have us go further in abandoning happiness as central to self-interest. In his view, happiness is overrated. We should not and "do not pursue happiness directly. We pursue worthwhile, meaningful, valuable, exemplary lives. If we are reasonably successful in that quest, happiness may follow. If not, we can still take pride and derive satisfaction from living well."[15] Belliotti overstates both the facts about motivation and the values worth pursuing. Most of us do actively seek happiness, typically in and through activities we find meaningful, and at least part of what makes those activities meaningful is their contribution to our happiness. Indeed, the notion of meaningful lives that bring no happiness whatsoever is problematic. Happiness and meaning are distinct but interwoven in ways that make it impossible to pry them apart as sources of motivation in good lives.

Properly understood, the paradox of self-interest challenges *excessive* and *exclusive* self-seeking. As such, it is an important corrective to self-preoccupation, but it is not a basis for rejecting all direct regard for happiness in conjunction with other values. Periodic self-reflection about whether we are sufficiently happy is entirely compatible with maintaining genuine interests in the world and zestful pursuits. Indeed, it seems likely to promote those interests and pursuits by ensuring they are meaningful and fulfilling.

The point is a general one about pursuing each dimension of self-interest. Thus entrepreneurs speak of a paradox of wealth: If you are preoccupied with maximizing your wealth you will fail, for that self-absorption deflects you from what is essential in producing wealth.[16] Instead, cultivate passions about particular goods and services that other people want and you take pride in; then wealth is more likely to follow. That outward focus is fully compatible, of course, with periodically monitoring our wealth. Likewise, becoming obsessed with our health can make us (unhealthy) hypochondriacs, but we should periodically monitor our health. Even the preoccupation with our character can lead to spiritual egotism, as John Dewey calls it, which deflects us from humane concern for others.[17] In general, to effectively pursue any aspect of our self-interest we should avoid becoming overly preoccupied with it, for doing so undermines broader commitments around values that impact others as well as ourselves. But of course we should have due regard for our self-interest and periodically attend to it. Indeed, our interest in paradoxes of self-interest presupposes we have direct interest in our well-being.

3. Paradox of Guidance

The paradox of guidance shifts from motivation to guidance. According to it, usually we lack a clear conception of what will make us happy, and hence in pursuing happiness directly we are pursuing a will-o'-the-wisp. There are too many complexities in the world interacting in too many unpredictable ways with individual psychology. The more we are deluded into thinking we know how to become happy, the more we suffer disappointments as we act on our delusions.

Immanuel Kant formulates the paradox in terms of practical reason: "The more a cultivated reason purposely occupies itself with the enjoyment of life and with happiness, so much the further does one get away from true satisfaction."[18] In general, "one can form no determinate and sure concept of the sum of satisfaction of all inclinations under the name of happiness."[19] Kant defines happiness in several ways, sometimes as uninterrupted pleasure, sometimes as satisfaction of all our desires (which is different, for not all satisfied desires yield pleasure—witness buyers' remorse), and sometimes as both.[20] In any case, his point is that usually we do not have an accurate idea of what will make us happy. Seeking riches can lead to troubles and anxiety; seeking knowledge can result in pained awareness of tragedy; seeking long life can lead to ill health in advanced age; and so forth.[21] Our aim in exercising practical reason should be to lead moral lives, and then happiness will hopefully come along the way, whether in this life or in some spiritual life after death.

Matters are not as bleak as Kant would have it, at least not today. Studies show that most people are mostly happy.[22] Undoubtedly our practical reason is highly fallible, but it serves us reasonably well in pursuing happiness, especially given our substantial capacities to adjust to disappointments. Kant gives a one-sided analysis of reason's role in seeking happiness because he has a philosophical ax to grind. He seeks to establish that the primary role of practical reason is to discern universal and absolute (exceptionless) moral duties, which in his view have little direct connection to happiness. Yet, contrary to Kant, the limitations of reason do not render the pursuit of happiness futile, and whatever flaws reason has carry over to morality. Few ethicists share Kant's belief that there are many absolute duties that reason can discern. Moreover, our practical reason is as flawed in discerning and integrating our various duties as it is in pursuing happiness. Whether in pursuing morality or happiness, we must make do with our flawed reasoning capacities.

Inspired by Kant, but deepening his skepticism, Nicholas White locates the paradox of guidance in the very concept of happiness, rather than the limitations of our practical reason. The concept of happiness, he says, is essentially the notion that there is a best or right way to harmonize our myriad desires, interests, aims, and values.[23] Each of us repeatedly faces conflicting aims, and the concept of happiness arises from the expectation of finding a guide about how best to harmonize our wants, akin to how the picture in a puzzle guides us in fitting together its pieces. This expectation is futile, and a unifying picture for an entire life is a chimera. Coordinating our desires, interests, and values is a matter of ongoing contextual decision making rather than applying a general guide to our lives overall.

In some passages, White seems to recommend abandoning the concept of happiness altogether because it is based on the "unrealizable hope for some kind of coherence of aims."[24] Surely that recommendation is unwise. Coherence is often possible through reasoned attempts to live good lives. Moreover, the fact that many of us lack clear and reliable *conceptions* of what will make us happy does not mean we lack a reasonably clear *concept* of happiness. That concept is subjective well-being, which I understand as loving our lives, valuing them in ways manifested by predominant patterns of enjoyment and meaning. I agree that coherence must emerge within practical situations rather than from grand schemas, but I do not share White's skepticism about finding sufficient coherence to make happiness possible.

4. Paradox of Constituents

Although most paradoxes of happiness make empirical claims, one paradox expresses a logical truth. According to the paradox of constituents, it is a matter of logic that happiness cannot be pursued as an exclusive end, for happy lives are comprised of other things that must be sought for their own sake. Elizabeth Telfer provides a charming statement of the paradox: "In the case of most ends, the means are logically separable from them: thus if I play the piano [solely] to earn money, it makes sense for a fairy godmother to say, 'Forget about the playing; here is the money.' But this does not apply to happiness. If I marry in order to be happy it would not make sense for her to say, 'Forget about the marriage, here is the happiness,' since the happiness I sought (the argument goes) was by definition happiness in marriage."[25] Because the marriage is a constituent of this individual's happiness, her happiness cannot be pursued as an independent end.

By underscoring that happiness is a response to meaningful and enjoyable activities and relationships, the paradox of constituents conveys an insight bearing on all the paradoxes of happiness. Nevertheless, as Telfer points out, the paradox does not provide a basis for denying that happiness can itself be pursued as an end in itself. For the activities and relationships that produce happiness are contingent matters for each of us, not matters of logic. It is intelligible for persons, young or old, to say they want to be happy even though they have yet to discover which activities and relationships will make that possible. And having discovered those activities and relationships, they can pursue them (in part) as means to (the sought-after end of) happiness.

To sum up, most paradoxes of aim convey insights that are half-truths. Yes, we should avoid excessive self-preoccupation and instead focus outwardly on people and projects, but in doing so we should not disregard our happiness, for it remains one important dimension of good lives, interwoven with moral and other values. Indeed, we do well to periodically review our primary endeavors and relationships to appreciate their meaning and to assess whether they are making us happy.[26] We do and should consider our happiness in making major life decisions, for example about whether to pursue a job offer or to marry a particular person. And even in situations where we must sacrifice some of our happiness for higher ideals, we do well to be clear that we are indeed sacrificing something of great value in order to achieve something of even greater value.

SUCCESS: GETTING, MONEY, AND STATUS

Shifting the focus from aims and intentions to results, *paradoxes of success* challenge widely held beliefs that obtaining certain things will automatically make us happy. The paradoxes caution against equating happiness with specific results, as distinct from the process of pursuing them. In one colloquial sense, success refers to obtaining material goods such as money and consumer products, as well as social status and other external rewards, by contrast with intrinsic satisfactions from what we believe to be valuable endeavors and relationships.[27] In another sense, with which I begin, success simply means getting what we seek.

5. Paradox of Getting

The paradox of getting is that happiness has less to do with acquiring what we seek and more to do with the journey in seeking it. By their very nature, desires promise pleasure (satisfaction) when they are fulfilled (satisfied), and we have a deep-seated tendency to think that happiness will come from reaching our goals. Yet there is no tight correlation between satisfying our desires and being satisfied with what we get. Hence the saying: Be careful what you wish for, lest you get it.

The paradox of getting conveys several insights. On the one hand, happiness has more to do with liking what we already have than with constantly getting more. On the other hand, happiness often comes more from making progress toward meaningful goals than from success in achieving them.[28] Sometimes, "anticipation is better than realization."[29] Even when realization brings satisfaction, the satisfaction is short lived, as we adjust and take for granted what we gained. Moreover, experiencing progress can promote happiness even when it is accompanied by feelings of frustration due to temporary setbacks and suffering, periodic exhaustion, and temporary depression. The experiences that most directly promote happiness come from what Mihaly Csikszentmihalyi calls "flow": engaging in valued activities that challenge and engage us, while providing immediate and positive feedback, whether or not episodic pleasures are involved.[30]

In addition to the enjoyments or gratifications obtained from flow activities, myriad everyday pleasures contribute to happiness, especially when we learn to savor them (by concentrating on them in ways at odds with the paradox of hedonism). So do long-term projects and periodic accomplishments. The pursuit of happiness, and more generally the pursuit of self-fulfillment, must often proceed by "crooked paths," to borrow Nietzsche's expression.[31]

6. Paradox of Money

The paradox of money is that money does not bring or buy happiness, contrary to the widespread illusion that it does. Insofar as money is pursued in the belief it will make us happy, the paradox of money is a special instance of the paradox of getting. But it warrants special mention in challenging our tendency to regard money as a general solution to our problems. Much money simply feeds the "hedonic treadmill": the more we buy and have, the more we want.[32] In macroeconomic terms, the paradox of money has been called the paradox of (economic) progress: Average incomes in western democracies have doubled over the last fifty years, but levels of happiness have remained virtually unchanged. Even after adjusting for rising costs, there is a genuinely surprising failure of increased wealth to increase happiness in the way we tend to expect.[33]

The paradox of money expresses only a partial truth, albeit an important one.[34] Money does contribute to happiness, although less than we usually believe. It increases happiness dramatically by moving individuals out of poverty, but thereafter it contributes little and haphazardly to happiness. Part of the explanation for this surprising result is that we tend to misuse money once we have it, becoming caught up in endless routines of getting and spending, rather than building wealth to increase freedom and peace of mind.[35] Also, we are made unhappy by envy and by feeling we are not making what we deserve compared to others, which brings us to the next paradox.

7. Paradox of Status

According to the paradox of status, our prestige-oriented comparisons with others do not promote happiness, even though we constantly act as if they do. It is not enough to have a comfortable life; we need to keep up with the Joneses and then surpass them. Insofar as having money is as much about status as survival, at least once beyond poverty, it is not surprising that the paradoxes of status and money overlap. When a group was asked whether they would prefer an income of $50,000 when others earned $25,000, or an income of $100,000 when others earned $200,000, they chose the $50,000—half of what they could have had, but preferable to half of what others have.[36]

Envy and snobbery partly explain this preference for lower amounts of money over lower status, but the primary explanation seems to be our need for self-esteem and our tendency to attach self-esteem to social status. Money, luxury cars, large houses, expensive jewelry, and virtually any conspicuous consumption that favorably sets us apart from others are symbols of personal significance.[37] Yet, insofar as we remain preoccupied with assessing well-being in terms of these shifting standards, driven by status anxiety, we place our happiness and perhaps our other values at risk.[38]

FREEDOM: SUBMISSION, CHOICE, AND SELF-CONFLICT

Paradoxes of freedom assert that (happiness-promoting) freedom is won by surrendering or limiting it. Like paradoxes of aim, the freedom paradoxes suggest we should not pursue happiness directly, but this time the emphasis is on liberation and choice. Usually we assume that our happiness increases as we increase our freedom, choices, and liberation from conflicting desires; the paradoxes of freedom call this assumption into question.

8. Paradox of Submission

The paradox of submission is that surrender can liberate us in ways contributing to happiness. We feel happily liberated not by maintaining complete control (or what we think of as complete control) but instead through loyalty to ideals, standards, and meaningful causes and relationships, as well as to experiencing ourselves as part of wider realities.[39] Harry Frankfurt asks, "How are we to understand the paradox that a person may be enhanced and liberated through being seized, made captive, and overcome? Why is it that we find ourselves to be most fully realized, and consider that we are at our best, when—through reason or through love—we have lost or escaped from ourselves?"[40] He answers that our very identity is shaped by deep caring for people and things beyond ourselves, and that deep caring has a selfless element, by contrast with our usual self-preoccupation. This selflessness contributes to a sense of meaning and self-respect and thereby indirectly promotes happiness. We are liberated by choosing freely and decisively to close some options, as for example when spouses promise to love, honor, and cherish each other, forsaking (adultery with) all others. Deep caring reshapes our will and identity, establishing a "volitional necessity" that makes it difficult or even impossible to abandon who and what we love. Happiness, as well as self-realization, comes from caring relationships and submission to standards and ideals of excellence.

The paradox of submission is also a familiar theme in religious conceptions of happiness that enjoin submission to a deity. The idea is also central in twelve-step recovery programs such as Alcoholics Anonymous that enjoin admitting powerlessness over our addictions and submitting to a "higher power" so as to become empowered to overcome the addictions. William James expresses the idea in nonsectarian terms: "Give up the feeling of responsibility, let go your hold, resign the care of your destiny to higher powers, be genuinely indifferent as to what becomes of it all, and you will find not only that you gain a perfect inward relief, but often also, in addition, the particular goods you sincerely thought you were renouncing."[41] Willa Cather memorably conveys a related experience in *My Antonia*: "I was entirely happy. Perhaps we feel like that

when we die and become a part of something entire, whether it is sun and air, or goodness and knowledge. At any rate, that is happiness; to be dissolved into something
complete and great."[42]

Although the paradox of submission makes a psychological claim, then, it is generally tied to normative claims about which loyalties, submissions, and sources of
meaning are desirable. The distinction is important and bears on all the paradoxes
of happiness in thinking about fully good lives. A sense of meaning is one thing; a
justified sense of meaning produced by valid ideals is something else. Terrorists provide a painful reminder of the difference. For this reason, the paradox of submission
expresses a partial and dangerous truth—a truth easily misunderstood and abused.
In general, the value of happiness increases insofar as it is interwoven with other
justified values.

Frankfurt tends to slide over the distinction between desirable and undesirable
loyalties, whereas Alan Gewirth highlights it. As noted in chapter 2, he distinguishes
two conceptions of self-fulfillment: satisfaction of our most strongly motivating
desires (aspiration-fulfillment) and effective pursuit of what is most worthwhile in us
(capacity-fulfillment). Corresponding, there are two conceptions of happiness:
satisfaction of our strongest desires (aspiration-happiness) and normative conceptions of developing what is best in us (capacity-happiness). The two go together ideally, but not always in practice. In some cases, "You may be made very unhappy if you
develop your highest talents; for example, a person who by intense concentration
and practice becomes a superb violinist may come to feel very discontented with his
life."[43] Alluding to the paradoxes of aim, Gewirth points out that aspiration-fulfillment and happiness are often best pursued indirectly by focusing on valuable activities and relationships. Yet, in light of his violinist example—suppose the violinist
turns to alcohol and abandons his talents altogether—Gewirth might have added
that capacity-fulfillment sometimes requires the pursuit of aspiration-happiness. In
any case, the two are interwoven and should be pursued together in good lives.

9. Paradox of Choice

The paradox of choice, as Barry Schwartz calls it, is that multiplying the number of
options sometimes lessens happiness, contrary to the belief that it increases our autonomy and thereby our happiness. In one study, 65 percent of people claim that if they
had cancer they would want to make their own treatment choices, yet only 12 percent
of people who actually got cancer wanted to make their treatment decisions.[44] As this
example suggests, too many choices can be burdensome because they place responsibility (and potentially blame) on us, but also because evaluating options takes time and
adds complexity and confusion. Thus President Bush's 2005 Medicare drug benefit

program gave senior citizens as many as sixty options, thereby initially causing confusion, anxiety, and "choice overload." In addition, the more desirable choices we have, the greater the "opportunity costs," such as regrets in having to turn down attractive options in settling for others. Again, having the options to return purchased goods would seemingly increase our happiness in making choices. Yet Schwartz marshals evidence that we are more satisfied when our decisions are not so easily reversible, probably because reversible decisions keep us anxiously alert to better options we have missed, and also because it distracts us from pursuing the valuable possibilities inherent in the choices we have made. Of greater consequence, the paradox of submission overlaps with the paradox of choice: When we commit ourselves in a spirit of permanence, as in getting married, we tend to be happier than if we feel free to walk away at any time.

In practice, the paradox of choice applies most directly to "maximizers," who habitually learn about and assess all options in order to make the very best choice. "Satisficers," in contrast, quickly locate a satisfactory choice and then act. Most of us do well to be maximizers in only the most important areas of our lives. In everyday choices such as buying food and clothes, we tend to be happier when we settle for what is good enough rather than worrying about the ideal choice.[45] The goal is to find the proverbial joys of a simple life while grappling with sufficient options to avoid boredom.

10. Paradox of Self-Conflict

Conflicting desires are so commonplace that most of them provide no basis for speaking of paradox, rather than simply dilemma, ambivalence, and indecision—unless we return to Kant and White's paradox of guidance. Yet some conflicts are so ubiquitous and intense that they deserve to be called paradoxes of happiness centered on self-conflicts. For example, we want to be thin and to exercise self-control, but we also want to eat and drink whatever we want; we desire financial security, but we also want to walk away from frustrating but secure jobs; we desire intimacy, but we also desire the independence that places intimacy at risk.

The last example is explored by Ziyad Marar as what he calls "the Happiness Paradox": we have elemental needs both to break free and to belong.[46] More fully, "it is not simply that these needs contradict one another, they are literally paradoxical in that the successful expression of the one requires the assertion of its opposite."[47] Thus we desire to be free from the constraining judgments of other individuals and groups and to choose our own values; simultaneously, as we exercise our freedom we seek justification in their eyes, which we know is attached to their values. The problem is inherent in human nature, but it intensifies in a postmodern world where belief in objectively defensible values is at risk or has evaporated.

I do not share Marar's postmodernist vision of endless and tortured oscillation between seeking freedom from other's values and obeisance to the values of our selected audiences whose approval we desire, with no anchor in reasoned moral judgments that apply to ourselves and others. I retain belief in the possibility of objectively justified values in terms of which we ground our identity, self-respect, and good lives. Marar powerfully illuminates, however, how our desires for individuality and intimacy are sometimes so sharply at odds that they reveal paradoxical aspects of our identity. He is also correct that at least some such conflicts can only partly be diminished through practical wisdom and reasonable compromise, not to mention therapy, so as to make happiness possible. Sometimes happiness requires accepting, rather than fully resolving, our conflicts. This acceptance brings us to the last set of paradoxes.

ATTITUDE: AFFIRMATION AND HOPE

Paradoxes of attitude assert that locating happiness in things we lack is futile; we already have everything we need to be happy—if we just change our attitudes. This idea, which generalizes the paradoxes of success, is paradoxical because we tend to assume that our happiness is derived from something we currently lack, some bluebird or enchanted garden that is always just beyond our grasp.[48] In addition, we overlook how much of our experience of the world is filtered through attitudes that are substantially up to us and that give us more control over our happiness than we usually believe. Happiness itself is defined in terms of attitudes of positive evaluation of our lives, and it turns largely on other attitudes that we can cultivate: self-respect and self-esteem, hope and optimism for a brighter future, gratitude for what we have received, humility in our expectations, relinquishing painful regrets, forgiving offenses, and working through our grief until we can accept tragedy. Paradoxes of attitude take various forms, two of which emphasize affirmation of the present and hope for the future.

11. Paradox of Affirmation

According to the paradox of affirmation, happiness lies in cherishing what we have already, who we are at present, and the way the world is now, rather than in pursuing future goals whose possession is always uncertain. The more we pursue happiness outside ourselves, the unhappier we become (a claim at odds with paradoxes of aims). Instead we need to change our attitudes from negation and self-denigration to affirmation and self-esteem.[49]

In smell-the-roses moments, affirmation seems the simplest of things, for goodness and beauty are everywhere if only we are attuned to them. Far more challenging, however, is the task of developing habits of appreciation that enable us to affirm the ubiquitous good despite the equally ubiquitous bad. Such habits might be cultivated through spiritual disciplines aimed at cultivating humility, gratitude, and love.

The Greek and Roman Stoics, for whom happiness meant serenity, proposed an even more demanding transformation of attitude. Epictetus advises, "Do not seek to have events happen as you want them to, but instead want them to happen as they do happen, and your life will go well."[50] Of great importance, we must accept the inevitability of the deaths of ourselves and people we love: "What upsets people is not things themselves but their judgments about the things. For example, death is nothing dreadful . . . but instead the judgment about death that it is dreadful—*that* is what is dreadful."[51] According to Epictetus, happiness comes from what we can control and from what we must otherwise accept.

12. Paradox of Hope

In tension with the paradox of affirmation, the paradox of hope suggests that happiness comes from positive attitudes concerning the future, such as hope, faith, and optimism—not from getting what we hope for, but rather from the impact of these future-oriented attitudes in the present. In particular, hope generates positive thoughts about the promise of goods that will emerge from the present. This theme permeates the writings of Norman Vincent Peale: "The happiness habit is developed by simply practicing happy thinking" and "we manufacture our unhappiness by thinking unhappy thoughts, by the attitudes which we habitually take, such as the negative feeling that everything is going to turn out badly, or that other people are getting what they do not deserve and we are failing to get what we deserve."[52] Peale is not quite as Pollyannaish as first appears. He emphasizes that changing attitudes requires discipline in changing habits, and he acknowledges that tragedies cannot and should not be brushed aside with superficially upbeat thoughts. Still, Peale's excessive emphasis on positive thinking is best supplanted by the more sober stance of tempering optimism with accuracy and honesty.[53]

In general, paradoxes of attitude convey only partial truths, for our happiness depends both on our attitudes and on actual events in the world—to which our attitudes are attuned when we are reasonable and truthful. Certainly Epictetus goes too far in advocating serenity-promoting attitudes by weakening our ties to people whom we love. This stance was appropriate amidst the horror and radical uncertainty of the Roman Empire, but it is unappealing in today's world where happiness lies in the kinds of deep love and caring that Frankfurt emphasizes, and that are incompatible with the Stoics' emotional distancing.

Furthermore, despite the insights contained in paradoxes of attitude, we lack complete control over our attitudes and hence our happiness. Indeed, many psychologists suggest that each of us has a largely fixed point or range of happiness. Studies of identical twins reveal they have comparable ranges of happiness, whether raised together or apart from each other, suggesting that our happiness range is part of our genetic inheritance.[54] This should not be surprising, given that roughly half of our personalities are genetically given.

The twin studies also help explain why some people are by nature and temperament happier than others. They are also compatible with some puzzling, indeed paradoxical, facts about good and bad fortune. Common sense tells us that our happiness would soar permanently if we won a multimillion-dollar lottery, and it would sink irreversibly if we became quadriplegics. These emotional highs and lows do occur, but only for a short time. In tune with our range of happiness, within a year of these events, levels of happiness usually return to about where they were before.[55] Although we are extremely sensitive to dramatic changes, we tend to adapt psychologically to the status quo, adjusting our expectations and desires to the situation before us.[56] To be sure, fixed-point and fixed-range approaches to happiness are themselves contested, and it seems that at least some major life events, for example marriage, divorce, and unemployment, do modify our happiness range.[57]

Finally, shifts in our attitudes can alter our assessments of when and how much we are happy during other periods of our lives. It makes sense to say, for example, "I thought I was happy when I was married (or single), but now I know I was not." Again, "I thought I could never be happier than I was in my youth, but now I know that was an illusion." As we live longer and more deeply, we acquire a wider range of comparisons to use in assessing our lives and our attitudes can shift. In this way, our conceptions of happiness are dynamic rather than static.[58]

CONCLUSION

The pursuit of happiness might be a simple matter for individuals blessed with a happy temperament, but for most of us it can be precarious and perplexing. The paradoxes of happiness help illuminate why this is so. All the paradoxes suggest that happiness is pursued indirectly as the by-product of meaningful activities and relationships. The paradoxes have different emphases, however, and each conveys one-sided truths that are sometimes in tension with each other.

Paradoxes of aim tell us that we should not focus narrowly on our pleasures (hedonism) and our personal good (self-interest); nor should we assume that we can have a pellucid picture of what will make us happy (guidance); nor should we conceive of happiness as separable from meaningful activities and relationships (constituents). Paradoxes of success remind us that getting what we want does not always lead to wanting what we get (getting), and that happiness is easily lost amidst illusions about material goods (money) and comparisons with others (status). Paradoxes of freedom emphasize that submitting to causes, loyalties, and standards can bring happiness-promoting liberation (submission), that too many choices can threaten happiness (choice), and that we can undermine our happiness when we fail to reasonably resolve or accept our conflicting desires for belonging and breaking free (conflict). Paradoxes of attitude tell us that pursuing happiness in things we lack can be futile unless we learn to cherish what we already have (affirmation) and derive peace from hope and faith (hope). Whereas the paradox of constituents conveys the logical truth that (subjectively) meaningful activities and relationships partly constitute happy lives, the other paradoxes use hyperbole to highlight psychological incongruities and empirical ironies that might warrant further empirical study. All the paradoxes contribute to understanding how happiness interweaves with meaning, morality, and self-fulfillment in good lives.

8

HAPPY TO HELP

The generous person . . . will give to the right people, the right amounts, at the right time, and [do] all the other things that are implied by correct giving.
He will do this, moreover, with pleasure or [at any rate] without pain.[1]
—Aristotle

If asked why we donate money or volunteer time, few of us would gush with Cotton Mather about the "incomparable" pleasure and privilege of giving.[2] Still, most of us do at times derive pleasure, meaning, and happiness from helping others, including strangers. Psychologists and social scientists have extensively studied why we give— "why" in the sense that calls for an *explanation* in terms of motives (desires, emotions, and attitudes), social influences, and situational factors. After taking account of these studies of why we do give, I discuss two moral questions pertaining to happiness and why we should give—"why" in the sense that calls for a *justification* of giving. First, what does happiness as a motive reveal about the character of donors and volunteers? Second, what role does happiness play in justifying decisions to give or not give?

HAPPINESS AS A MOTIVE IN GIVING

Philanthropy is voluntary giving for public purposes, whether the gift is money or time, or material goods or expertise, and whether the purpose is humanitarian, educational, environmental, religious, political, or mutual aid.[3] We tend to think first of large donors, such as Bill and Melinda Gates, who endowed the richest foundation in the history of philanthropy, and Warren Buffett, who donated an even greater amount to the Gates' foundation because he trusted them to distribute his money more effectively than he could. We also celebrate the contributions by people who devote their lives to humanitarian service: for example Clara Barton, founder of the American Red Cross; Jane Addams, creator of Hull House, the community center in Chicago; Albert Schweitzer, who spent fifty years providing medical care to Africans; Paul Farmer, the Harvard professor of medicine who devoted much of his life to fighting disease and poverty in Haiti; and Muhammad Yunus, the Nobel laureate who pioneered micro-loan programs to support entrepreneurship in Bangladesh and other developing countries. Yet such dramatic gifts constitute only a small percentage of philanthropy. Most philanthropic dollars come from modest gifts contributed by millions of donors, and most donated time comes from vast numbers of volunteers in schools, museums, art programs, libraries, and religious organizations.

Probing the motives of philanthropists might seem inappropriate. It invites sentimental exaggerations of human goodness and purity. It also invites cynicism from discovering unsavory motives, or perhaps from projecting our own unsavory motives (including envy) on philanthropists who receive recognition from others. What matters, it might be urged, is the actual good achieved, or not achieved. Philanthropy goes awry when donors support bad causes, as well as when fundraisers deceive donors or receive exorbitant salaries, and when recipients are made dependent in unhealthy ways. Yet even then it seems best to criticize philanthropists for poor judgment and shortsightedness rather than for their motives. In any case, can we really know what motivates others, or even ourselves, in giving?

In reply, I agree that motives have less significance than the actual good accomplished. Nevertheless, motives matter. They are important in understanding character, which concerns desires and commitments just as much as conduct. Insofar as philanthropy brings about good, we need to understand what leads people to engage in it so that we can encourage it in others and foster it in ourselves. Furthermore, insofar as philanthropy does harm, we need to understand how misguided motives distort giving, whether through arrogance or desires to manipulate. We also need to understand the ideals of character relevant to philanthropy, for they too might be justified or unjustified. Let us begin, then, with a brief overview of what psychologists have discovered about philanthropists' motives.

Psychologists confirm that philanthropy and happiness are correlated, with the correlation involving causality in both directions: happiness increases giving and giving increases happiness.[4] On the one hand, happiness tends to promote giving. As David Myers summarizes, "In experiment after experiment, happy people are more willing to help those in need. It's the feel-good, do-good phenomenon."[5] For example, in a famous set of experiments, Alice Isen elevated the mood of individuals by such simple acts as leaving dimes in pay phones.[6] She then arranged for another person to drop some papers just as the caller left the phone booth. The dime finders tended to help the paper droppers more often than members of a control group did. Similar results have been found using a wide variety of mood elevators, from candy to viewing happy pictures. Isen focused on momentary mood elevation (episodic happiness), but a major study of long-term patterns confirms that a disposition to happiness (life satisfaction) is one of the aspects of well-being manifested in voluntary service.[7] These studies also reveal that unhappy and depressed individuals tend to be more self-preoccupied and hence less responsive to the needs of others.

On the other hand, giving tends to increase donors' happiness. Usually the happiness comes as a side effect rather than a direct goal, in tune with the paradoxes of happiness. We first care about people and the causes we donate to, desiring to benefit them. Then, in giving, we indirectly derive enjoyment, a sense of meaning, and happiness. Simple giving can also elicit or deepen caring, as we experience meaning and joy in being able to lessen the hardship of others. Graham Greene provides an illustration of this in *A Burnt-Out Case*.[8] Querry, the protagonist, had been a famous architect who cared only for the aesthetic features of his creations. In despair following an unhappy love relationship, he finds himself restored to happiness by constructing simple buildings on behalf of a philanthropic group that brings immediate aid to impoverished and sick people.

Philanthropy, I should add, provides many counterexamples to psychological egoism, the view that ultimately we are only motivated by the desire to get things for ourselves. By definition, we always act on our own desires; *our* acts are motivated by *our* desires, together with *our* beliefs about how to satisfy our desires. What matters is that some of our aims are to contribute to the well-being of others because we care about them for their sake. This is true even if self-interested desires are more potent than other-regarding desires, as typically they are.[9]

Admittedly, whatever our direct aims, in the background there is generally a hope or even an expectation of some pleasure and meaning from giving. Moreover, by experiencing happiness in giving we will be more likely to give in the future, with a tacit expectation of increased happiness. Here, too, most studies focus on episodic happiness, but a few studies take a longer-term perspective. For example, Jane Piliavin explored the relevance of philanthropy to happy lives by studying individuals who serve as blood donors over many years.[10] She found that donors not only experience momentary good feelings after making donations, but they tend to have a longer-term disposition to feel better about themselves, as persons who care. She found this result confirmed by an extensive review of the literature on volunteering and happiness: "On many levels—psychologically, socially, and even physically—one indeed does 'do well by doing good.'"[11]

This generalization needs to be contextualized by age, for happiness in helping is connected to the life cycle. The elderly tend to benefit most dramatically in terms of happiness, especially individuals who have lost loved ones and who find volunteering a way to create new social networks in light of their values. Young and middle-aged adults also show a general rise in happiness on average, although largely when volunteering does not violate time required for work and family commitments.[12] Adolescents (high school students) tend to benefit from service learning in many ways, including an increased sense of community and reduced behavioral problems, but their overall happiness is largely unaffected, perhaps because they are still forming the mature value commitments to which their happiness will become connected.

Why does philanthropy tend to promote givers' happiness? Several dynamics are at play, including moral ones.[13] In particular, givers' happiness is tied to their values, and hence to their integrity and self-respect. Philanthropy is an immediate and practical way to put our values into practice, whether by writing a check or volunteering. Because philanthropy is voluntary, it offers a vast array of opportunities to translate ideals into actions that express close identification with causes and organizations.[14] In addition, giving heightens our sense of meaningful connection to others.

Self-esteem is a closely related and overlapping dynamic: Giving tends to support an image of ourselves as being compassionate and caring individuals, and it contributes to our sense of being useful and effective. Social feedback augments self-esteem as recipients express appreciation and observers express admiration. In the case of large public gifts, recognition can be dramatic, such as having one's name placed on buildings and programs, but even thank-you letters convey recognition.

Giving provides additional benefits such as alleviating our distress in seeing others suffer, making us feel empowered by being able to help, and developing skills through volunteering that we use in our careers and elsewhere. Sometimes helping just gets our minds off our troubles, as Eleanor Roosevelt observed: "If you can get hold of something that you feel is going to help the people around you, you'll find that you're so busy trying to add one more thing to it that you won't have time to be sorry for yourself or to wonder what you're going to do with your spare time."[15]

Robert Stebbins discovered that most of the happiness-promoting features of work also apply to voluntary service.[16] Volunteering often involves caring and commitment, community involvement, the need to make some effort in applying our knowledge and skills, persevering in the face of difficulties, ample opportunities for flow experiences, the achievement of positive outcomes for others and in terms of self-fulfillment, and even progress in something like a career of involvement in helping others.[17] Serious leisure activities generally have the same features of what Stebbins calls "devotee occupations," which are forms of work that provide meaning beyond money: (1) substantial knowledge and skill is required, (2) variety of activities, (3) opportunities for innovation and personal expression, (4) significant degrees of control over how time is invested, (5) aptitude for and personal interest in the activities ("fit"), and (6) ample opportunities to pursue the work without handicaps such as excessive workload or paperwork.[18]

Admittedly, philanthropy does not always contribute to givers' happiness. It can have the reverse effect when the giver perceives it as ineffective and hence a waste of time and resources. Again, bitterness and cynicism are caused by learning that we have been duped by con artists. Less than 5 percent of charitable organizations are fraudulent, but that adds up to a sizable number. Moreover, it is essential to pursue types and amounts of philanthropic involvement that we are suited to, that fit our individual nature, our particular interests and talents. For example, most of us are not well suited for volunteering to help AIDS patients, and one study showed that among those who do help, half drop out within a year because the work is emotionally debilitating.[19] Instead, we can fight AIDS by contributing money to effective organizations. Even if we are suited to a particular type of helping, we must cope with compassion fatigue and donor burnout.[20] And it is a safe generalization that we will not continue volunteering if we find that helping makes us miserable.

Finally, although thousands of studies confirm the correlation between philanthropy and episodic happiness, few studies examine how philanthropy ranks in comparison to other factors that promote our happiness. Robert Wuthnow did conduct such studies. He asked donors and volunteers to rank the sources of their overall happiness, in order to answer the question of how their helping activities contribute to their overall happiness and sense of fulfillment compared to other sources.

> And the answer is: the fulfillment we receive from doing things for people does not figure very importantly in our overall happiness. In order of importance, the sources of fulfillment that best predict differences in their happiness . . . are: fulfillment from family, fulfillment from leisure activities, fulfillment from religion, fulfillment from being good to themselves, fulfillment from doing things for others, and fulfillment from work. Caring behavior does not rank high on the list.[21]

Even if philanthropy is not the primary source of happiness for most people, happiness is a significant motive that helps explain why people engage in philanthropy. The exact strength of happiness as a motive is an empirical matter reported by psychologists and social scientists in the form of statistical averages, but the overall averages reveal that philanthropy is one important source and expression of happiness.

DESIRABLE MOTIVES AND IDEALS OF CHARACTER

What does happiness as a motive reveal about the character of donors and volunteers? Deriving happiness, or at least some pleasure and meaning, from helping others is generally regarded as a key mark of good character. David Hume writes, "The epithets sociable, good-natured, humane, merciful, grateful, friendly, generous, beneficent, or their equivalents, are known in all languages, and universally express the highest merit, which human nature is capable of attaining."[22] To warrant such epithets, individuals are presumed to find pleasure, meaning, and happiness directly from helping others and from contributing to good causes, and in this regard we speak of an element of selflessness. Deriving happiness from giving indicates, rather than cancels out, this element of selflessness. That is, deriving happiness, enjoyment, and meaning directly from helping others carries with it a presumption that we care about them.

We withhold or qualify praise of donors when their happiness in giving does not come in part from caring about others, but instead exclusively from satisfying "ulterior motives" such as seeking applause, gaining a tax break, or exerting power in manipulating philanthropic organizations in objectionable ways. Furthermore, when people volunteer solely in order to polish their resumes, gain work-related experience, fulfill an academic requirement for service learning, or make job contacts without caring a whit about the people they help, we might praise them for their prudence and savvy but not for their compassion and generosity. Implicitly, then, we look beneath philanthropists' happiness for evidence that they care about people and values for reasons beyond narrow self-interest. "Beyond" narrow self-interest means in addition to self-interest, not to the exclusion of all self-interest. We quite reasonably accept the presence of self-interest in philanthropy, as virtually everywhere in life, so long as it is not dominant and does not threaten promoting the good of others.

To elaborate, selflessness is slippery. Properly understood, it suggests using one's time, money, creativity, or other resources for the good of others because we care about them. It is compatible with additional concern for our own well-being as long as that self-concern does not distort caring and helping. Philanthropy typically springs from multiple motives that blend self-interest (caring for ourselves) and altruism (caring for others). In general, as Mary Midgely reminds us, we have evolved as creatures with mixed motives that constantly dovetail, with only occasional severe conflicts: "The structure [of human nature] must consist of a number of motives which are genuinely distinct and autonomous, but which are adapted to fit together, in the normal maturing of the individual, into a life that can satisfy him as a whole."[23] Mixed motives in giving are usually desirable, insofar as they strengthen a commitment to helping others. It remains important, however, that the mixture of motives includes caring for others, for their sake. As the paradoxes of happiness suggest, our own happiness will then come indirectly as we "forget" ourselves in service to others. In this way, deriving happiness from helping others is entirely compatible with selflessness; indeed, selflessness is shown in deriving happiness directly from helping others.

Selflessness is sometimes understood in terms of ideals of purity that seem to rule out mixed motives. To be sure, everyday standards for purity of motivation in helping others are vague and flexible, something like "Care more about people you help than about your own ego." But religious traditions tend to emphasize ideals of greater purity in the form of completely selfless giving that emulates God's love. "Purity of heart is to will one thing," Kierkegaard tells us, the one thing being love, with God as its perfect exemplar. Such talk easily slides into ideals of selflessness as self-disregard and self-indifference, although there is usually a background motive of concern for rewards in heaven.

Kant sets forth another problematic ideal of purity, one centered on doing what is right entirely from a sense of duty: "To be kind where one can is duty, and there are, moreover, many persons so sympathetically constituted that without any motive of vanity or selfishness they find an inner satisfaction in spreading joy and rejoice in the contentment of others which they have made possible. But I say that, however dutiful and amiable it may be, that kind of action has no true moral worth."[24] According to Kant, such actions "deserve praise and encouragement but no [moral] esteem." Moral esteem is owed only when individuals meet responsibilities to others motivated by a concern to do what is right, thereby expressing recognition of recipients' and our own dignity as rational beings capable of following universal principles of duty.

If Kant merely meant that good motives are not sufficient for good conduct, he would be making an important point. For a person might spread joy and happiness but do so in morally objectionable ways: giving to immoral causes; giving time or money that is owed to someone else, perhaps one's family members; failing to meet other responsibilities, such as at work; and so on. As Aristotle suggests, generous giving, to be virtuous, requires good motives but much else as well, including giving appropriate amounts at appropriate times to worthy causes.[25] But Kant is not simply reminding us that good motives are insufficient to accomplish good. He is setting forth an ideal of moral purity that restricts morally worthy motives to conscientiousness, in the sense of meeting duties because they are duties. He calls for a kind of moral purity of motivation: our commitment to universal principles of duty is the only morally admirable motive, and it should be salient and sufficient (if not exclusive) as the motive in doing what is right.

Like Kant, Iris Murdoch reminds us of the power of ideals of purity and even moral perfection: "What of the command 'Be ye therefore perfect?' Would it not be more sensible to say 'Be ye therefore slightly improved?'"[26] She answers, "The idea of perfection moves, and possibly changes, us (as artist, worker, agent) because it inspires love in the part of us that is most worthy. One cannot feel unmixed love for a mediocre moral standard." Yet Murdoch fails to appreciate that ideals of purity can be as dangerous as they are inspirational, and she gives only passing mention of how neurotic perfectionism leads to depression and anxiety. Ideals of purity of motive and accomplishment generate unrealistic expectations that quickly lead to disillusionment and hence to apathy. Demanding too much can discourage us from doing even a little, and unrealistic expectations invite apathy and "compassion fatigue." Worse, ideals of perfection and purity can generate loss of moral perspective and dangerous self-absorption.[27]

Ideals of purity can make perfection the enemy of the good. That does not mean that we shouldn't care about ideals of character, but it does call for realism about those ideals. In particular, ideals of purity need to be balanced by ideals of wisdom in locating and pursuing the reasonable middle ground between perfection and mediocrity.

HAPPINESS AS A JUSTIFICATION FOR GIVING

In saying that helping makes them happy, philanthropists might mean that happiness is their reason (justification) for giving, in addition to their motive (explanation). This appeal to happiness is ambiguous. On the one hand, it sounds humble and self-effacing: "I'm as selfish as anyone; I just happen to get a kick from helping others." On the other hand, it is self-flattering: "Good people derive pleasure from helping others, and that's true of me." Let us set aside this ambiguity and concentrate on whether the philanthropist's happiness can be a justification for giving—a sound justification, not merely a proffered one. A number of social critics find any hasty reference to happiness problematic. In their view, the subjective-leaning language of personal happiness and fulfillment masks and threatens responsibilities of compassion, beneficence, and loyalties to communities.[28]

Justification might refer to (1) moral permissibility, (2) moral goodness, or (3) moral obligation. Let us consider each possibility. First, the question of justification might mean, Is a particular philanthropic act or activity morally permissible to engage in? In the abstract, the answer is straightforward. Within wide boundaries, we have the right to pursue happiness by giving to others. Yet there is an implicit caveat: our right to pursue happiness is limited by other moral reasons. Simply appealing to the givers' happiness is not sufficient to justify philanthropy. Thus giving to immoral causes, such as racist or terrorist groups, is unjustified, regardless of whether it makes racists and terrorist supporters happy. Supporting grossly inefficient and wasteful causes is generally unjustified, if only because many worthy causes desperately need resources. And Bernard Madoff was unjustified in donating stolen money to good causes. Justification of specific acts and practices of philanthropy, then, centers primarily on recipients and third parties, and secondarily on givers' happiness. But once it is established that the cause is morally permissible and that we are not violating other overriding obligations, philanthropic service is justified in the sense of morally permissible.

Even when the giving is permissible, the mere appeal to the happiness of givers is unsatisfying, or at least incomplete, as moral justification. It misses the primary moral point of helping others. Usually there are innumerable other options available for pursuing our happiness and self-fulfillment.[29] The question is, What is good about choosing philanthropy over other options? Moreover, if happiness were the primary reason for engaging in philanthropy, it would also be the primary reason for never helping others if we happen to find greater happiness elsewhere, perhaps in a life of utter self-indulgence. The attitude here might be: "If helping others makes you happy, fine, but I find happiness by spending my money and time in travel, expensive restaurants, and time with my family. So fundraisers stay away, and stop assuming there is anything better about helping others than enjoying fine wines."

Second, asking about justification might mean, Is a particular philanthropic endeavor morally good or desirable, although not obligatory? Showing that an act of philanthropy is good requires taking into account the donor's character, impacts on recipients, and effects on third parties and the wider society. Regarding the donor's character, giving might manifest an array of virtues, such as generosity, compassion, gratitude, and a sense of justice. The giver's happiness might enter here, as we noted earlier, as evidence for the presence of these virtues. Regarding the impact on recipients, justification might involve appeals to a wide range of values, including beauty (giving to the arts), cultural (giving to politics or to historical heritage), religious, and so on. Occasionally the happiness of recipients is salient, for example, in Make-A-Wish Foundation's promotion of the happiness of a seriously ill child. More often recipients' basic needs are supported by the philanthropy, whether the needs concern humanitarian goals (e.g., relieving poverty and suffering), political goals (e.g., promoting democracy), artistic goals (e.g., producing a creative work of art), cultural goals (e.g., sustaining libraries and museums), or educational goals (e.g., creating scholarships). In this context, needs encompass the requisites for survival but also worthy desires for valuable things.

Regarding effects on the happiness of third parties and the wider society, there are many things to consider. One effect is to encourage others to give to good causes, which is especially important for "lead donors" and "matching donors," who make generous contributions designed to spur many additional smaller gifts. An important general consequence is the fostering of caring relationships between givers and receivers that carry wider ripple effects, especially in fostering a wider sense of community based on caring. Some philanthropic relationships are highly personal, for example those fostered in Big Sister and Big Brother organizations, and Girls Club and Boys Club programs. But philanthropy provides avenues for ongoing caring relationships between givers and groups of recipients who do not know each other personally. Either way, caring relationships enrich giver and receiver alike, and often facilitate ways in which givers receive as much as they give, whether in terms of self-esteem and social recognition or in terms of integrity—of being able to put their values into practice.

Finally, the question of justification might mean, Is a particular philanthropic act obligatory, or at least one way to fulfill a general moral responsibility? The general issue of philanthropic obligations is complex and much contested, and I will merely illustrate what is at stake with regard to obligations to alleviate world hunger. Here again the happiness of donors is not the primary justification, although it is relevant. Primary justifications include obligations of compassion and gratitude. Both obligations were highlighted by Schweitzer in referring to his personal experience: "It struck me as inconceivable that I should be allowed to lead such a happy life while I saw so many people around me struggling with sorrow and suffering. . . . I must not accept this good fortune as a matter of course, but must give something in return."[30] Schweitzer insisted that exactly how we show gratitude and compassion through philanthropic giving, however, is largely a matter of personal choice, as are the amounts that we give.

Peter Singer disagrees with this degree of personal discretion. For three decades he has argued that we should concentrate our philanthropy on alleviating world hunger, and that we should be giving vastly more than most of us give. Recently he reasserted his central argument in *The Life You Can Save*:

> First premise: Suffering and death from lack of food, shelter, and medical care are bad.
>
> Second premise: If it is in your power to prevent something bad from happening, without sacrificing anything nearly as important, it is wrong not to do so.
>
> Third premise: By donating to aid agencies, you can prevent suffering and death from lack of food, shelter, and medical care, without sacrificing anything nearly as important.
>
> Conclusion: Therefore, if you do not donate to aid agencies, you are doing something wrong.[31]

In responding to the criticism that his view is unrealistic, given the psychology of happiness, Singer admits that most of us will not give in amounts anywhere near to what the argument requires. So, without altering his view that the argument does indeed identify our obligation, he advocates that most of us donate 5 percent of our income and the rich much more. Doing the math carefully to ensure that extreme poverty is completely overcome, he has worked out a fine-tuned set of wealth brackets that require, for example, people whose income is in the range of $105,000–$148,000 should give 5 percent, and those making above those amounts much more.[32] As for happiness, he admits it is a powerful motive, though not part of the justification of philanthropy. He also contends that giving 5 percent (or more) of our income will not lower our happiness level at all and might actually increase it because we know we are engaged in a good cause; more than that, you are doing what you ought to do.[33] Singer cites studies showing that philanthropy and happiness are correlated, many of which I cited earlier. Yet those studies are about philanthropy in general, with individuals choosing to give in ways they see fit, rather than of massive giving to fight world poverty. As a result, his happiness-based justifications for focusing our resources on world hunger are open to challenge.

The central question, however, is whether Singer makes his case that our giving must be on the scale and with the focus on fighting poverty. His moral intuition centers on Premise 2, which expresses the ethical theory of act-utilitarianism. It requires us to maximize good consequences, or in the negative version applicable here, to prevent bad. Since few things are worse than extreme poverty, most of our resources beyond those needed for survival should be redirected to alleviate that poverty. For most of us, this requires sacrificing virtually all luxuries in our lives because they are not nearly as important as saving another person from extreme poverty and death. It also requires not paying for our child to attend expensive schools, such as Princeton University where Singer teaches, except where doing so carries the promise that the university's degree will indirectly lead one's child to alleviate world poverty. And the premise requires abandoning all forms of philanthropic giving other than those directed toward alleviating extreme poverty. That includes giving to the arts, to religious organizations, to the sciences, and so on, except in the selected areas where the giving serves to alleviate poverty, such as religious organizations and applied scientific research aimed at fighting poverty.

One reply to Singer, then, is to reject act-utilitarianism and to invoke a more plausible ethical theory than act-utilitarianism. Candidates for such a theory include rule-utilitarianism, duty ethics, virtue ethics, and rights ethics. For example, rights ethics typically emphasizes our right to pursue our happiness and our rights to use our property as we see fit so long as we do not violate other people's rights.[34] Libertarians generally deny that the rights of impoverished people make a claim on our property. Most versions of human rights ethics, however, grant that other people's rights to life make a claim on the resources of the wealthy: the right to life of the starving person creates a duty for us to help them. But how much we are required to help depends on balancing our duties to our families, ourselves, our employers, as well as with our rights to use much of our property as we judge best—taking into account our personal happiness and self-fulfillment, as well as our sense of morality.

Rights ethics provides a powerful counterbalance to Singer, although it is only one component of a sound ethical theory in my view. Virtue ethics is equally essential, with its emphasis on good persons and good lives—lives that are morally decent, fulfilling, and happy. Virtues (and ideals) such as compassion (caring responses to suffering), generosity (giving liberally on behalf of good causes), justice (doing our fair share), gratitude (giving back to communities in a spirit of thankfulness) enter into understanding morally good judgment in exercising rights in morally decent lives. Taken together, these virtues support philanthropic giving, in addition to the claims of the rights of people in extreme poverty to receive aid from communities. At the same time, there are the virtues and duties of authenticity and self-respect in having due concern for our self-realization and happiness, and these virtues might well lead us into forms of philanthropy in addition to alleviating poverty. There are virtues of caring and responsible conduct in helping family and friends, and virtues of prudence (caution, efficiency) and wisdom (morally good judgment) in balancing responsibilities.

To conclude, exactly when and why philanthropy is obligatory, or otherwise desirable, are complex matters. They require exercising good judgment in assessing specific programs and activities, establishing priorities among philanthropic options, and balancing philanthropy with other personal responsibilities and rights—including our right to pursue happiness. Happiness is important in justifying philanthropy, as well as in motivating it, but it is interwoven with additional moral values and manifested in practical wisdom rather than abstract ethical theories.

9

SHARED PURSUITS IN LOVE

Love is that condition in which the happiness of another person is essential to your own.[1]
—Robert Heinlein

Marriage partners pursue happiness together. This means three things. First, they pursue a happy marriage, a marriage that both partners are happy with and happy in. Second, they pursue the overall happiness of both partners, not only their domain happiness within their marriage. Third, and even more inclusively, they undertake a shared pursuit of happiness, that is, happiness in a shared life pursued together in love—with shared activities and agency, shared intimacy and identity, shared virtue and luck, and shared enjoyment and meaning. In all these ways, happiness plays a major role in justifying decisions to sustain or abandon marriages. So do other moral values; indeed, marriage is the most moralized of all love relationships, with the possible exception of parenting. Most spouses make moral commitments to share a life "until death do us part," and to be guided by ideals such as caring, honesty, fairness, and fidelity. As a consequence, nowhere is the interplay of happiness and morality more complex than in love and marriage.

HAPPY MARRIAGES AND SHARED PURSUITS OF HAPPINESS

Focusing on marriage might seem to privilege one type of love and one way of life. That is not my intention, and much of what I say is relevant to all forms of love. Moreover, I understand marriage broadly, in a moral sense, to include all committed partnerships, whether gay, straight, or bisexual, and whether or not formalized in legal or religious ceremonies. I focus on monogamy rather than polygamy, however, and on chosen rather than arranged marriages. Although most people marry at least once, marriages take innumerable forms that reflect individual personalities and social customs.[2] Marriage is an evolving set of practices, and historically even the cultural ideal of love-based marriage is relatively young. It became dominant around 1800; before that time marriages were driven mainly by economics, power, and status.[3] Then, for 150 years the dominant model for love-based marriages remained economically lopsided, with a male breadwinner and female homemaker. Only since the 1960s have most marriages in Western societies involved two wage earners, expectations of equality and fairness, and relatively easy access to divorce.

Psychologists point to several typical features of happy couples and happy marriages.[4] Happy couples spend more time together, on average five hours per week more than troubled couples. Each day they express appreciation and affection four to five times more often than they communicate criticism. They experience delight when something good happens to their spouse, rather than feeling destructive envy. Especially important, happy couples manage conflict better, not necessarily by fighting less but by fighting in ways that minimize hostile escalations and sweeping denigration. In addition to enjoying many activities together, spouses share goals and values that create a common or overlapping sense of meaning. They do not agree on everything, but they respect each other's convictions. Above all, marital happiness is rooted in an abiding and deep friendship—most spouses report that their partner is their closest friend. In all these ways, spouses maintain a shared inner life: "You grow together, explore new directions and take risks together, challenge your assumptions together, and take responsibility together."[5]

Psychologists also study how marital (domain) happiness contributes to the overall (global) happiness of spouses. Studies show that married people tend to be happier overall than unmarried ones: "The married person will be 18 percentage points more likely than the unmarried person to say he or she is very happy," and that is now as true for women as for men.[6] Explaining this connection between marital and overall happiness is complicated. Frequently, individuals are already happy and carry their happiness into the marriage, which is not surprising given that happiness is usually an attractive feature in potential mates. Again, exceptionally happy marriages might or might not suffice to make persons happy overall.

In addition to domain happiness and its contribution to overall happiness, I am interested in *shared pursuits of happiness*. Marriage involves the coordinated pursuit of the overall happiness (not just domain happiness) of two people who share a life. With varying degrees of intimacy, spouses typically connect their lives with the goal of pursuing their mutual overall happiness. They do so through shared affection, shared identification, and shared agency in pursuing shared long-term plans that are open-ended and evolving.

To illustrate shared pursuits of happiness, consider the marriage between Jack and June Bingham, as June Bingham depicts it in *Braided Lives*. Braiding is an apt leitmotif for their love, as is the image of two "love trees" that they saw in the forests of the

Forbidden City in Beijing, China. The trees were so named because they "so thoroughly wrapped themselves around each other year after year."[7] The trees had distinct lives and yet were intertwined and in places fused. June portrays their marriage as based on emotional intimacy, a sense of adventure, great fun, and a moral core of friendship, mutual respect, and mutual responsibility.

The Binghams are well educated and both have accomplished careers, she as a versatile writer (playwright, biographer, and columnist) and he as a politician (nine-term U.S. Congressman and U.S. Ambassador to the United Nations). June portrays their marriage as peaceful, with rare fights. Yet their shared life is anything but boring, either to them or the reader. They face major illnesses and the death of one of their four grown children. They also confront anti-Semitism in society and within Jack's family: June is a secular Jew and Jack was raised in a conservative Christian family. Although their families eventually accepted their marriage, other tensions prove intransigent: "Some interpersonal problems are not soluble, and one may simply have to learn to live with them."[8]

June and Jack take steps to protect their marriage. For example, infidelity is occasionally a temptation for each of them, and they are proactive in preventing it. Both are physically attractive, enjoy sex, and move in a world where power is an aphrodisiac. They operate with their private version of nuclear mutually assured destruction (MAD), knowing that if one partner has an affair the other will do the same and the marriage will likely unravel.[9] Once when Jack was drunk and tried to return to a party where a beautiful woman had tried to seduce him, June forcibly took his car keys. On another occasion when June was enchanted by President-elect John Kennedy, who approached her with lust in his eyes, she declined an invitation to accompany her husband to a White House social gathering.

The couple remained devoted to each other until Jack's death. June expresses their unity in the final words she speaks to him: "You have nothing to worry about. We have lived our love, and loved our life."[10] Death ends the marriage but not her love, which continues during an agonizing period of grieving, both in private with her family and throughout public memorials to Jack. Gradually she begins a time of renewal, learning to write with a computer and participating in off-Broadway productions of her plays. She also enters a second happy marriage to a longtime friend of Jack's, whose wife had died recently after a forty-six-year marriage, coincidentally the same duration as June's marriage to Jack.

The Binghams illustrate how shared pursuits of happiness require shared agency: cooperative endeavors, mutual decision making, compromise, and adjustment. Of course, so do many other activities in life, including business transactions. Marriage is distinguished by a foundation of deep affection, long-term commitments based on love, and caring for the happiness of one's partner. Shared pursuits of happiness combine caring about one's own happiness with caring about the partner's happiness. More generally, shared pursuits of happiness blend self-interested and altruistic desires, as well as a third category of desires: desires to promote the happiness and well-being of both partners. Let us look more closely at these aspects of shared pursuits.

SHARED IDENTITY IN PURSUING HAPPINESS

Recent philosophical discussions of love emphasize themes about personal identity rather than shared pursuits of happiness, but the themes are closely connected. Aristophanes' speech in Plato's *Symposium* is a familiar starting point in these recent discussions. According to a myth recounted by Aristophanes, human ancestors were round creatures with double appendages, including double sexual organs in three variations: male–male, female–female, and male–female. These rebellious and powerful creatures angered Zeus, provoking him to slice them in half. Wounded psychologically and physically, they yearned to be reunited with their other half, driven by what today we call gay, lesbian, and heterosexual desires: "This, then, is the source of our desire to love each other. Love is born into every human being; it calls back the halves of our original nature; it tries to make one out of two and heal the wound of human nature."[11] When soul mates have the good fortune of discovering each other, "something wonderful happens: the two are struck from their senses by love, by a sense of belonging to one another, and by desire, and they don't want to be separated from one another, not even for a moment."[12] In spiritual terms, many couples live with the hope that the god of love might "restore to us our original nature, and by healing us, he will make us blessed and happy."[13]

Aristophanes' image of completely fused identities is charmingly romantic but decidedly unappealing in some respects. It assumes there is only one ideal soul mate for each of us, and it assumes the soul mate is identical to us—but what about "opposites attract"? Worse, fused identities threaten individuality, and thereby threaten the contribution of individuality to happy marriages. Shared identification needs to be rethought as a singular emotional attachment to one's partner, manifested in dispositions to care deeply for them. In this connection, Robert Solomon agrees with Aristophanes that "love is shared identity" and that "'merging' and 'union' are not just metaphors but deep insights into the nature of the self and the transformation of the self in love."[14] Love is a process that involves much talking (conversation, arguing, negotiating), but it is defined primarily in terms of the emotional chemistry and alchemy between partners that literally creates a new self shared by them, a "we." At the same time, love typically involves "a dialectical tension" between the desires for individuality and unity with the beloved. Ultimately, however, Solomon emphasizes concern for oneself: "The primary motive for love is . . . a sense of self-worth. . . . To put it very crudely, when love succeeds, each lover feels better about him or herself than would otherwise be conceivable; when love fails, it is . . . because one no longer likes or can no longer tolerate the person he or she has become."[15] Insofar as lovers' self-esteem is reshaped through their partners, love creates new selves mutually defined by the lovers.

Solomon insightfully explores conflicting desires for intimacy and individuality, but his talk of "dialectical tension" captures only the problematic aspects of this conflict. In healthy relationships, partners remain two distinct persons who cooperate and complement each other. They share a life in quite familiar ways summarized by Irving Singer: "the casual spending of time with one another, the enjoying of each other's presence, the desire to give and receive pleasure, the exchange of judgments and impressions, the reaching of decisions that affect them both, the cooperative struggle for goals they care about, the rearing of a family as a combined expression of themselves, the participation in a society to which they each contribute, the feeling on various occasions of reciprocal excitement, joy, or sorrow."[16] I would add to Singer's list the common pursuit of happiness, with each partner experiencing the happiness of their partner as integral to their own.

Robert Nozick sheds light on how this shared pursuit involves shared identifications, well-being, and autonomy. First, agreeing with Solomon, Nozick emphasizes that partners form a shared identity, Solomon's "we," in which they significantly but not entirely define themselves in terms of each other. In healthy relationships individual identity is not lost, as it sometimes is in pathological relationships. Typically, partners do come to think of themselves as transformed by being part of a couple living a common life. The deeper their love, the deeper their mutual identification. More than anywhere else, in love we are what and who we care about most deeply.

Second, two individuals pool their autonomy and decision making. They make many decisions together, often on the basis of negotiation, compromise, or agreements to delegate areas of authority. Partners in marriage and in love "limit or curtail their own decision-making power and rights; some decisions can no longer be made alone."[17] These decisions range from the mundane, such as what to have for dinner and which movies to watch, to the momentous, such as whether to have children and when to sacrifice a job in order to advance a career.

Third, love blends individual well-being with that of one's partner, not only in terms of economics and social status, but especially in terms of emotional well-being and vulnerability: "If a loved one is hurt or disgraced, you are hurt; if something wonderful happens to her, you feel better off."[18] I would add that marital love interweaves the partners' pursuits of happiness as an important aspect of their overall well-being. Indeed, finding a significant degree of happiness in the relationship is one sign that the partners love each other, at least in any honorific sense of love as valuable caring. Shared well-being, together with shared autonomy and shared identity, means that the happiness of spouses depends greatly on the delight, fun, and joy they find together, and that they give to and accept from each other.

These aspects of sharing, especially the last one, explain why it is largely impossible to pry apart self-interest and caring for the beloved. Love has a selfless aspect, in that it involves direct concern for the interests of the beloved—for her sake, not just from ulterior reasons of narrow self-interest. At the same time, love redefines self-interest in terms of the relationship and the well-being of the beloved. This is true in all forms of love,[19] but especially marital love.

Robert Heinlein highlights the altruistic aspect of love in terms of caring about the happiness of the beloved: "Love is that condition in which the happiness of another person is essential to your own."[20] That is, our happiness is tied to caring about the partner's happiness, caring for the partner's sake as well as for the sake of self-interest. But it is equally true that love is that condition in which our happiness depends on being loved by our partner. In fact, the love that forms the basis for a shared pursuit of happiness typically fuses self-interest with altruism. It intertwines (braids) caring for the happiness of the beloved with wanting the beloved to reciprocate by caring about our happiness. The success of shared pursuits of happiness depends on both luck and the virtues.

LUCK AND LOVE'S VIRTUES

Although we have considerable control about whether to pursue relationships, "falling" in love feels more like acquiescence than choice. Moreover, staying in love involves a large element of luck. Martha Nussbaum itemizes some of the factors not entirely under our control: "two people of similar character and aspirations who also find each other physically, socially, and morally attractive and who are able to live in the same place for an extended period of time."[21] Then there is the need for them to sustain each other's trust despite jealousies and temporary separations, to remain constant in their love amidst inevitable conflicts and quarrels, to cope with innumerable problems, and to adjust to changes that include illness and growing old. The virtues help in meeting all these challenges, but virtues provide no guarantee of success. And the challenges lie within, as well as coming from the world. Specifically, happiness in love is not entirely under our control.

Granting the role of luck, however, does not diminish the contribution of character to shared pursuits of happiness in love. Traditional moral perspectives on marriage emphasize *conscientiousness* in meeting responsibilities established by wedding vows. We do better to focus on a wider range of virtues, while appreciating their connections with being responsible.[22] Most central is the virtue of *benevolence*, as focused and magnified in the caring, affection, empathy, and sensitive support for the beloved. Mutual *respect* is equally essential. *Faithfulness*—taking seriously the responsibilities created by marital commitments—aims at sustaining love, with the more specific virtue of sexual fidelity contributing to constancy in love. *Honesty* makes possible emotional intimacy. *Fairness*, the virtue highlighted in feminist views of love, is vital to a couple's attempts to sustain mutually beneficial relationships. *Gratitude*, not just for specific gifts but for the contribution of the love to our happiness, is also important. These and additional virtues partly define the nature of a couple's love, and the structures of marriages, while other virtues such as courage and gratitude also enable relationships to survive as couples face difficulties together. These virtues and their accompanying ideals are embodied in people and relationships in many ways.

The Binghams' marriage illustrates love's virtues, but let us introduce a second illustration. The relationship between the philosopher Hazel Barnes and her partner Doris Schwalbe was officially guided by an existentialist ethics, published in Barnes's philosophical writings, according to which all values are the product of personal freedom. Certainly their relationship is a creative and mutually defined one. Nevertheless, Barnes is emphatic that the virtues (which they embody but do not invent) help their love to flourish: "independence, self-sufficiency, individualism, but also personal responsibility, empathic concern for others, the importance of justice, and, above all, accountability, absolute honesty and integrity: all those old-fashioned virtues that sound so dreary but turn out to be life-sustaining in a relationship."[23] Consider fairness (justice) in their relationship. For them, fairness makes clear and justified claims that both partners will pursue their self-development. This means that each is allowed to carry on with their careers as professors. In more mundane matters, they display great flexibility but still meet the demands of balance. For example, household chores are handled by each playing to their strengths and interests, with Doris cooking and Hazel doing most of the cleaning. Again, they pursue many shared interests, such as literature and opera, nature and travel; yet they also allow and encourage each other's separate pursuits, such as Doris's interest in fishing and Hazel's interest in film. They also leave room for expressing temperamental difference while sustaining intimacy without suffocation.

Moving beyond case studies, psychologists provide more systematic evidence of the virtues' contribution to love. To begin with, couples confront a variety of generic challenges in addition to more unique problems (such as anti-Semitism or impotence). Those challenges include tasks emphasized by Judith S. Wallerstein and Sandra Blakeslee: sustaining areas of both intimacy and autonomy, being empathetic and emotionally nurturing, maintaining a satisfying sex life, keeping their life together fun and exciting, making the marriage safe for expressing differences (for example by learning how to argue respectfully), reshaping relationships with the couple's extended families, dealing with adversities such as illness and financial crises, keeping alive a sense of shared history in the values that brought the couple together, and (for many) parenting.[24] The virtues are needed in grappling with these problems.

The virtues are concealed in cognitive psychologists' talk of "emotional intelligence," but they are given explicit attention by positive psychologists. For example, Martin Seligman emphasizes virtues of hope and faith in sustaining a couple's shared pursuit of happiness. He acknowledges the problem of reverse correlation in studying the role of these and other virtues. That is, in addition to the virtues contributing to happiness in marriages, happy persons are more likely to marry because their happiness is an attractive feature to potential partners. Seligman also emphasizes caring as manifested in nuanced skills in expressing attention and valuing of the beloved.

TROUBLED SHARED PURSUITS

"All happy families are alike; each unhappy family is unhappy in its own way," according to Tolstoy's opening to *Anna Karenina*.[25] Yet the claim is doubly mistaken. Happy marriages do tend to share certain features and virtues, as we have seen, but those features and virtues take many forms. Likewise, unhappy marriages tend to share certain features, with many variations. In studying these features and variations, psychologists are refining common sense and developing useful techniques to improve relationships.

Unhappy couples do not necessarily fight more often than unhappy couples, but they fight in ways that degrade each other.[26] Unhappiness-tending argument patterns are harsh, accusatory, sweepingly critical, contemptuous and sneering, rife with defensive blaming and at some point stonewalling. Instead of sensing when fights have turned ugly and require efforts at truce and repair, spouses inflict as much emotional injury as possible and sometimes physical injury as well. Furthermore, in unhappy relationships one or both people might lack skills and attitudes of emotional intelligence, especially of empathy in understanding and appreciating the nuanced needs of each other— something much more complicated than skills in "communication," whose importance therapists once rated too highly. At a deeper level, they have lost what first brought them together: shared identification, shared enjoyment, shared meaning, and shared desires to pursue their lives and their happiness together.

In contrast, creative marriages allow partners to grow. Growth carries risks. Sadly, sometimes one or both partners outgrow the marriage. Even happy marriages can burn out. For good reason, we maintain the right to leave a marriage that becomes hopelessly miserable. As Andrew Cherlin observes, we live in "a society in which marriage is still valued, but an unhappy married couple is almost expected to divorce," at least after seeking marital counseling.[27] The expectation combines our valuing happiness and additional moral values, as does marriage itself. Of course, conservative critics who defend "family values" decry a culture in which happiness plays a dominant role in ending marriages, but in their own lives they are just as vulnerable to divorce as any other political or religious groups.

Ben Bradley, the distinguished editor of the *Washington Post*, is frank in reflecting on his three marriages, the last of which was a creative partnership with journalist Sally Quinn. He writes, "I think the conscientious pursuit of happiness by itself can validate decisions to change, to try again, especially when failure to change will lead to lives of duplicity, dishonesty, and deceit."[28] The "especially" provides an important qualification. Responsible divorce generally blends concern for happiness with additional moral values, including values of what we owe to ourselves and the honesty we owe to our partners.

Divorce frequently causes terrible suffering, and sometimes cynicism. After going through a painful divorce that ended a two-decade marriage, writer and radio commentator Sandra Tsing Loh recommends: "Avoid marriage—or you too may suffer the emotional pain, the humiliation, and the logistical difficulty, not to mention the expense, of breaking up a long-term union at midlife for something as demonstrably fleeting as love."[29] Her argument strikes me as an argument for humane ways of divorcing, not for abandoning marriage. To be sure, some divorces result from irresponsible ways of pursuing happiness. And sometimes divorce is a wrong choice that might be prevented with greater moral commitment, good luck, spiritual guidance, or therapy. To add to the complexity, a couple's perspectives on their marriage might change over time, so that at times one or both partners regard the marriage as doomed but later are grateful they stayed with it.

As an example of this perspectival complexity, consider in more detail Rafael Yglesias's *A Happy Marriage*.[30] The novel closely mirroring Yglesias's own relationship that began in 1975, was formalized in legal marriage in 1977, and ended with the death of his wife in 2004. Yglesias names his protagonist Enrique Sabas but retains his wife's name, Margaret, for the wife in the novel. The book rotates between the joyous early years of their marriage, providing glimpses of their marriage often in reversed order, and Margaret's death from bladder cancer. It is an attempt to unravel the mystery of how two very different individuals could find their love, however troubled, the most important thing in their lives.

Eager to write, and to gain fame from writing, Enrique dropped out of high school to complete and publish his first novel at age seventeen. When he meets Margaret he is twenty-one and about to publish his third novel. He is not a happy person, having imbibed his mother's neuroticism, formed unrealistic literary ambitions, and been tortured by self-pity and self-doubt. When he later finds himself unable to support his family by publishing novels, he turns to writing movie scripts, which he regards as a self-betrayal that cheapens his talents, even as it makes him and Margaret multimillionaires. As a result, the unhappiness he brings to the marriage is both refracted and intensified.

In sharp contrast, Margaret is a happy person, at peace with herself and the world. She earned a Cornell degree, and comes from a wealthy family. Although she is talented artistically, she lacks the kind of ambition so essential to Enrique. From the beginning Enrique is captivated by her slim body and "depthless blue eyes," and also by her intelligence, charm, confidence, maturity—and happiness. When they first have sex, however, Enrique finds himself impotent, for him an uncharacteristic and traumatic event that he awkwardly tries to explain as due to his love for Margaret. Margaret gently reassures him, suggesting it is too early to call their friendship love. When the impotence recurs she cares enough for him to insist they just have sex without thinking about affection, exactly the invitation Enrique needs. Their love and their shared pursuit of happiness progress, bringing joyous sex and emotional intimacy that make marriage a natural choice for both of them.

A crisis occurs seven years into the marriage, shortly after the birth of their first son. Margaret is working sixteen-hour days that combine child care with a job that pays as much as Enrique makes. She is exhausted and largely loses interest in sex. Enrique falls in love with one of Margaret's closest friends from college. Convinced that he no longer loves Margaret, he tells her their impoverished sex life is threatening their marriage and suggests couples therapy, secretly expecting it to be a first step toward divorce. Margaret is devastated. Fortunately, a trusted therapist helps them restore some of the intimacy that first drew them together, although only some. When Enrique decides to end the adultery he is motivated more by the fear of losing his son than by his troubled love for Margaret. Still, the therapy forces him to grapple with his general unhappiness, not just his unhappiness in the marriage.

It takes many years before he appreciates that whatever value and lasting happiness he found in life centers on Margaret and their sons. The catalyst for that understanding is Margaret's diagnosis of cancer. Only the prospect of losing her makes him certain "that he would do whatever was necessary to keep her alive," including sacrificing his writing and their money.[31] Against this backdrop of a troubled but generally happy relationship we understand Enrique's capacity to take care of Margaret during her three-year struggle with cancer, and also his retrospective struggle to understand and be grateful for their relationship. Everything in the past is cast in a new light, including periods of misery and joy.

As an example of a miserable period, he rethinks his year of adultery with Margaret's friend. The primary cause of the affair and the unhappiness, he now recognizes, was not the lack of sex. To be sure, that lack did matter, but he could have dealt with it by talking more honestly with Margaret. The affair connected with his general unhappiness. In retrospect, as he is able to place events in a longer illuminating perspective, the adultery seems to him largely irrelevant to his marriage. I would challenge this as rationalization, for the adultery, which he never confesses to Margaret, nearly had ended the marriage. Nevertheless, it is plausible to see his general unhappiness during their young adulthood as distorting his appreciation of what Margaret meant to him even at the time of the adultery.

As an example of a happy period, Enrique and Margaret celebrate their twenty-year anniversary with a trip to Venice, linking it to his work on a movie. Enrique never understood Margaret's perplexing combination of reticence and confidence. There was the time, for example, when she seriously began a career in painting but quickly became discouraged, despite promising critiques of her work. She reveals that she simply lacked Enrique's ambition and was happy with their life together as it is, but that she had avoided telling him that because she feared her lack of artistic fervor would lessen his interest in her. Again, during therapy he objects to her constant control over the details of their daily life, for example concerning which friends to see and which parties to attend. Upon voicing his dissatisfaction, he realizes that he actually enjoys that kind of control, and certainly has benefited from it. Again, some reflections concern his frustrated attempts to express his love with perfect gifts, failing each time to capture her taste. (It is not until she is dying that he finds the perfect gift in a pair of earrings.) He comes to appreciate "that what he had extracted of true value out of life was the life she had given him."[32] Yet even this insight fades somewhat, until Margaret's diagnosis with cancer reminds him that he had failed to keep such joyous episodes salient during the unfolding of their marriage.

All of love's virtues are manifested in the Enrique–Margaret marriage, albeit imperfectly, as in most relationships. The couple care deeply about each other, are good parents, enjoy countless daily interactions, and support each other's major interests. They respect each other, including accepting each other's foibles, and they establish a fair and balanced relationship. For the most part they faithfully nurture their love. In the main they embrace the ideal of sexual fidelity as important in protecting their love, although of course Enrique's adultery is a betrayal of that ideal and a betrayal of Margaret. Honesty, too, is compromised by the affair, but in most other respects they are exceptionally honest in ways that move toward a deepened mutual understanding. Both come to know with certainty that their love for each other and for their children was what most made their lives worthwhile.

To conclude, marriage is at once a moral relationship and a shared pursuit of happiness, and the two are intertwined in ways that highlight the moral importance of happiness. The pursuit is conducted with shared agency based on shared identification and caring. It is aimed not only at a happy relationship but also at the overall happiness of both partners. Virtue cannot guarantee happy marriages, although as elsewhere it is a good bet. Luck enters at all the usual junctures of individual lives, compounded by luck in being able to sustain love and to receive it in return. Hence love's perplexing mixture of strength and fragility.

10

BALANCING WORK AND LEISURE

We have gone beyond the work ethic, which endowed work with moral value, and now dangerously depend on our jobs to be the primary source of our identity, the mainspring of individual self-esteem and happiness.[1]

—Joanne Ciulla

Balance is generally considered a mark of wisdom in pursuing happiness and good lives, especially balance between work and leisure. Today we hear the complaint, from workers and social critics alike, that lives have become unbalanced, lopsided in the direction of work owing to longer hours, demands for higher productivity, less job security, loss of pensions and health care coverage, and encroachment of work into leisure via email and other electronic devices.[2] At the same time, most Americans voluntarily choose to work more than is necessary to meet their needs and take fewer vacation days than offered—in part to please employers but in part because they are deeply invested in their work.[3] This investment is excessive and dangerous, according to critics like Joanne Ciulla.

What is balance between work and leisure, why is it valuable, and how does it contribute to happiness in good lives? I doubt we have a clear idea of balance that we apply in identifying good lives; at least I don't. It seems to me largely the other way around.[4] We have some fairly rough criteria for good lives and apply them in understanding balance. One criterion is happiness, suggesting that balance is not an entirely independent guide to happiness (paralleling what was said about authenticity in chapter 4), although it remains an important guide in pursuing happiness in good lives overall. I also discuss health and morality as criteria for balance, and along the way I allude to additional criteria, specifically self-fulfillment and meaning as measured in terms of the full range of values, including such values as beauty, wealth, athletics, and scientific understanding, as well as morality. All these criteria are multifaceted and sometimes conflict, although they also overlap, interweave, and support each other. In this way, the concept of balance mirrors the practical challenges in pursuing happiness in good lives.

WORK, LEISURE, BALANCE

For my purposes, *work* refers to activities providing economic benefits, including paid employment, entrepreneurship, and the unpaid housework and child care by home-makers. *Leisure* refers to voluntary nonwork activities, excluding time spent on chores and obligations that we find unpleasant and onerous.[5] As Michael Argyle writes, lei-sure activities are what "people do in their free time, because they want to, for their own sake, for fun, entertainment, self-improvement, or for goals of their own choosing, but not for material gain."[6] These descriptive (morally neutral) definitions of work and leisure are somewhat vague—for example, just what are "economic benefits" and "free time"? Nevertheless, they have proven useful in the empirical studies I draw upon.

Balance can also be given descriptive (value-neutral) meanings, for example what-ever de facto allocations of time and effort individuals devote to various aspects of their lives. The predominant use of "balance," however, is normative (value-laden) when applied to human lives and to the work-leisure relation. Balance suggests reason-able and desirable allocations of time, energy, emotional engagement, commitment, and responsibility. Balance might be judged from a subjective perspective—what the individual considers reasonable allocations of attention and effort.[7] Alternatively, it might be assessed from a more objective perspective—what is reasonable in terms of justified values that define good lives.

In thinking about balance we need to take account of stages and cycles of life. Usually I have in mind *synchronic balance*, which is balance during a time slice of a life. Such balance is much celebrated, for example, by Aristotle and the Stoics who call for mod-eration in all things. But there is also *diachronic balance*, which concerns allocations over a lifetime, as when Ecclesiastes speaks of a time for every purpose under heaven. Diachronic balance might be compatible with synchronic imbalances, including lop-sided immersion in work or leisure during some periods of life.

Such lopsidedness might be required, for example, in some creative pursuits. Dar-win, Einstein, and Watson and Crick were engrossed in the work that led to their momentous discoveries, even at the expense of other important goods. We also know that engrossment in science (or any other activity) can be creative and yet be based on dangerously narrow Faustian bargains.[8] In developing what he calls a "bal-ance theory of wisdom," Robert Sternberg emphasizes that creativity may have little to do with wisdom and balance.[9] He has in mind synchronic balance, but I would recast his point: There can be wisdom in allowing some synchronic imbalances in a life that is diachronically balanced. As Robert Nozick observes, "Completely balanced and proportional judgment might inhibit youth's forceful pursuit of partial enthusiasms and great ambitions, through which they are led to intense experiences and large accomplishments."[10]

As a final preliminary remark, I note that although work-leisure balance is of enormous concern to some people, it is of little concern to others. The latter group includes many people who are retired, too sick or disabled to work, wealthy enough not to work, and so desperately strapped for money that discussions of balance strike them as a luxury for the privileged. At the same time, we should bear in mind that work is not exclusively about gaining economic benefits. Especially in America, as Ciulla emphasizes, identity and social recognition are strongly tied to work, and work also provides opportunities for personal development, the pursuit of meaningful activities and relationships, keeping our minds alive, staying healthy, making moral contributions—and pursuing happiness.

HAPPY WORK, HAPPY LEISURE, AND HAPPY LIVES

According to the first criterion, balance is any work-leisure allocation of time and energy that supports happiness. This includes being *happy that* our work and leisure are the way they are (propositional happiness). But primarily it consists in having a *happy life*. Bear in mind that I have set aside normative definitions of happy lives that build virtue into happiness, possibly begging important questions in thinking about balance. In contrast, I understand happiness as subjective in that it centers on an individual's emotions, attitudes, desires, and values, regardless of whether the values are justified. Specifically, our lives are happy insofar as we love them, valuing them in ways manifested by high levels of enjoyment and a robust sense of meaning (whether or not that sense of meaning is justified). Although happiness is subjective in this way, it is one of the genuine values characterizing good lives.

Recall, too, the distinction between global and domain happiness. Global happiness is loving our lives overall, in their entirety or during large time segments; domain happiness is happiness in particular areas such as work and leisure. Global happiness is what matters most in assessing balance. There are myriad ways to achieve it. For example, some individuals dislike their work but find that the leisure it makes possible suffices to bring high degrees of overall happiness. Conversely, some people love their work so much that it makes their lives happy overall, even though they are not especially happy during leisure. Perhaps for most of us, global happiness requires substantial happiness in both work and leisure. In any case, these variations make it impossible to generalize about "correct" work-leisure combinations that promote global happiness. Even so, statistical generalizations about happiness are possible, and they are much pursued by psychologists.

Happiness within the domain of work has many sources, summarized by Peter Warr in *Work, Happiness, and Unhappiness*. Warr defines happiness as a combination of satisfaction (pleasure, enjoyment) and "self-validation" (self-fulfillment, authenticity, meaning).[11] His idea of self-validation blurs the subjective *sense of meaning* with *objective meaning*, understood in terms of justified values, but primarily he has in mind subjective meaning. Hence his definition of happiness is close to mine, although I would add that the enjoyment and sense of meaning must add up to a life we love.

Warr sorts happiness-promoting factors into three categories: work environment, individual personality, and alignment (balance) between work environment and personality. First, *environment-centered factors* include personal control over our work, opportunities to employ our personal skills (expertise, knowledge), challenging and manageable goals imposed by the workplace, variety of activities during the day or across longer time periods, clarity about work expectations and the consequences of work, opportunities for meaningful contact with other people, satisfying amounts of money and other economic benefits, physical safety and security at the workplace, and recognition for one's social worth and status within an organization.[12]

Second, *person-centered factors* include temperament and general personality traits, such as optimism, enthusiasm, extraversion, and agreeableness. As in all domains of life, happiness at work is especially threatened by neurotic tendencies to experience excessive depression, anxiety, and hostility. Other personality factors are more attuned to situation and context. For example, how do we compare ourselves to others? Are we grateful for being relatively well-off in our work, or do we envy what others derive from their jobs? Are we relatively effective in our work, or is our job performance below par, both in our own eyes and those of others?

Third, *alignment-centered factors*, such as flow and fit, pertain to congruence between personality and work environment. Flow, drawing on Mihaly Csikszentmihalyi's conception, refers to activities whose intrinsic features motivate and engage us, require concentration, involve clear goals and provide immediate feedback about how well we are performing an activity, manifest our sense of competence and control but without self-consciousness, and create a sense of time passing quickly.[13] Warr thinks of happy work as typically involving ample and recurring opportunities for flow, usually on a daily basis, thereby greatly contributing to enjoyment and especially to a sense of meaning.

Other researchers are less sure about the connection between flow in work and (global) happiness, and they suspect that the term smuggles in values. Daniel Nettle observes: "People with a lot of flow in their lives are less bored and apathetic than others, but they score absolutely no higher in their responses to questions about how happy they are. . . . Studies of high-flow professions such as musicians, artists, and writers show that these individuals are prone to deep dissatisfaction, which moves them forward in their quest, as well as bouts of depression and addiction."[14] For his part, Csikszentmihalyi speaks of flow as "optimal experience," which is clearly a normative expression. He then blurs the contribution of flow to happiness: "When we are in flow, we are not happy, because to experience happiness we must focus on our inner states, and that would take away attention from the task at hand."[15] Perhaps his point is better made by saying that we are not thinking about our happiness (or ourselves) during flow, but that flow experiences tend to contribute to loving our lives. In any case, I understand flow subjectively, as activities that deeply engage us, regardless of whether the activities are desirable.

The term "fit" refers to being well suited for particular jobs and for types of work. Russell Muirhead helpfully distinguishes between personal and social fit. Personal fit occurs "where work contributes to our own development and expression," whereas social fit is a good match "between individual aptitudes and the [morally legitimate] tasks society generates."[16] Muirhead focuses less on happiness and more on self-fulfillment, understood normatively in terms of "an individual's best purposes." But in places he is aware that developing the best in us is not the same as being happy, and he seems to appreciate that both these values are important aspects of "fit."[17] In fact, these two aspects—developing the best in us and being happy—can conflict. A musical prodigy might be miserable in her work, perhaps owing to the pressures accompanying the pursuit of excellence in her field, or perhaps she simply enjoys leisure more than working at perfecting her talent.[18] I believe we should celebrate happiness, along with the pursuit of excellence, as a criterion for fit. Loving our work matters, both as an aspect of personal fit and because personal fit is important for social fit—for the contribution we can make to community through our work.

What about happiness during leisure? Does leisure tend to promote happiness in entirely different ways than work does? Of course, there are obvious differences. Work provides money, which contributes to well-being by providing economic support for leisure and also status and pride. Leisure typically provides more free time and personal control. It also includes time with family and friends. But an interesting theme is emerging in the empirical literature: Sources of happiness at work and in leisure are far more similar than dissimilar.

Leisure should not be stereotyped as idling away time, much less as vegging out in front of a television, although a good life can leave room for that, too. Leisure sometimes becomes predominantly or even exclusively passive when work leaves us exhausted and with little interest besides watching television. But active leisure is enormously important in most good lives. It includes what Robert Stebbins calls *serious leisure*, for example committed pursuits as amateurs, hobbyists, and volunteers.[19] Stebbins found that most of the happiness-promoting features of work also apply to serious leisure (as noted in chapter 8). Like work, happiness-making leisure can involve caring and commitment, community involvement, the need to make some effort in applying our knowledge and skills, persevering in the face of difficulties, ample opportunities for flow experiences, the achievement of positive outcomes for others and in terms of self-fulfillment, and even progress in something like a career of philanthropic involvement.[20]

Serious leisure activities often meet what Stebbins regards as the six primary features of "devotee occupations"—those forms of work that provide meaning beyond money: 1) substantial knowledge and skill is required, 2) variety of activities, 3) opportunities for innovation and personal expression, 4) significant control over how time is invested, 5) aptitude for and personal interest in the activities ("fit"), and 6) ample opportunities to pursue the work without handicaps such as excessive workload or paperwork.[21] Work and leisure strongly overlap along these lines. Of course, leisure also involves less unstructured activities, including "casual leisure" such as play and watching television, and "project-based leisure" in the form of occasional structured projects such as taking a major vacation and throwing a wedding party. But happy leisure typically requires some structure made possible by serious leisure. When that structure is lacking, leisure can become a source of malaise rather than happiness.

Despite the presence of money in work and greater control in leisure, then, much work and leisure are sources of happiness for similar reasons. Individuals who choose heavy involvement in their work often do so because the work itself is deeply engaging. Reminding ourselves of the intrinsically attractive features of work is important in thinking about work-leisure balance for individuals who have freedom to choose, albeit not for the economically desperate who have little choice but to work more than they would like.

Finally, in addition to work-leisure balance, there is a need for happy balance among work activities themselves, and also among leisure activities. For example, the work of most professors includes teaching, research, and service, and tenured professors have considerable leeway in working out happy balances among these subdomains at different stages of their careers.[22] Sometimes the primary way to increase happiness at work is to locate areas, however modest, that we can control, enjoy, and derive meaning from. Thus, Martin E. P. Seligman's advice to lawyers, who tend to be less happy than many other professional groups, is to reshape their jobs in directions offering greater flow (for example, writing or research time in a library), as well as finding ways to prevent the pessimism needed in pursuing their work from spilling over into their personal lives.[23] He phrases his advice as finding areas of our work where we can build on our personal strengths and virtues in ways we find personally satisfying and meaningful.

As for imbalances within the domain of leisure, for example, too much time at the pub or watching television can lead to family problems, and overinvolvement in some types of volunteering can lead to burnout.[24] In turn, family brings stresses of its own that pose challenges to happiness and meaning. Some studies reveal that, on average, child rearing lowers satisfaction levels. As Daniel Gilbert reports, child-rearing "couples generally start out quite happy in their marriages and then become progressively less satisfied over the course of their lives together, getting close to their original levels of satisfaction only when their children leave home."[25] Gilbert concludes that fortunately for the human race prospective parents have the illusion that this will not occur to them. More recent studies suggest that the average drops in happiness occur primarily with "couples who slid into being parents, disagreed over it or were ambivalent about it."[26] I would add that in having children parents often seek meaning (in the form of love) more than enjoyment. Women who bear the primary responsibility for most child rearing often report greater levels of satisfaction at work than at home. It is not even true that leisure always provides greater control than work, as parents taking their child to an emergency room know well.

HEALTHY BALANCE

Health is the most familiar criterion for balance. It interweaves with health but is distinct from it, and like happiness it can be understood in many ways. Today health is widely understood as biopsychosocial—as physical, mental, and social well functioning. It encompasses general capacities, actual functioning of persons in their present circumstances, and preventive measures to avoid threats to health before they arise. Furthermore, health can be defined either negatively, as the absence of disease and disorders, or positively, as effective or optimal functioning and self-development.

Negative definitions of health, to begin with, have the most traction in thinking about balance. According to them, lives are imbalanced when their relative allocations of time and energy contribute to unacceptable levels of sickness and disorder. To be sure, we might disagree about exactly what counts as sickness and disorder, and our therapeutic culture constantly expands these categories in controversial ways. But certainly physical sickness includes work-generated chronic fatigue, frequent colds, and carpal tunnel syndrome. Mental disorders include pathological depression and anxieties caused by chronic stress, which is generated as much by tight deadlines and tyrannical supervisors as by long hours.[27] Additional psychological problems include battered self-esteem and excessive anger caused by unfair labor practices or toxic colleagues.

Leisure can involve its own health problems, which interact with those at work. Physical and mental disorders include alcohol and drug abuse, and pathological spending and gambling. Quite apart from disorders, there are anxieties arising from inadequate day care for children. And needless to add, depression can be caused by miserable marriages, painful divorces, conflicts with friends, and other tensions during leisure time that affect happiness overall. Some of these problems are alleviated by new computer technologies and enlightened management policies that permit more flexible work arrangements, including work at home, and take seriously the need for workers to spend time away from work. But many workers still find it difficult to integrate work and leisure in healthy ways.

Work-leisure imbalances are much discussed in self-help books that popularize ideas such as workaholics, compulsive shopping, and affluenza, which has been defined as "a painful, contagious, socially transmitted condition of overload, debt, anxiety, and waste resulting from the dogged pursuit of more."[28] Problems of imbalance also show up in the offices of professional therapists. By far, the worst impacts on health come from forced unemployment—forced imbalance in the direction of leisure. Ilene Philipson orients most of her psychotherapy practice in Silicon Valley around work-related problems in the aftermath of the millennial tech bust. She deals with hundreds of clients devastated by layoffs from companies they loved and trusted. Clients cry out in pain about being betrayed by companies they thought cared as deeply for them as they cared for the company. Philipson sees her clients "marrying" their jobs, seeking from their workplaces the kinds of unconditional affirmation once reserved for marriage. Echoing Ciulla, she writes that work "is colonizing our emotional lives"; "as our identities verge on becoming corporate constructions, we lose our capacity not only to be actively engaged family members, but citizens."[29] Philipson urges greater attention to family and community, and setting clear boundaries for work—for example, by turning off pagers and e-mail during family time. No doubt that is sound advice for many individuals, but others seem to thrive on blurred boundaries.

Next consider conceptions of positive health, which have become prominent in thinking about balance. Invariably, they conceal moral values and often allude to happiness, thereby overlapping with the other two criteria for balance.[30] Most famously, the World Health Organization defines health as "a state of complete physical, mental and social well-being, not merely the absence of disease or infirmity."[31] Mental well-being, as understood today, includes healthy self-esteem—the reasonable mean between self-debasement and narcissism, as discerned in light of the moral virtue of self-respect. Perhaps it also includes concern for self-fulfillment, an idea that at some points alludes to moral values defining capacities "worthy" of development. And "complete mental well-being" seems to include happiness, or at least the capacity for happiness under normal circumstances.

Plato founded a long tradition of linking healthy functioning to morality and happiness. Yet his conception of health, as reason governing the appetites, is too vague to help us in balancing work and leisure in contemporary society. Closer to our time, Lewis Mumford sets forth a more nuanced and multifaceted conception of organic balance.

According to Mumford, balance means developing different aspects of the personality, including biological rhythms such as exercise and rest, psychological stability and richness, cognitive understanding and appreciation of beauty, individualism and group participation, perspectives sensitive to both transitory and enduring goods, and economic productivity and recreation. All these aspects of balance contribute to healthy personal development: "Balance is valuable as an aid to growth: it is not the goal of growth."[32] Balance contributes to our ability to respond to "novel situations, unexpected demands, emergent opportunities," and thereby promotes survival and mental health.[33] Mumford seems to think that we can identify the requirements of balance prior to identifying healthy growth in particular individuals, and then we use those requirements to guide us in promoting growth. There is a problem with this view that becomes clear when we ask: Exactly which capacities require development and in which combination, so as to specify balance between work and leisure? I believe Mumford has it backward. We first develop some idea of what healthy growth is in particular contexts and instances, and then we apply that understanding in understanding balance. It might turn out that for some people work largely answers their personality needs, while for others work plays at most a supportive role for rewarding leisure activities.

Regardless of which conception of healthy balance we employ, applying it to work and leisure is not straightforward. Ideas of healthy balance apply in different ways at three different levels: societal (public health), organizational (healthy versus toxic workplaces), and personal decision making in allocating time and energy (individual health). At the first two levels, the standard will be health for the average person, but at the third, personal level, there is considerable variation. As John Dewey suggests, "How to live healthily or justly is a matter which differs with every person. It varies with his past experience, his opportunities, his temperamental and acquired weaknesses and abilities."[34]

MORAL BALANCE

Moral balance is usually understood as giving work and leisure their moral due in terms of meeting important responsibilities in both domains. As such, balance would come into play only after these responsibilities are established, for example by making commitments to an employer and a family (in addition to general responsibilities to oneself and others). Alternatively, and more plausibly, moral balance involves forming and implementing life plans that contain morally desirable patterns of moral goods and virtues as well as responsibilities. Balance is morally valuable when and because it promotes goods and virtues, and prevents vices such as fanaticism, tunnel vision, callousness, and negligence.

Some thinkers understand moral balance hierarchically and propose general rankings of work and leisure. Gilbert Meilaender, for example, contends that we should work in order to live, rather than live in order to work. Good lives, he urges, are centered on meaningful personal relationships with family, friends, community, and God: "When work as we know it emerges as the dominant idea in our lives—when we identify ourselves to others in terms of what we do for a living, work for which we are paid—and when we glorify such work in terms of self-fulfillment, it is time for Christian ethics to speak a good word for working simply in order to live."[35]

I am suspicious of such rankings. Insofar as work is meaningful and fulfilling, we live to work just as much as we work to live. Work and leisure are both vital ingredients in most lives, and balancing them is less about general rankings and more about contextual judgments aimed at integrating them. Even for those who make family paramount and hence are willing to sacrifice particular jobs when they threaten family, work remains essential insofar as it provides economic resources for family. And abstract rankings of family over profession invite responses such as the following:

"Which is more important to you, your [professional] field or your children?" the department head asked.

She replied, "That's like asking me if I could walk better if you amputated my right leg or my left leg."[36]

Moral balance needs to be understood contextually, as people confront life crises and moral dilemmas (akin to how "healthy balance" becomes salient in responding to unhealthy imbalance). Often there is more than one morally reasonable way to allocate priorities among responsibilities, and certainly among moral and other goods. For example, early in his fifty years of humanitarian service in Africa, Albert Schweitzer had to decide whether to abandon his mission in order to return to Europe with his wife, a nurse who was unable to adjust to the harsh climate. He chose to stay in Africa, even though doing so created tensions in his marriage and made it impossible for him to share fully in raising his daughter. I would have chosen otherwise, but then I would never have undertaken anything like his extraordinary humanitarian commitment in the first place. In any case, I do not think there is a justified moral ideal of balance that shows he made the wrong choice by putting his work and service ahead of his family (especially in light of the apparent consent of his wife).[37] Moral balance requires taking into account personal moral priorities. And even if there were a clear moral ideal of balance here, the ideal itself would need to be contextually refined in light of the dilemma, as we gained clarity about what moral reason implies in that situation.

Complicating everything, morality includes duties to ourselves—to maintain our health, to be authentic, to pursue self-fulfillment, and perhaps to take heed of happiness. Kant understands most duties to ourselves as general duties, such as to take care of our health and preserve our lives, but he also includes the highly individualized duty to develop our talents. Mill celebrates Wilhelm von Humboldt's suggestion that "the end of man . . . is the highest and most harmonious development of his powers to a complete and consistent whole."[38] Schweitzer, applying such themes to work– leisure imbalances during the 1920s, warned that long hours (truly long then) imposed on workers betrayed "the ideal of a man well and truly developed as a spiritual personality."[39] Even Adam Smith, after celebrating specialization in the marketplace, cautions that "the man whose whole life is spent in performing a few simple operations . . . has no occasion to exert his understanding" and hence "becomes as stupid and ignorant as it is possible for a human creature to become."[40] For all these thinkers moral balance is an important, albeit secondary, value that serves self-fulfillment and moral responsibility.

A useful framework for thinking about moral balance will avoid general rankings of work and leisure while inviting integrations of the moral goods and responsibilities in both domains. Alasdair MacIntyre provides such a framework in *After Virtue*, at least with a few modifications. He famously introduces the idea of social practices: complex, shared activities aimed at distinctive internal goods, and guided by standards of excellence that tend to expand human achievement and fulfillment. Internal goods are those that partly define activities as particular social practices, in contrast with external goods like money, power, and fame that might be acquired through many different practices. The professions are paradigms of social practices, with medicine aimed at the internal good of health, law at justice, and teaching at education. I would broaden social practices to include all forms of work that contribute to community goods and meaningful lives, not just the professions, which require extensive advanced education.[41] Internal goods also include personal goods in the form of meaningful ways of life for professionals and other workers. Both types of internal goods, public and personal, contrast with generic goods like money and power that can be acquired through many different practices.

Many leisure activities also qualify as social practices. As one example, MacIntyre lists "the making and sustaining of family life" as a social practice.[42] He also allows that amateurs, hobbyists, philanthropists, and others, not just professionals, can participate in social practices in the arts, sciences, sports, and games. Indeed, some engage in social practices as varied as entertainment, sports, or scientific inquiry with commitment comparable to professionals, but without payment or with token payment. Hobbyists include such things as collectors, mountain climbers, bird-watchers, voracious readers in history or philosophy, and even avid audience participation in the arts. Much volunteering and philanthropy qualify as participating in social practices in the form of giving money, time, and talent for public purposes, whether the purposes are humanitarian, cultural, political, environmental, or any number of causes.[43]

Good lives typically involve participation in multiple social practices, which need to be integrated and balanced, along with integrating their internal and external goods. Lives must make sense, morally and personally, as narrative (historical) unities. The virtues play a key role—wisdom in discerning reasonable emphases, courage and self-discipline in pursuing responsibilities, love and commitment in cherishing goods, etc. They enable us to meet the standards of excellence at work and to restrict the tendency for money and power to distort the internal goods of work. That is a deep and recurring concern, although we can also agree with free-market celebrants that capitalism not only creates wealth but also fosters virtues such as prudence, responsibility, self-control, and collegiality.[44]

Like Aristotle, MacIntyre assumes the (cardinal) virtues are genuine only when they apply across all social practices we participate in. More recent studies, however, emphasize that virtue is highly contextual; for example, we can be courageous or kind in the domain of family life but less so at work, or vice versa.[45] MacIntyre would root the virtues in Christianity, whereas I would celebrate a much wider range of traditions. And most important, MacIntyre moves too far in the direction of accepting traditions as the final word in applying the virtues, rather than emphasizing that traditions themselves are open to criticism in terms of the virtues and other values.[46] Nevertheless, he provides an insightful framework for integrating the internal and external goods of the various practices in which we participate.

I also note that MacIntyre says little about happiness, and he is a critic of the therapeutic emphasis in our society that tends to approach moral issues in terms of mental health. Except where he discusses Aristotelian *eudaimonia*, he tends to think of happiness in terms of pleasures whose worth is linked to satisfying desires for internal and external goods. He remarks, for example, that our guide in good lives should be desirable goods, not happiness.[47] In contrast, I regard happiness as integral to fully good lives, as essential as health and morality in understanding balance between work and leisure.

PRAGMATIC BALANCING

I have suggested that balance cannot be understood prior to and apart from general criteria for good lives, in particular happiness, health, and morality. Each of these criteria has both generic and personal dimensions, and hence needs to be applied contextually and in a spirit of ethical pluralism. Moreover, the criteria can conflict. For example, a parent might risk her health by working more than she should and do so out of both a sense of moral responsibility for her children and because her happiness centers on them. Because of this conflict, integrating work and leisure requires reasonably integrating these three criteria as well. Maintaining balance between work and leisure is a personal matter but it requires setting reasonable priorities and making reasonable compromises and adjustments. Granted, where obligations are involved we can make some clear-cut judgments: It is wrong, for example, to use excessive work as a way to escape responsibilities for one's children. But even these judgments are made in light of commitments that individuals have already made, for example commitments to have children.

Each of us makes rankings in particular contexts based on our personal commitments. We structure our lives around commitments having fundamental importance to us, such that to violate them will cause deep psychological and moral harm, with other commitments being more defeasible and malleable.[48] Commitment to a particular workplace, for example, might be highly defensible, although commitment to a particular profession might be as fundamental in defining us as our personal commitments to friends and family. Usually concerns about balance arise in response to stress, stain, and dilemmas as we integrate or modify our core commitments in changing circumstances.

In one regard, however, moral criteria for balance emerge as paramount, as connected with procedures in maintaining balance more than in the content of balance. Confronting imbalances requires virtues such as prudence, courage, fairness, and a sense of responsibility, each manifested in a pragmatic spirit. By "pragmatic," I mean the decisions will be highly practical, contextual, and personal.[49] Typically the decisions arise from and seek to minimize tensions, frustrations, and anxieties. We are concerned, for example, about how to meet demanding work schedules while providing adequate (or excellent) day care for our children, especially when our child is sick or we cannot find child care on days when schools close for vacations. We are concerned with how our marriages or relationships are put at risk by allowing work to claim most of our energy and interest. We are alternately stressed in unhealthy degrees by work pressures and bored by work that has lost its challenge. We need to be aware of the risks of layoffs and sensitive to when it is time to risk changing jobs.

"Pragmatic" also alludes to American pragmatism, of course, which provides some of the most illuminating depictions of practical reasoning (although I do not endorse it as a stand-alone moral theory). In particular, John Dewey portrays most occasions for moral reasoning as prompted by "as *excess* of preferences" whereby "we want things that are incompatible with one another," or at least appear to be, and we must seek "what we *really* want" by constructing "a unified preference out of competing preferences."[50] At a general level, our competing preferences might be equally clear and important to us, as with work and family. We seek to integrate them, aware that the goods they make possible are mutually enriching: work providing economic support for families, families providing emotional support for work, and both work and family providing opportunities for self-expression and meaning. Intelligent moral reasoning "coordinates, organizes and functions each factor of the situation which gave rise to conflict, suspense and deliberation" bringing "order, perspective, proportion . . . out of a diversity of earlier incompatible preferences."[51]

Integrating work, family, and other leisure activities is guided by reasonable practical judgment that gets us through the day, the week, and the year, with an eye to the horizon of our long-term plans and hopes. Mary Catherine Bateson calls it an improvisational art, akin to jazz, in which we creatively find ways to integrate multiple commitments, "discovering the shape of our creation along the way, rather than pursuing a vision already defined."[52] Pursuing good lives is less like putting a puzzle together guided by a picture on the box than creating a picture by putting together various pieces at hand.[53] It is dynamic process, not a static one, and it integrates moral reasoning with prudent attention to health and happiness.[54]

All this makes it difficult to generalize about (reasonable) balance and (unreasonable) imbalance in the direction of work, simply in terms of the number of hours consumed by work or, recalling Ciulla and Meilaender, the extent to which an individual's identity is linked to their work. Should we then abandon the idea of balance? Surely not. Balance between work and leisure, reasonable allocations of time and commitment remains an important diagnostic tool in thinking about how good lives go awry—assuming we adopt a pluralistic and pragmatic value perspective that tolerates, and celebrates, a variety of good lives.

11

SIMPLICITY

There are two kinds of simplicity—one that is akin to foolishness, the other to wisdom.[1]
—Henry David Thoreau

"Simplicity, simplicity, simplicity!"—that is the catalyst which transforms "lives of quiet desperation" into an "irrepressible satisfaction with the gift of life."[2] Thoreau's conviction reverberates through many moral traditions and thinkers, including Confucius and Buddha, Socrates and the Stoics, the Quakers and Shakers, modern environmentalism and contemporary self-help books. What is voluntary simplicity? If it is merely removing complexity by narrowing the range of our concerns, then it might be wise or foolish. If instead simplicity is centering our lives on what is most important, keeping it salient by eliminating damaging distractions and waste, then by definition it is a virtue manifesting practical wisdom. Happiness is a crucial part of what matters most, but it is only a part because good lives embody additional goods. As a result, simplicity is not altogether simple to understand, let alone achieve. I begin by sketching a concept of simplicity as a virtue, then identify some ways simplicity promotes happiness, and conclude by subsuming simplicity under the broader rubric of coping with complexity in good lives.

DEFINITIONS OF SIMPLICITY

Definitions of simplicity vary according to how we answer four questions. First, is the concept and definition of simplicity descriptive (value-neutral) or normative (value-laden, honorific)? Descriptive definitions typically specify that simplicity is reducing complexity, whether by restricting activities, removing clutter and debt, or cutting back on stressful activities such as long hours at work. So defined, simplicity might be unwise. For example, reducing time spent at work might result in losing a good job; downsizing to a less stressful but lower-paid job might result in financial distress later on; and spending more time watching television might cause boredom and alienation from our family. In contrast, normative definitions specify that simplicity consists of reducing complexity in desirable ways—in ways that center our lives on what is most valuable and to that end remove undesirable distractions and waste. This centering can be specified in terms of the generic aspects of good lives, and it can be specified in terms of the particular values that give meaning to an individual's life, for example, engagement in sports, the arts, or science. Accordingly, whether a given instance of reducing complexity instantiates the virtue of simplicity turns on whether it expresses practical understanding about how to pursue happiness in a good life. I adopt a normative definition of simplicity as a virtue.

Second, regarding normative definitions, are the values that specify "what is important" understood subjectively or objectively? Subjectively, simplicity might mean seeking what we believe will increase our happiness by satisfying preferences, adding enjoyments, and enriching a sense of meaning. Objectively, simplicity means seeking and achieving what is genuinely important in terms of justified values that include happiness but also the other dimensions of good lives—authenticity, self-fulfillment, health, moral decency and goodness, and meaningfulness in terms of justified values. As such, simplicity manifests wisdom. I adopt an objective conception of simplicity that highlights the generic features of good lives, while still acknowledging the importance of subjective elements such as what makes us happy and what we care about most deeply.

Third, is simplicity understood in absolute or flexible terms? Absolute definitions, as we might call them, specify a canonical conception of *the* simple life, perhaps as all or nothing and with an emphasis on purity. Such a life might have a rigid and authoritarian cast, as in Puritan and Amish societies. In contrast, flexible definitions assume a pluralistic view of good lives, a view that celebrates wide variation in what Thoreau calls experiments in simple living, and many degrees and kinds of simple lives. Such definitions accent the verb "to simplify" rather than any particular pattern of results defining "the" simple life. They can proceed at many different levels, in many different ways, and with many different goals in mind. I intend a pluralistic and scalar definition of simplicity, congruent with a pluralistic conception of good lives.

I include, for example, all three categories of simplifiers distinguished by Amitai Etzioni: moderate, strong, and holistic.[3] Moderate simplifiers are wealthy individuals who maintain a relatively rich lifestyle while downshifting in some areas of their lives, in particular by buying far fewer luxuries than they could easily afford in order to use their financial resources to help others. Strong simplifiers give up high-paying and high-stress jobs, such as corporate attorneys and investment bankers, in order to live on far lower income and have a lower socioeconomic status. Holistic simplifiers go further, adjusting every aspect of their lifestyle in light of ideals promulgated in the "simple living movement," for example, moving to a smaller house, relocating from urban to rural settings, and being conscientious about types of food and energy usage. I agree with Etzioni that instead of focusing exclusively on holistic simplifiers we should think of simplicity as a wide-ranging virtue that can be manifested in many different ways.

Fourth, is simplicity defined formally or substantively? Formal definitions specify, in abstract terms, that a simple life is centered on what is most important and eliminates what is inessential and wasteful. Substantive definitions go further in outlining a conception of what is important and worthwhile, and what is inessential and wasteful. Obviously, substantive definitions can be more or less detailed. I favor a definition of simplicity in which the aim is to center lives on "what is important" as understood in terms of happiness, authenticity, self-fulfillment, health, moral decency and goodness, and meaning in terms of justified values. In addition, I am especially interested in three moral emphases familiar in the contemporary conceptions of simplicity: focus, frugality, and ecological responsibility.[4]

More Focus, Less Distraction. As Thoreau reminds us, the search for a simpler life often begins with the desire to become happier, or to reduce unhappiness in the form of excessive stress, anxiety, anger, depression, or despair. Many of us are overextended. We lead hectic lives, often feel anxious and overwhelmed, and have too little time for what we find meaningful and enjoyable. The ideal of simplicity enjoins making more time for activities and relationships that are both personally satisfying and morally desirable. There are many possibilities from which to choose: increase leisure by cutting back on hours spent at work; focus on aspects of work that are more enjoyable and meaningful; change jobs; change careers; change our obsession with promotions and status at work; retire early; slow the pace of our days to allow more time for mindfulness and relaxation; develop healthier habits of exercise and diet; adjust our attitudes; etc. A simpler life involves setting boundaries and frees time for what is inherently valuable. Exactly what that involves must be understood in relation to individuals and in light of an array of justified values, such as worthwhile relationships, meaningful work, and valuable forms of service to others.

More Frugality, Less Waste. Once beyond the economic level of bare subsistence, frugality means living below our means in order to save and invest in the future— for ourselves, our family, and our community. Frugality does not imply poverty; indeed, frugality is a familiar recommendation to people aspiring to become millionaires.[5] But frugality has many variations and aims. The goal might be to work less and make less money in order to allow more time with family and friends. Alternatively, the goal might be to save more money in order to get out of debt and achieve financial independence, freeing our family from the anxieties of living from paycheck to paycheck.

More Conserving, Less Consuming. Cherishing and being attuned to nature is a central theme in the history of voluntary simplicity. Certainly it was at the heart of Thoreau's rural and rustic version of environmentalism that emphasized aesthetic and spiritual connectedness with nature. Contemporary approaches to simpler living might be urban or rural. Yet a central theme is awareness of the environmental crisis, not only as a social policy issue but in terms of reducing our personal use of carbon energy sources. One ideal is reducing automobile commutes to work, either by shifting to public transportation or by living closer to work, ideally within walking or biking distance. Additional emphases include living in a smaller house, using energy-efficient lightbulbs, insulating better, using solar power, and recycling. Other emphases are more controversial, for example food issues: Is there a moral imperative to become a vegetarian, and of what sort, or is it all right to eat free-range chicken and genetically modified salmon?

In sum, as a virtue, simplicity is not exactly simple. I understand simplicity (1) normatively, as the virtue of reducing complexity, distraction, and waste in order to center our lives on what is most important; (2) objectively, by specifying what is important in terms of justified values characterizing good lives, while acknowledging the importance of subjective elements such as deep caring and personal sources of happiness; (3) flexibly, as allowing many variations and degrees, and as inviting tolerance for diversity in experiments in simple living; and (4) substantively, both in specifying what is important in terms of the main dimensions of good lives and in highlighting the reduction of complexity and waste via focus, frugality, and ecological responsibility.

REDUCING COMPLEXITY TO INCREASE HAPPINESS

Does simplicity promote happiness? To repeat, the answer depends on the value criteria used to specify what is most important and should be kept central in our lives. If happiness were the sole value used to specify what is important, then the question of whether simplicity promotes happiness would be almost rhetorical: "Does a life centered on happiness promote happiness?" (I say almost, because there is the issue of whether centering our lives too directly on our happiness is self-defeating, as the paradoxes of happiness suggest.) If instead, as in my view, "what is important" includes all aspects of good lives—including moral decency and goodness, authenticity, genuine meaning, health, and fulfillment, as well as happiness—then much of this book is relevant to answering the question. In this section I limit discussion to how focus, frugality, and environmental responsibility contribute to happiness.

Most psychological studies of how focus, frugality, and environmental responsibility contribute to happiness rely on self-reporting of two things: (1) happiness, understood as subjective well-being (as life satisfaction and high levels of enjoyment), and

(2) simplicity (as self-defined). Tim Kasser and his colleagues adopt this approach while integrating two additional variables they suspect are important: mindfulness and intrinsic motivation. Mindfulness is attention to our behavior and mental states; it implies receptive and perceptive responses, and is manifested in such activities as savoring and flow. Intrinsic motivation means being motivated primarily by the value we perceive as inherent in activities and relations, rather than the material (and other "external") rewards they bring. This line of research is especially helpful because, in tune with the paradoxes of happiness, it invites consideration of how happiness is often best pursued indirectly, through mindful engagement in activities and relationships that we find intrinsically worthwhile.

More fully, Kasser and his colleagues employ a value-orientation questionnaire designed to contrast intrinsic motivation and materialistic (extrinsic) motivation. Materialistic value orientations place a high value on external rewards such as money, possessions, and social image and status. In contrast, intrinsic motivation orientations emphasize the "intrinsic value" of activities and relationships, pursued as worthwhile even if they do not bring additional (external) rewards. Three categories of intrinsic values are explored: personal growth, such as developing one's interests and talents; affiliation, such as caring and intimate personal relationships; and community feeling, manifested in service aimed at making the world better.[6] In one set of studies, Kasser and Kirk Brown studied people who identify themselves as voluntary simplifiers and asked questions about their happiness levels and about fifty-four environmentally responsible behaviors, such as recycling and involvement in environmental causes.[7] Control groups were average Americans. Kasser and Brown found some correlations between happiness and simpler lifestyles: "People who reported being more satisfied with their lives and experiencing more pleasant than unpleasant emotions were also more likely to report doing more ecologically sustainable behaviors and having lower ecological footprints."[8] The strongest correlations with happiness, however, were mindfulness and intrinsic value orientation.

Simplicity, via mindfulness and intrinsic motivation, contribute to happiness by providing valuable forms of focus: focus of attention to, interest in, and engagement with what is valuable. To begin with, focus implies attention to the activities, relationships, possessions, and other things that matter most to us in light of values we have carefully reflected on. This clarity contributes to a sense of who we are, for what we value is integral to our identity. Equally important, focusing on what we value most dearly tends to increase our chances of obtaining it, rather than constantly being distracted from it.

Typically we have more desires than we can satisfy, higher expectations than we can meet, and a multiplicity of values that cannot all be fully implemented. Simplicity implies concentrating on our basic needs and our most valuable desires. That is no easy task, for we tend to conflate luxuries and necessities, and the line between them shifts in a rapidly changing world. Thus, computer access is now a necessity for most people, but many people think cable and satellite dish entertainment is also a necessity. After meeting basic needs, we can turn to our desires and set priorities among them. Simplicity frees up resources—of time, energy, wealth—that add to our abilities to obtain what we most want. It prevents us from frittering away our lives with trivia. It removes or reduces anxiety about debt and economic insecurity. It helps foster passions that unfold our talents and valuable capabilities.

Aims (and priorities) are set at different levels: overall aims, general aims in domains such as work, and aims in specific situations. The skill sets required at these different levels are not identical. For example, an individual might be effective in setting reasonable boundaries between work and family, but less successful in overcoming an addiction. Again, a person might be effective in making short-term priorities such as maintaining a weekly budget, but less effective in making long-term plans such as saving for retirement. Of course, obtaining our particular goals does not guarantee happiness. Our aims might be based on error and illusion, and our efforts at simplification might hit a wall of bad luck. Nevertheless, reasonable attempts at focus usually have greater likelihood of success than just muddling through with no sense of priorities. Quite apart from success in obtaining what we value most highly, the pursuit of what is most important tends to be more meaningful and enjoyable. It tends to produce a life we love. And it contributes to self-esteem from knowing we are doing what we can to live a good life.

Focus is more than cognitive. It combines attentiveness with good judgment, commitment, and self-control. This implementation includes effort and courage in the face of temptations, but more important it includes forming habits that preclude the need for expending great energy in disciplining desires in particular situations. Self-control makes a double contribution to happiness. It increases our ability to satisfy important desires and meet important goals. It also increases the subjectively felt sense of control, which contributes directly to our sense of well-being and happiness.

Focus also contributes to flow and savoring. Flow means immersing ourselves in activities that we find inherently engaging, which provide immediate feedback, and which yield a sense of meaningful and enjoyable activity. Savoring implies attending to and appreciating the good things in our lives, taking interest in the moment and taking time to smell the flowers and enjoy their beauty. Savoring is a source of enjoyment and often expresses a sense of meaning, thereby contributing doubly to happiness.[9] In addition, both dimensions of savoring might be complex. For example, savoring the experience of reaching a mountain summit after a long climb might bring a sense of accomplishment, serenity after long struggle, thrill at the spectacular view, feeling the chill in the air, noting the special flora and fauna, etc.[10] Again, savoring the completion of writing a book might bring a variety of enjoyments, for example, in the process of making final revisions, in a sense of accomplishment, in enjoying looking at and holding the book, and in enjoying recognition from peers.

In sum, psychologists confirm that simplicity contributes to happiness in a variety of ways. We need to bear in mind, however, that psychological studies report statistics rather than universalities. Kasser's main conclusions are that people who voluntarily adopt simpler lifestyles are as happy as or happier than people who do not do so. But there is no guarantee that all of us would be as happy, let alone happier, if we adopted a simpler life. Many people enjoy very complicated lives, thriving on challenges and complexities that do not cause them as much stress as others experience. Moreover, most people enjoy and derive meaning from their materialistic goods, including their new car, large house, and sophisticated entertainment center.[11] If the case for a simpler life is exclusively an appeal to happiness, then it fails for many people. The case for focus, frugality, and environmental responsibility needs to be grounded in a wider range of moral values than just happiness. More generally, simplicity needs to be understood and defended in terms of good lives in all their dimensions—and in all their complexity.

COPING WITH COMPLEXITY IN GOOD LIVES

Reducing complexity is celebrated in discussions of happiness; *coping with complexity* is highlighted in discussions of good lives. The themes are compatible, for reducing complexity is a way to cope with complexity. Yet they constitute different emphases. On the one hand, coping with complexity is much broader and might involve maneuvers in addition to reducing complexity. On the other hand, good lives include dimensions in addition to happiness: a life might be simple in ways contributing to happiness but not to other goods. Tolstoy says that Ivan Ilyich's comfortable and contented life "had been most simple and commonplace—and most horrifying."[12] Ilyich's life was relatively happy, but it lacked the deep love for other persons that Tolstoy regards as essential to morally good lives. Morally good lives might involve complexities that we must learn to cope with, rather than to simplify with an eye to maximizing happiness.

In general, the theme of reducing complexity needs to be subsumed under the broader rubric of coping with complexity in good lives. Doing so allows us to approach simplicity and complexity as potentially complementary or conflicting, rather than polarized from the outset. Depending on the situation and on our personal resources, coping with complexity in the pursuit of good lives might best be done by reducing complexity or by accepting and managing necessary complexity in other ways.

To begin with, centering our lives on what is most important requires integrating myriad values in good lives. Morality by itself involves multiple virtues, rights, responsibilities, and goods that might conflict and need to be integrated. Each needs to be given due consideration and balanced with the others, and some might have to be overridden and set aside in particular situations. There are additional categories of values that need to be given a fair hearing, including values that shape personal meaning and fulfillment—everything from love and friendship to aesthetic appreciation to athletic excellence. Identifying what is most important in practical situations, and more broadly in composing a good life, requires exercising good judgment in integrating multiple values within multiple categories. It requires the kind of morally committed pragmatic thinking discussed in chapter 10.

This complexity of values in good lives is often obscured in discussions of simplicity. For example, in *Voluntary Simplicity* Duane Elgin slides between understanding simplicity as (a) entirely subjective in promoting happiness and (b) a more complex virtue promoting a wider range of values in good lives. In some passages, he tells us that "To live more *simply* is to live more purposefully and with a minimum of needless distraction. The particular expression of simplicity is a personal matter."[13] In other passages he characterizes simple lives as good in much broader ways—as honest, authentic, compassionate, environmentally responsible, healthy, and rich in love and service.[14] Rather than clearly indicating that good lives have multiple dimensions, some of which are subjective (happiness, enjoyment, sense of meaning) and others that include a fuller array of defensible values, Elgin blurs the two dimensions.

If good lives were reducible to happiness, then the exclusive aim would be to promote our own happiness, making our value orientation egoistic. We could still acknowledge that love, friendship, and community contribute to our happiness, but all these other dimensions of good lives would be bent and distorted in an egoistic direction. Likewise, compassion for the suffering of others, or even for our own suffering, would be limited in directions that maximize our personal enjoyments and sense of meaning. Honesty would be rethought to expand all happiness-producing illusions. Authenticity would shift entirely to what makes us happy, rather than including the challenge of developing our talents. In general, our lives would systematically be distorted in selfish directions, and that of course is a genuine danger in contemporary culture.

The multiplicity of values and the variety of good lives reflect the complexity of human psychology and the world. That complexity needs to be managed, sometimes by limiting it but other times by embracing it. Regarding human psychology, we are enriched by focus and limits but also by embracing complexity. Not all instances of simplification are desirable, even as ways to advance happiness, and complexity has its own charms in sustaining our interest and preventing boredom.

We can easily recast what was said earlier about reducing complexity under the broader rubric of coping with complexity. Good lives are often richly variegated, and with myriad interests pulling in different directions. To manage that complexity, we must selectively reduce some complexities, such as unproductive distractions, in order to allow grappling directly with complexity in other areas of life. Thoreau simplified the time spent earning money so that he could maximize time spent grappling with the complexities of writing, moral reflection, and the study of nature. Einstein lived a simple life so that he could grapple with the complexities of physics. In addition, these thinkers approached complexity in their intellectual work with an eye to uncovering simplicity amidst complexity. $E=mc^2$ is a strikingly simple formula that encapsulates an astonishing complex feature of the universe. The emotional intelligence required in human interactions contains complexity mixed with some underlying simplicity of its own.

Depending on the context, complexity might be managed using a host of tools, far too many to summarize. To mention just a few categories, the tools might include habit formation, technology, or therapeutic approaches. Consider the mundane matter of forming and modifying habits in order to economically structure our lives. Finding it difficult to make time for exercise, we fix time to get to the gym or to go for a walk. We protect the ritual in order to reduce the need for constant decision making about an important contribution to health and vigor. The habit is simple, but it helps manage the complexity of maintaining health. Likewise, we develop habits to structure many of our activities at work or in leisure, while allowing more flexible chunks of time.

Habits include setting default structures that we can then largely ignore, apart from periodic reviews. Consider financial planning, which can be so complicated that we end up doing nothing. Even if we never took a single business course, the traditional ideal of fiscal responsibility of living below our means need only be extended to a few new minimal steps that we then build upon. As the ideal of coping effectively with complexity, simplicity enjoins learning the basics, implementing them, and allowing refinements to emerge along with our comfort level. The basics include, for example, enrolling in the retirement plan offered on our first job so as take advantage of matching contributions our employer offers. They also include knowing that additional investing can be done automatically by investment companies. Frugality becomes less a matter of deliberate attentiveness, of the sort celebrated in the simple living movement, and more a matter of managing financial complexity with simple routine.

Turning to technology, when simplicity is defined descriptively as merely removing complexity, there is often a bias against new technology and a preference for minimal and small-scale technology.[15] In fact, technology offers the most dramatic ways to cope with complexity, even as it simultaneously adds to complexity. Most technologies are Janus-faced, producing both benefits and burdens, removing some complexities but adding others. For example, cell phones and email greatly increase productivity, but they also remove boundaries between work and leisure in ways that might reduce or add to stress, depending on how we choose to use it. Many advocates of simple living choose, in a Thoreau-like spirit, to minimize their purchases of new technologies, as a matter of personal taste and value. Most of us, however, do better to heed Lewis Mumford's observation: "Simplicity does not avoid mechanical aids: it seeks only not to be victimized by them."[16] In tune with the simplicity movement, Mumford favored conscientious consumerism: "Buy nothing merely because it is advertised, use no invention merely because it has been put on the market, follow no practice merely because it is fashionable."[17]

As aids, technological devices and systems are increasingly complex, but they need to be user-friendly. The friendliness begins with easily understandable knobs, buttons, clicks, and other operational features. Donald A. Norman spent his career seeking ways to make technology operationally simpler even as its power and workings become increasingly complicated. Efficient and effective technology is both simple and complex: "Good design can help tame the complexity, not by making things less complex—for the complexity is required—but by managing the complexity."[18] Why must remote controls for entertainment devices be so complicated? They don't have to be, and gradually capitalism moves toward ways to remove irritating needless complexity. For that matter, why do brochures explaining how to use the devices have to be so complicated? Again, they do not have to be, and here the fault often concerns writing simple and direct prose in ways to introduce basics clearly and relegate complexities to later for connoisseurs of complexity and innovation.

As for therapy, our health-oriented culture provides a treasure trove of options for increasing our ability to cope with complexity—in the world and in our emotional lives. Therapy is understood broadly to include healing sickness and enhancing function. There are formal therapies, such as counseling and medications, aimed at coping with psychological disorders and dysfunction. These resources are often abused, but that should not lead us to underestimate their contribution. What Thoreau saw as ubiquitous "quiet desperation" includes a variety of genuine disorders for which the health sciences provide help: depression, anxiety disorders, addictions, and a host of other disorders in many degrees of severity. These afflictions might be alleviated by reducing complexity in our activities. They might also, however, be best dealt with by introducing new complexities, such as honest explorations during psychotherapy, and in general an understanding of how morality and mental health are interwoven.[19]

Complexity is often most troublesome because of the stress it generates, and psychologists identify a host of everyday techniques for coping with daily hassles with less stress, while embracing complexity. They include identifying meaningful patterns beneath the complexity, making more reasonable appraisals of undesirable events, focusing on the good, meditation and relaxation techniques, greater mindfulness, exercising a sense of humor, not "catastrophizing" and procrastinating, forgiving ourselves and others, maintaining greater balance between work and leisure, adjusting the pace of our daily activities to allow more time to enjoy them, etc.[20] Moving beyond this emphasis on coping with the stresses of complexity, positive psychologists are studying ways to prevent stress ("proactive coping") rather than coping with stress after it occurs ("reactive coping").[21] They study what might be called "best practices" in living—the effective ways in which healthy people cope with complexity by making reasonable appraisals of what is important, efficient organization, and prioritizing. Clearly there is a strong overlap between reducing complexity and embracing complexity while coping with it effectively. But we do well to place the emphasis on coping with complexity, and to think of reducing complexity as only one of many tools used to manage complexity.

Finally, advocates of simplicity contend that simplicity tends to contribute to all aspects of good lives, not just happiness. For example, Etzioni highlights how simplicity contributes to protecting the environment, by lowering consumption and waste. He highlights how simpler living tends to orient us to love, family, community, rather than to excessive careerism aimed at maximizing wealth and status. And he even expresses optimism that simpler lives will result in greater socioeconomic equality: "Voluntary simplicity, if more widely embraced, might well be the best new source to help create the societal conditions under which the limited reallocation of wealth needed to ensure the basic needs of all could become politically possible."[22] Perhaps he is right, but much depends upon what "limited reallocation" requires. Much depends as well on the potentially negative side effects of reduced economic growth that became so vivid during the economic downturn beginning in 2007. And much depends on whether "what is important" is understood in the altruistic manner that Etzioni emphasizes, and on whether democracies can effectively nudge people toward greater concern for community. Complexity indeed!

To conclude, the virtue of simplicity involves more than simply reducing complexity. It consists of centering our lives on what is most important, keeping salient what is of most importance in practical situations, and removing distractions and waste that threaten that salience. What is most important includes happiness and much more. Simplicity has great value in pursuing happiness, but it also needs to be understood in terms of a wider range of values characterizing good lives. To that end, we do well to think of reducing complexity as part of coping with complexity in good lives.

12

FELICITY IN *FRANKENSTEIN*

Any adequate psychology of character will presumably include the truth, in some scientifically presentable form, that many people are horrible because they are unhappy, and conversely: where their unhappiness is not something specially defined in ethical terms, but is simply basic unhappiness—misery, rage, loneliness, despair.[1]
—Bernard Williams

"Happiness writes white," according to a literary maxim, meaning that extended depictions of it are bland and boring.[2] For writers and readers alike, the struggle to become happy is far more interesting than the state of being happy. Engrossing narratives are driven by tension and turmoil, and even episodic happiness should emerge on a background of suffering. Although hopes of "happily ever after" might provide an upbeat ending to a novel or screenplay, or appear early and be dismantled as a way to get the action underway, dwelling on happiness risks sentimentality (read: dishonesty).[3] No doubt there is much truth in all this, but mainly as it pertains to happiness as bovine contentment. If instead we understand happiness as loving our lives, valuing them through ample enjoyments and a rich sense of meaning, then depictions of happy lives can employ writers' full palette of conflict, challenge, and catastrophe. Examples include most of the novels, movie scripts, and memoirs cited in this book, including *Walden*, *The Old Man and the Sea*, *Happy-Go-Lucky*, and *Braided Lives*. Having said this, we can learn much about happiness from depictions of unhappiness, and in this chapter I discuss one example in detail, Mary Shelley's *Frankenstein*.

This iconic novel is usually approached as a cautionary tale about creative overreach and male hubris, but it also expresses and critiques Romantic conceptions of happiness (as good) and suffering (as transformative).[4] In doing so it explores the moral psychology surrounding what I call the happiness principle, or hypothesis: Happiness promotes virtue, unhappiness produces vice. More fully, happiness, which is made possible by satisfying natural desires for social acceptance and self-esteem, promotes virtue, and unhappiness, which is caused by social ostracism and self-hatred, produces vice. Although the principle is shared by the two protagonists, Victor Frankenstein and his unnamed creature, Shelley explores its dangers as well as its element of truth. Specifically, Shelley challenges our tendency to invoke the principle in justifying excessive demands for happiness and in excusing wrongdoing.[5] I begin with the creature's understanding of the principle, then Victor's understanding of it, and then how creature and creator alike use the principle to evade responsibility. I conclude by linking the discussion to the work of positive psychologists, who tend to be more sanguine about the principle but whose conclusions are consistent with Shelley's insights.

MALICIOUS BECAUSE MISERABLE: THE CREATURE'S VIEW

"I was benevolent and good; misery made me a fiend. Make me happy, and I shall again be virtuous" (103).[6] So pleads the creature in his first conversation with Victor. Within minutes Victor reflects that as creator "I ought to render him happy before I complained of his wickedness," thereby tacitly agreeing that the creature's misery contributes to his malice (104). Creature and creator apparently agree that happiness promotes virtue and misery produces vice, and this agreement plays a key role in the novel. In particular, the creature invokes the principle twice to defuse Victor's anger: once in getting Victor to listen to his life story (103–104) and once in eliciting Victor's promise to create a companion for him (147–150). Later Victor breaks his promise, not because he abandons his belief in the happiness principle, but because he comes to doubt that a companion would guarantee the creature's happiness and hence his virtue. The broken promise provokes the creature to murder Victor's closest friend, Henry Clerval, and Victor's bride, Elizabeth. In turn, these murders incite Victor's campaign to destroy the creature, which leads to Victor's own demise. In a final discussion with Captain Walton, who had tried to save Victor's life, the creature invokes the happiness principle yet again to explain and partly excuse his murders (222).

To elaborate, let us begin with how the creature comes to believe the happiness principle. Two years before his first conversation with Victor, the creature jerks to life possessing extraordinary physical and mental capacities, advanced skills of self-preservation, and a disposition to goodness. He also has an appearance more hideous than an animated mummy—gigantic stature, yellow and sallow skin, watery and dun-colored eyes, shiny white teeth and straight black lips that open to a demonic grin. Horrified and disgusted, Victor flees from him and literally jumps with joy when he vanishes (62). The creature spends two years covertly observing the De Lacey family and other villagers and, after mastering their language, he reads Milton's *Paradise Lost*, Goethe's *Sorrows of Young Werther*, and Plutarch's *Lives*. These books provide a moral education, but his moral understanding is shaped even more by reflecting on his own responses to the villagers. In particular, he notices that he is happy when sympathetically attuned to the De Laceys, but he explodes in rage when they react to him with horror and violence. He redirects his rage to Victor, whom he learns about from reading Victor's lab notes, which he found in the clothes he put on when he fled the laboratory where he was created. Comparing himself to an unjustly punished Satan in *Paradise Lost*, when he deserved to be God's beloved Adam, he feels justified in inflicting suffering on Victor. He murders William, a mere child who is Victor's youngest brother. Then he orchestrates the death of Justine, William's caregiver, by planting evidence that falsely blames her for William's death. These murders bring the creature momentary glee, but they do not yield the happiness he derived from sympathy for the De Laceys. Reflecting on this difference, he concludes that society caused his misery by frustrating his innate benevolence and need for social connection, as well as by eroding his self-worth. In turn, his misery caused his malice by generating a sense of injustice and indignation. He infers that he can be restored to happiness, and thereby to virtue, if Victor creates a female partner who is loving toward him and like himself in being physically repulsive (147).

Controlling his vengeance, the creature confronts Victor with a series of moral appeals, punctuated by threats if the appeals are ignored. Initially he appeals to reciprocity: "Do your duty toward me, and I will do mine towards you and the rest of mankind" (102). Next he makes several virtue-oriented appeals to the creature's self-respect, love for life, and loyalty toward Victor for creating him. He also appeals to Victor's general sympathy, compassion, mercy, decency, and sense of justice. His most poignant appeal, however, is to the happiness principle: "Misery made me a fiend. Make me happy, and I shall again be virtuous" (103).

The words calm Victor's emotions and stimulate his moral understanding. Feeling compassion and curiosity, but also "for the first time" that he has duties as creator to render the creature happy before complaining of his wickedness, he agrees to listen to the creature's narrative and follows him to his hut (104). There, in a scene left to the imagination, Victor sits by a fire with the creature he had found unbearable to look at, listening attentively over an entire day to his detailed life story, including how he came into the world inclined to benevolence, manifested that benevolence toward the De Laceys and other villagers, and grew malevolent only when his acts of kindness were met with hatred. These experiences led the creature to believe the happiness principle, which he reasserts and elaborates on at the end of his narrative: "I am malicious because I am miserable" (147). He also traces his misery to social rejection: "My vices are the children of a forced solitude that I abhor; and my virtues will necessarily arise when I live in communion with an equal" (150). Again he appeals to the happiness principle to support his demand for a companion, recasting that demand as a right. The appeal elicits a promise from Victor to accede to the creature's demand.

The happiness principle is set forth in a context of negotiation. It is essential to the moral framework in which the creature offers a contract and a conditional pledge: If you meet your duties to me (which include respect and social acceptance needed for happiness), then I will meet my duties to you and other humans (which happiness enables me to do). The happiness principle is not itself a promise to return to virtue on the condition that Victor makes him happy. Instead it is a psychological claim that has clear moral relevance to the creature and to humans: Misery (unhappiness) promotes malice, happiness promotes virtue. The principle is invoked as a background belief to support the reasonableness of entering into a contract that creates particular reciprocal duties, as well as affirms general duties of reciprocity and mutual respect.

Notice that the creature appeals to virtue rather than to self-interest. He calls for happiness *in order to* return to virtue. He demands, "by the virtues that I once possessed" and by the virtues that Victor currently possesses, that Victor listen to his narrative with an eye to restoring his happiness in order to restore his virtue (104). The creature's appeal to happiness as promoting virtue assumes that the creature retains a desire for virtue. At least, it does so if the creature is speaking in good faith, and the end of the novel affirms that he is (222).

Exactly how does the creature understand the happiness principle? The answer turns on his understanding of three things: happiness (versus misery), virtue (versus vice), and the pathway by which happiness "necessarily" produces virtue. First, the creature's narrative suggests that he understands happiness as a subjective, enjoyable state of mind. Moreover, he accents a particular form of enjoyment, tranquility (133). He locates the primary sources of tranquility in mutual sympathy with others, attunement to nature, and self-esteem. Consistent with the novel, we can distinguish happiness as short-lived enjoyment (episodic happiness), such as the glee the creature feels in murdering William, versus longer-term dispositions to enjoyment and meaning, such as the creature manifested during his early observations of the De Laceys. Misery, then, is unhappiness (episodic or dispositional) in the sense of experiencing negative emotions such as self-hatred, sorrow, despair, rage, hatred, and vengefulness.

Second, the creature understands virtue by reflecting on his natural sympathy toward the De Lacey family, together with his equally natural self-affirmation as someone deserving justice and respect from others. In doing so he relies on the three books he reads, all of which are revered by the romantics. Goethe's *Sorrows of Young Werther* refined his grasp of lofty sentiments of love. Milton's *Paradise Lost* evoked deeper emotions of anger and envy when misery replaces bliss in Satan's war against God. Plutarch's *Lives* made him feel "the greatest ardour for virtue rise within me, and abhorrence for vice, as far as I understood the signification of those terms, relative as they were, as I applied them, to pleasure and pain alone" (132). This passage might suggest that the creature reduces virtue to pleasure and vice to pain, as a philosophical hedonist would, but that is not altogether clear. The hedonistic reduction would be a simplistic reading of the books he mentions, whereas his narrative and his conversation with Victor reveals a more sophisticated moral sensibility. The hedonistic view is also at odds with the creature's understanding that pleasure can be derived from vice as well as from virtue, as when his heart swells with "hellish triumph" in murdering William (144).

Third, the creature regards virtue as produced by happiness, as something distinct from it, in the way a motive is distinct from its effects. Virtue consists of excellence of character, especially love, sympathy, justice, and self-respect. The happiness principle asserts that virtue and happiness are correlated psychologically, rather than fused as a matter of definition. Happiness motivates virtue, just as misery motivates vice. The creature's way of linking happiness and virtue turns on a particular assumption about his personal nature, and about human nature. He exemplifies Rousseau's natural man, who comes into the world with strong desires for sociability and self-preservation.[7] Satisfying these desires tends to bring pleasure and happiness. Simultaneously, the desires naturally unfold in the direction of virtue. In the creature's understanding of the happiness principle, then, happiness and virtue have a common source in innate benevolent and prosocial desires, the expression of which requires a supportive society.

Finally, the creature's demand that Victor make him happy is not the demand that Victor directly put him into a state of bliss, perhaps by programming him in a manner that removes his freedom to make choices. Instead it is the demand to be given the prerequisites for acting on his naturally good desires, especially for self-esteem and social interaction. Developing and expressing these desires generates streams of pleasure, enjoyment, and joy, along lines largely congruent with self-regarding and other-regarding virtues. The creature is born with survival skills he can exercise independently. But both his self-respect and his ability to exercise sympathy depend on having at least one companion with whom he can give and receive sympathy, love, and respect.

VIRTUOUS BECAUSE HAPPY: VICTOR'S VIEW

Victor sputters with rage as he begins his first conversation with the creature, who he knows murdered William and caused Justine's death. Within minutes, however, he realizes for the first time that he has duties to the creature. Shortly thereafter he agrees to listen to the creature's narrative over the course of an entire day. When the narrative culminates with the murder of William, Victor again explodes in rage. Once again his rage is quickly defused, and he accedes to the creature's demand for a mate. These abrupt reversals cry out for explanation.

One suggestion, later offered by Victor in justifying his decision to break his promise to make a female companion for the creature, is that he is duped by the creature's sophisms and "struck senseless by his fiendish threats" (171). That explanation does not ring true. In fact, Victor listens to the creature with curiosity and compassion; he reflects on the creature's arguments and threats rather than being overwhelmed by them; he calmly reasons that he owes the creature "the small portion of happiness" that is in his power to bestow (149). A second explanation, then, is that the creature's appeals to his innate goodness, as well as to Victor's compassion and justice, suffice to defuse his anger. That view is equally implausible, for Victor would have no reason to believe that these values outweigh the creature's proven monstrosity. At least, he would have no reason unless he accepts the happiness principle as a crucial background condition grounding virtue in happiness, and vice in misery. A third explanation, then, is plausible: Victor's quick reversal results from his ready embrace of the happiness principle once the creature articulates it. That is, Victor's sudden openness to the creature's needs turns on acknowledging the happiness principle, in some very personal way.

Shelley carefully sets the stage for Victor's ready embrace of the happiness principle when the creature articulates it. Just before his first conversation with the creature, Victor is in a state of utter misery himself. He is emotionally isolated, tortured by guilt for having created a monster, pathologically depressed, and grappling with suicidal impulses—clearly a state in which his unhappiness threatens harm to himself and thereby to his family. His father cautions him against excessive grief and urges him to overcome the misery that prevents him from meeting his duties to himself and others (94). Victor regards the advice as sound but inapplicable to him, given that he suffers more from guilt than grief. At the same time, he affirms his natural goodness in pursuing his scientific career: "Yet my heart overflowed with kindness, and love of virtue. I had begun life with benevolent intentions"—words that foreshadow the creature's parallel narrative (93). In his own eyes, Victor had benevolent motives in discovering how to create life, then in planning to create a human being, and finally in creating the prototype for an entirely new species of "happy and excellent natures," hoping as well to learn the secret of restoring human corpses to life (55). Of course he also had self-interested motives to gain recognition from society and gratitude from members of the new species, but he regarded his self-interest as aligned with his morally good intentions.

Victor understands the happiness principle much like the creature does, including his definitions of happiness and virtue, and the pathway by which happiness produces virtue. His understanding, however, emerged from markedly different experiences. Like the creature, Victor thinks of happiness as a subjective state of enjoyment, whether episodic or dispositional. In light of his disastrous adventures in creativity, he voices a decided preference for a style of happiness centered on tranquility: calmness, serenity, peacefulness. Tranquility is found by participating in domesticity (family and friends) and communing with nature. He renounces the passion and ecstasy of great creative discovery because it undermines wisdom (moderation, caution) in exercising virtue.

His creative endeavors severed him from his family, friends, and nature. And they produced a monster that causes death and misery.

Virtue, like happiness, is the manifestation of a serene mind: "a human being in perfection ought always to preserve a calm and peaceful mind, and never to allow passion or a transitory desire to disturb his tranquility" (56). For Victor, then, the happiness principle means that happiness as tranquility tends to promote the virtues, including intellectual virtues like prudence, wisdom, and rationality. Happiness and virtue are linked to stability of mind found through family, friends, and communion with nature. Indeed, he makes the extraordinary suggestion that if everyone pursued happiness through "the tranquility of his domestic affections" there would be no slavery, violence, and colonial oppression (56). In the same vein, he celebrates "how much happier that man is who believes his native town to be the world, than he who aspires to become greater than his nature will allow" (54). This dichotomy omits a crucial third possibility, besides parochial illusions and unrealistic ambitions: namely, creative striving based on realistic hopes and due care.

The conviction that happiness as tranquility promotes virtue has roots in Classicism, Stoicism, Romanticism, and common sense. Although she sympathetically dramatizes this belief, Shelley also critiques it. She is well aware that tranquility by itself can lead to complacency. Some of the greatest benefits to personal excellence and to humanity also require strong passions. Victor is untrue to his own experience when he downplays his "delight and rapture" in making extraordinary discoveries (53). He is more authentic when, on his deathbed, he recalls the joy and promise of creativity. After advising Captain Walton to "seek happiness in tranquility and avoid ambition," he immediately questions his own advice: "Yet why do I say this? I have myself been blasted in these hopes [in being creative], yet another may succeed" (220).

A balanced view, of the sort the novel endorses, acknowledges that strong passions sometimes distort morally responsible reflection but other times motivate moral engagement and morally valuable creativity. In general, Victor's notion that tranquility by itself is a key to wisdom is wrongheaded. The pursuit of virtue requires wise balancing and integrating of moral (and other) reasons. Tranquil moods cannot guarantee wisdom. Nor can any other emotional tone. Only good moral judgment, sound moral reasoning, and moral imagination can yield insight. And sometimes they are accompanied by emotionally heightened engagement, while other times tranquility serves us better.

As an example, consider Victor's two most extended moral reflections, one leading to his promise to make a female companion for the creature and the other leading to his decision to break the promise. Despite his subsequent denials, he makes the promise calmly, after lengthy deliberation about the creature's arguments and threats (150). His decision to break the promise is made with equal equanimity, but this time in response to a wider range of reasons (170). In particular, he comes to appreciate that the couple might not get along, might even hate each other, and that the female partner might herself experience malice. Or they might get along but have children who are sufficiently strong and malicious to destroy the human race. Victor changes his mind not because of greater tranquility but because he places the possibilities and dangers in a wider moral perspective. On this one occasion, he exercises moral imagination and good moral judgment.

Admittedly, Victor's decision to break his promise, and to destroy the partially completed female creature, is morally ambiguous. It can be seen as misogynist, the culminating manifestation of a male psyche obsessed with abstract reasoning about duties in disregard of personal relationships.[8] Or it can be seen as Victor's most rational moment in appreciating the dangers inherent his work, especially the dangers of creating a species that could destroy humanity.[9] The important point is that in evaluating Victor's reasoning we do not focus on the calmness of his mood. Instead we focus on his actual reasons—what he considers and does not consider, and how he balances and integrates conflicting considerations.

In sum, Victor tacitly agrees with the happiness principle articulated by the creature. That agreement explains why he is easily convinced by the creature to apply the principle in justifying the creation of a female partner. When he later breaks his promise it is not because he abandons the happiness principle. Instead it is because he questions whether the female partner will make the creature happy, and also because he comes to appreciate that the well-being of humanity overrides the happiness of the creature. By the end of the novel, neither creature nor creator abandons the happiness principle, although they apply it in different ways according to their view of the facts.

RESPONSIBILITY FOR WRONGDOING

The happiness principle invites abuse. If unhappiness promotes vice, then misery easily becomes a rationalization for malice. And if happiness is necessary for virtue then unhappiness becomes an excuse for violence, especially when individuals have few prospects for happiness. The rationalization and excuse is especially tempting when we blame others for depriving us of essential resources for happiness. And the rationalization is even more tempting if we assume that our natural desires are good, that society is blameworthy for frustrating them, and that we are largely powerless to combat society's influence. But even without these additional assumptions, the happiness principle is a ready-made excuse for wrongdoing, given how much we cherish happiness.

Both the creature and Victor use the happiness principle to evade moral responsibility, albeit in different ways. To begin with the creature, we must acknowledge he is an extreme case—a thought experiment that provokes reflection on everyday moral psychology. His terrifying physical deformity deprives him altogether of a vital resource for happiness—sympathetic human contact. Human contact is essential to satisfy his inherent dispositions to sympathy and sociability, and thereby produce happiness and virtue. As a result, it is natural for him to blame Victor and the villagers for his malice. Nevertheless, the creature is not as innocent as he claims, and he abuses the happiness principle when he invokes it to excuse his malevolence and murders.

The creature is not a sociopath who lacks any sense of right and wrong. Instead, perhaps like many of us, he possesses a distorted sense of morality that mixes moral concern with malice. His distorted morality is demonstrated in his belief that Victor's harm to him justifies, or at least excuses, killing innocent third parties: William, Justine, Clerval, and Elizabeth. In committing these murders, the creature retains some sense of moral decency. This is made clear at the end of the novel, in his discussion with Captain Walton following Victor's death. There the creature expresses genuine grief and guilt for causing the deaths of Clerval and Victor, whom he praises as generous and noble and begs forgiveness (221). The creature manifests a radically divided moral consciousness. In admitting he is a wretch, however, he does not unambiguously accept moral responsibility. At a crucial juncture, he alludes again to the happiness principle: "My heart was fashioned to be susceptible of love and sympathy; and when wrenched by misery to vice and hatred, it did not endure the violence of the change, without torture such as you cannot even imagine" (222).

The phrase "wrenched by misery to vice" suggests his vice was beyond his control, that it emerged from his unhappiness without the possibility of moral choice. In turn, this suggests he should be excused for his wrongdoing (excused, though not justified). These suggestions constitute moral evasion, and the evasion is further elaborated in the passage and elsewhere. Earlier he said that he stopped trying to control his malicious impulses, allowing himself to be "borne away by the stream" (140). Now he adds, with remarkable duplicity, "I had no choice but to adapt my nature to an element which I had willingly chosen" (222). He portrays himself as the victim of others and simultaneously the victim of his own passions that he could not control: "I was the slave, not the master, of an impulse, which I detested, yet could not disobey" (224). Had he said "refused to obey," he would move closer to accepting responsibility. Although he compares himself to Milton's Satan, he shifts from Satan's active "Evil be thou my good" to the passive "Evil thenceforth became my good" (222). Evil happened to him, against his naturally good disposition, after society rejected him.

It might be objected that he finally accepts moral responsibility in his final confession that he is a despicable wretch, "a malignant devil" who has "murdered the lovely and the helpless" (223, 224). The confession is authentic, or at least we have no reason to doubt that it is. He feels remorse and sees himself as a monster, as he prepares to end his life in self-immolation. Nevertheless, it remains doubtful, or at least ambiguous, whether he accepts even partial moral responsibility for his actions. In condemning his character he engages in what John Dewey calls spiritual egoism: concern with his own character more than with the harm he causes others.[10] His revulsion toward his own character parallels his horror in seeing his physical image reflected in a pool of water (116). In both instances he sees his hideousness and is horrified by it, but his self-assessment is more a matter of feeling shame than of accepting guilt and remorse for harming others.

In short, by invoking the happiness principle the creature does not establish that misery forced him to be malicious. Like any normal person with strong passions, he had some choice. Yet he never unambiguously admits he made choices and accepts moral responsibility for them. If he had, he would have renounced his earlier belief that his misery by itself causes his viciousness, or even that happiness would restore him to virtue. And always he is preoccupied with his own suffering rather than the suffering of his victims.

Victor's use of the happiness principle to evade responsibility is equally devious. In many ways Victor is admirable and heroic, respected by everyone who knows him. Furthermore, he explicitly accepts guilt for causing the deaths of William, Justine, Clerval, and Elizabeth. He does so, however, in an oddly convoluted way that ignores his failures of common sense and focuses entirely on his creativity. Repeatedly he disregards his failures to foresee danger and to warn potential victims. He lets loose a gigantic creature and alerts no one to its possible dangers; as a result William is murdered. He knows Justine did not kill William but fails to reveal the full truth to authorities, fearing they would think him a madman (90); as a result Justine is executed. He knows the danger to his friends but takes only impulsive and inconsistent steps to protect them (118); as a result Clerval is murdered. He is several times warned that the creature will be with him on his wedding night, but he obtusely assumes only his own life is at risk; as a result Elizabeth is murdered.

We cannot explain these astonishing failures merely by pointing to his arrogance, although of course it is a major factor. Some deeper, unconscious motivation is present. Psychoanalytic readings of the novel highlight unconscious motives that surface in premonitions and dreams that he fails to act on. The most dramatic example, coming immediately after the creature stirs to life, is his Oedipal dream of kissing Elizabeth and seeing her shrivel into the corpse of his mother (59). From the very beginning he senses the dangers of the creature to his family and friends, yet he negligently avoids taking adequate precautions. There is something monstrous here, but I think its crux is not Freudian. Instead it pertains to Victor's attitudes about both creativity, happiness, and the happiness principle.

In constantly centering his guilt on his creativity—on his discoveries of how to create life and how to create a new species of life—Victor shifts responsibility to society. Creativity, after all, is hugely celebrated by society, especially when it occurs on the scale of Victor's triumphs. It is as if Victor is saying: "Yes, I went astray, but only because I accepted society's glorification of creativity, in which I excelled and for which I selflessly sacrificed my personal happiness." His sacrifice leads to his misery, certainly to the loss of tranquility, which he understands as happiness. In turn, his unhappiness undermines his judgment, leading to excesses for which he denies guilt. His self-excuses abuse the happiness principle, as if he unconsciously tells himself: In nobly serving society, I sacrificed my happiness; my vices flow from my unhappiness, but I am less to blame than society. His excuses are a disguised variation of Rousseau's blaming society for undermining innate goodness, but they depend crucially on his abuse of the happiness principle.

Further downplaying his guilt, Victor repeatedly depicts his creativity as pathological, as a "fit of enthusiastic madness," thereby further shifting blame to society's glorification of creativity (188, 219). Although he does not excuse his actions on the grounds of insanity, he does try to lessen blame by casting his creativity as misguided and due to a lack of tranquility, rather than as willful misconduct. He lacks even minimal moral imagination about possible dangers, and he fails to institute even minimum safeguards in bioengineering his creature. And he arrogantly goes it alone, with no collaboration or peer review by colleagues.

In making the creature, Victor never contemplates, much less accepts, his obligation to provide the minimum necessities for the creature's life. If we think of him as a parent, he fails completely to love and nurture his offspring. Here it is interesting to note Shelley's later essay on Rousseau in which she harshly criticizes him for abandoning his five children to orphanages, an act tragically illustrating—as does Victor—"that a father is not to be trusted for [grasping and acting on] natural instincts towards his offspring."[11] Rousseau, she says, violates the first duty of parents: "Our first duty is to render those to whom we give birth, wise, virtuous, and happiness, as far as in us lies."[12]

It is debatable whether Victor is literally a father, and hence whether he is morally culpable as a parent who cannot love his child. In some ways he is comparable to the geneticist who performs in vitro fertilizations (perhaps for hundreds of clients). The geneticist is not blameworthy for failing to love all these children, although of course he is blameworthy when he fails to exercise due care. In any case, Victor's creation of a new type of rational being is a singular event, comparable in only limited ways to paternity. But that singularity does not diminish his responsibility to foresee dangers, implement safeguards, and be prepared from the outset to provide at least minimal nurture.

Additional ambiguity surrounds Victor's decisions to break the promise to create a partner for the creature, the act that sets in motion the demise of Clerval, Elizabeth, and Victor himself. Initially he believes the best course is to create a partner for the creature, but subsequent reflection convinces him he must kill the creature before the creature kills him or other people. On his deathbed, however, he tells Captain Walton that he finds his past conduct not blameable (219). I doubt that Victor is claiming blanket absolution for all his actions, in particular for creating the creature. The context is explicitly about justifying his attempt to kill the creature: "I feel myself justified in desiring the death of my adversary" (219). Nevertheless, his very calmness in deciding to break his promise to the creature, together with his sentimentalizing of serenity, encourages him to be excessively certain about the decision. At the very least, he might have sought advice from Clerval and his own family.

RESPONSIBILITY FOR HAPPINESS AND VIRTUE

Although the happiness principle invites abuse, it contains an important truth: Often happiness does contribute to virtue and unhappiness to vice. Misery does not justify or excuse murder, but it does help us understand it and sometimes prevent it. In articulating the principle, the creature expresses insight into moral psychology (the psychology of morality): Misery caused by social rejection inclines us to envy, hatred, and revenge. Parents are especially attuned to the happiness principle when they nudge their children toward moral responsibility using inducements of happiness, and Victor's early failures to consider the happiness of his creature is integral to his moral failures as creator and caretaker. Even Kant, the ethicist who most downplays the moral significance of happiness, admits that happiness contributes to conscientiousness, the virtue at the heart of his duty-centered ethics. As noted in chapter 2, he believes that duties to others imply an indirect duty "to attend to one's happiness, partly because happiness (to which belong skill, health, wealth) contains the means for the fulfillment of one's duty and partly because lack of it (e.g., poverty) contains temptations to transgress one's duty."[13] Kant insists this duty is only indirect and only owed to others, not to oneself. More plausibly, Victor's father says there is a duty to ourselves, as well as to others, to give due attention to our happiness. In comforting and counseling Victor during his depression, he urges that overcoming his "immoderate grief" is a duty owed to others and to himself, "for excessive sorrow prevents improvement or enjoyment, or even the discharge of daily usefulness, without which no man is fit for society" (94).

Exactly how much truth is contained in the happiness principle is an empirical matter. When and to what degree happiness promotes virtue and unhappiness promotes vice needs to be explored scientifically, and positive psychologists have undertaken that task. In doing so, they too must begin with an account of what the happiness principle means: What is happiness (and unhappiness), what is virtue (and vice), and how does happiness promote virtue (and misery promote vice)—as a cause over which we have no control, or as an influence that we can voluntarily embrace or resist? The novel's conception of happiness is consistent with positive psychologists' definition of happiness as "subjective well-being," rather than in terms of "objective" goods (like money) or normatively in terms of virtuous living. I understand subjective well-being as loving our lives, valuing them in ways manifested in predominant tendencies to experience enjoyment and to have a robust sense of meaning. Positive psychologists approach virtue in terms of myriad specific virtues, rather than a monolithic overall moral goodness. In turn, they understand the virtues as moral excellences, as morally desirable ways of relating to other people, to ourselves, and to the natural world. Accordingly, they study the happiness principle in terms of how subjective well-being contributes to an array of specific excellences of character.

With this understanding, positive psychologists confirm that happiness contributes to many specific virtues, as noted in earlier chapters. For example, happiness tends to promote helping others, as documented in numerous studies of philanthropy and simple everyday kindness.[14] Again, happy people tend to be more attractive partners in friendships and love relationships that foster the virtues of intimacy. Conversely, unhappiness manifested as depression, chronic anger, and extreme envy, tend to make us less able and willing to engage with others in morally desirable ways. The happiness principle is not a universal truth; there are no such truths in psychology. Instead, psychologists chart all these connections as typical patterns, tallied as statistics about groups of people rather than universal claims or claims about particular individuals.

As both the novel and positive psychology reveal, the happiness principle invites abuse when and because it is not balanced by other important truths about how happiness and the virtues are related. Specifically, the principle needs to be integrated and balanced with three additional truths. First, virtue makes its own claims on us, as responsible moral beings, independently of our happiness, and to some extent we have capacities to respond to those claims despite our unhappiness (envy, rage, depression). Certainly that is true of minimal levels of decency and duty. The creature's belief that he is justified in murdering a child because Victor has made him unhappy is, quite simply, monstrous. Equally monstrous are Victor's failures to take adequate safeguards in pursuing science and bioengineering, in meeting his responsibilities to his creature, and in warning others of dangers. His reflections on tranquility as the proper way to pursue happiness are shallow evasions.

Second, we are largely responsible for our happiness, within limits set by our individual nature. Positive psychologists begin with the fact that half of our personalities, including our capacity for happiness, is genetically determined, and another 10 percent determined by our circumstances. This leaves about 40 percent within which we can increase happiness through choices and effort. The idea that happiness is a gift from outside us, whether from our parents or society, is a self-indulgent refusal to accept responsibility for pursuing happiness.

Third, the converse of the happiness principle is true: The virtues tend to promote happiness, and they are a good bet in pursuing happiness. Jonathan Haidt calls this the virtue hypothesis: "Cultivating virtue will make you happy."[15] This is an ancient theme embedded in proverbial wisdom, and psychologists have confirmed it in many directions, as I have emphasized throughout this book. Indeed, it qualifies as one of the founding themes in positive psychology.[16] Most psychological studies have focused on specific virtues. For example, the virtue of gratitude enriches pleasure and meaning by highlighting the good we have received from others. The virtues of hope, faith, and loyalty help sustain enjoyable and meaningful relationships. The virtues of creative striving and perseverance in accordance with standards of excellence promote flow experiences that contribute to enjoyment and feelings of accomplishment. And so on, for dozens of other virtues as illustrated in chapter 3.

Although positive psychologists highlight the positive aspects of human nature, they generally avoid Rousseau's (and the creature's) oversimplification that human nature is inherently good and that satisfying natural desires "necessarily" promotes virtue unless society intervenes. Human nature contains potentials for both good and bad, and much turns on personal choices interacting with genetic inheritance and social settings. A long history of human cruelty amply demonstrates that "natural" human desires include desires for vengeance and envy, of the sort that motivate the creature. Applying the happiness principle also presupposes we can identify and revive those natural desires, and then act on them within the societies we must now live within. In any case, we are social creatures who must act within the societies we live in, both in pursuing happiness and in exercising moral responsibility. Within social contexts, any one-sided emphasis on the happiness principle is a recipe for irresponsibility.

Finally, within wide limits we legitimately pursue virtue with motives that blend concern for our happiness with moral concern for others. This mixture of motives is inherent in human nature, which constantly requires blending and integrating different types of motives—both for the sake in maintaining personal unity and in order to marshal the greatest motivational strength in pursuing activities. We seek and enjoy satisfaction in respecting ourselves and esteeming our character, and also in being esteemed by others. This ubiquitous mixture of motives contributes to the difficulty in knowing exactly what motivates us in many situations. It is clear that both the creature and Victor had only limited understanding of their motives. Happiness and virtue were closely linked in their experience, but the order of causal influence might largely be reversed. It might be virtue that tends to promote happiness, and vice that promotes misery. Or the lines of influence might go both ways, perhaps with a dominance of virtue to happiness.

Thus, the creature derived pleasure, joy, and happiness from participating in the De Lacey's community, both as an observer as an active helper. Initially he had stolen food from the family, but he stopped this practice after discerning how his theft inflicted suffering on the family (114). He took pleasure in secretly providing firewood for the family, and additional pleasure in seeing the cottagers' delight in this gift and in the extra time it provided them to engage in other activities. The creature is a happy helper—happy because he helps, as well as helping because he is happy. Conversely, the creature's misery comes not only from his rejection by the villagers but primarily from his giving into the emotions and vices of envy, revenge, hatred. As for Victor, equating of happiness with tranquility, especially domestic tranquility, combined with the misery resulting from his creativity, make it easy for him to exaggerate the contribution of happiness to virtue.

In sum, the happiness principle and the virtue hypothesis need to be balanced: Developing and exercising virtue tends to promote happiness, and in turn happiness tends to promote virtue. Moreover, these claims only state general tendencies, and continuing studies by positive psychologists will determine exactly how strong the tendencies are. Pursuing happiness and virtue from mixed motives, combining self-interest and morality, is natural and acceptable within wide limits. In addition, virtue makes its own valid claims, quite apart from happiness. To excuse murder and other serious immorality on the grounds of unhappiness caused by others is a monstrous abuse of the happiness principle, as the creature illustrates. To think of happiness states, such as tranquility, as the key to virtue is equally muddled and dangerous, as Victor illustrates. Happiness and virtue need to be pursued in tandem and occasionally in tension with each other, with each making its distinctive claims on us as aspects of good lives.

13

PERSONAL AND POLITICAL

Dare to be happy.[1]
—Goethe

Benjamin Franklin observed that "Human Felicity is produc'd not so much by great Pieces of good Fortune that seldom happen, as by little Advantages that occur every Day."[2] Thus, giving a lad a substantial amount of money usually results in his squandering it, leaving nothing but painful regrets all around, whereas teaching him how to shave gives him a daily pleasure and frees him from annoying dependence on barbers. The illustration reflects Franklin's celebration of self-reliance and personal responsibility, yet it is noteworthy that he introduces it in discussing philanthropy. Specifically, the context is a plan to clean and light the streets of Philadelphia, services that Franklin initiated and government later expanded, thereby ensuring "little advantages" that increase the daily enjoyments of citizens. For Franklin, the pursuit of happiness interweaves the personal and political.

Although I linked personal happiness with public practices such as philanthropy, I have said little about governments' contribution to happiness. In this concluding chapter I relate my themes to the call for a "politics of happiness," that is, for applying scientific studies of happiness to government policies. I support the call, but with the strong proviso that happiness is only one of many factors relevant to public policy, and not the most important one. I reject the view that happiness should be the paramount aim of governments.[3] That aim is to protect democratic freedoms, including rights to pursue happiness in good lives, while promoting economic opportunity and security. Actual pursuits of happiness, however, remain highly personal because the ingredients of happiness vary enormously and can be integrated into good lives in myriad ways. I conclude with a brief overview of my themes about happiness in good lives by drawing on Goethe, who, like Franklin, appreciated the connections between the personal and political dimensions of happiness.

POLITICS OF HAPPINESS

The right to pursue happiness is an important democratic value, appropriately high-lighted in the Declaration of Independence. Citizens' concerns for happiness have always been expressed in voting, political polls, and satisfaction surveys. Applying happiness studies to government policy debates promises to make citizens' choices more informed. Hence it is appropriate for government to be informed about happi-ness research, to support it, and to help distribute information about happiness to its populace and politicians. When the information points in a clear direction, it should inform public policy. This information-oriented version of a politics of happiness is the shared ground in proposals made by an ecumenical group of economists, psycholo-gists, sociologists, and political scientists, both conservatives and liberals. Its lumi-naries include Daniel Kahneman, Ed Diener, Martin E. P. Seligman, Richard Layard, David Halpern, Arthur C. Brooks, Derek Bok, and even British Prime Minister David Cameron and French President Nicolas Sarkozy.[4] Reflecting on the accelerating inte-gration of economic theory and psychology in the new field of behavioral economics, David Halpern predicts that within a decade "large areas of government policy will be routinely subject to a subjective well-being cost-benefit analysis."[5]

An early reference point in the call for a politics of happiness is the Easterlin Paradox, named after Richard Easterlin who identified it in 1974: During the past half century personal income in the United States has doubled but happiness levels have remained the same.[6] This disparity is paradoxical for economists who largely assumed that in-creases in income and wealth promote happiness—an assumption made especially easy when economists simply define happiness as satisfying desires in the marketplace. The Easterlin Paradox is much less puzzling for psychologists, who remind us that satisfying a desire, even a very strong desire, does not automatically increase overall satisfaction (happiness). In particular, there is little puzzle about why happiness is only moderately affected by increasing income and wealth once individuals and societies move beyond poverty. We simply habituate to our new economic situation. Moreover, relative wealth matters more to our happiness than absolute income. Comparing our-selves to people who are richer than us might elicit admiration and inspire us to work harder, but more likely it makes us envious and frustrated. Again, comparing ourselves to people who have less than us might elicit compassion and a desire to help, but more often it makes us feel pride and pleasure in our success. As a result, increasing dispar-ities in wealth tend not to increase overall happiness.

It follows that attempts to increase or to sustain the average happiness in a society require a broader framework than simply increasing income and wealth. Positive psychologists have much to contribute to that framework. In a short time they have already uncovered a number of happiness-promoting proposals: increase the levels of trust in society; support marriage and discourage divorce by implementing more family-friendly practices in the workplace; increase taxation on consumption of material goods (which merely keep consumers trapped on hedonic treadmills); encourage active social interactions rather than passive television viewing; prohibit advertising to children who are not able to make rational assessments of it; improve education; maintain a supportive atmosphere for religions; improve health care and especially mental health services; increase employment and meaningful work (as well as unemployment compensation); decrease the use of harsh performance appraisal reviews at work (which cause much grief and little improvement in productivity); and lessen the huge and growing disparities between the rich and poor.

In making these proposals, British economist Richard Layard writes, "The authors of the American Declaration of Independence had the right idea. This means that public policy should be judged by how it increases human happiness and reduces human misery."[7] Unfortunately, Layard conflates protecting the right to pursue happiness with directly promoting happiness. We can agree that governments should respect citizens' rights to pursue happiness, and even that happiness is *one* important criterion for sound public policy. But Layard makes happiness the paramount and even sole criterion: "It is thus self-evident that the best society is the happiest."[8] He does so because he is a utilitarian who regards Jeremy Bentham as the final word in ethics and value theory. For Layard, as for Bentham, all moral imperatives reduce to one: maximize happiness, understood in terms of quantities of pleasure, taking everyone into account equally, both in everyday life and in setting public policy.[9] If we reject this hedonistic utilitarianism, as I do, it is not self-evident that maximizing happiness is the primary goal for a good society, or for a good person, nor that happiness is reducible to large quantities of pleasure. Good societies have multiple dimensions that do not neatly dovetail with maximizing happiness. Thus a society might be happy overall, as scored in cumulative averages of individual happiness, but shallow and backward, or unjust and evil.

Good societies reflect, indeed magnify, the complexity and variety of good lives. An individual good life has multiple value dimensions that include happiness but also moral decency and goodness, authenticity, self-fulfillment, health, and meaning in terms of additional justified values such as artistic achievement, aesthetic appreciation, professional skill, and athletic excellence. Good societies make possible a variety of good lives in all their dimensions. Similarly, valuable forms of government and public life need to be understood in terms of an array of values that cannot be reduced to those of hedonistic utilitarianism. The best societies are morally just in respecting and safeguarding human rights; they are compassionate, honest, and support excellence in a wide array of activities; they respect and support a variety of authentic and fulfilling lives; and so on, for a range of moral values that are not reducible to maximizing pleasure and happiness. This suggests that applying happiness studies to make societies better is far more complicated than Layard envisions.

Fortunately, most advocates of a politics of happiness are sensitive to the complexity of values and the variety of good lives. These advocates begin with democratic themes that affirm ethical pluralism, the view that there are many types of good lives, and that good lives have multiple dimensions that include but do not reduce to happiness (as subjective well-being). I have in mind, for example, Derek Bok in *Politics of Happiness* and David Halpern in *Hidden Wealth of Nations*, both of which books appeared in 2010. Although Bok and Halpern are sympathetic to many of the general policy directions outlined by Layard, they do not reduce all values to maximizing pleasure. They call for taking happiness seriously in assessing public policies, but only as one of many morally relevant values. Specifically, they favor using happiness studies primarily as tiebreakers in areas where public officials have areas of discretion that are not decided by group preferences.[10]

At the same time, Bok and Halpern believe that applying happiness studies to public policies might help reduce political polarization. This is because happiness is a widely shared value that cuts across a range of value disagreements. For example, amid America's culture wars, the mention of "family values" immediately sent up red flags, with liberals seeing it as concealing antigay bigotry, not to mention hypocrisy about divorce and dishonesty about the great economic pressures on families. Positive psychologists document significant correlations between happiness and marriage, with causation going in both directions: marriage contributes to happiness and happy people tend more often to marry. These studies might be used to strengthen marriage as a social practice, while inviting greater tolerance for gay unions and marriages that contribute to happiness.

As Bok and Halpern are well aware, however, there are dangers in government becoming heavily involved in directly promoting the happiness of citizens. The dangers include confusion, political bias, injustice, and excessive paternalism. To begin with confusion, there is worry about different researchers using different definitions of happiness, and thereby yielding results that have different implications for public policy. Although positive psychologists largely share a concept of happiness as subjective well-being, they define subjective well-being in different ways. Some researchers understand it as satisfaction with our lives and highlight overall cognitive self-appraisals of lives. This understanding of happiness relies heavily on questionnaires that ask individuals about their levels of happiness. Other researchers define happiness as high overall levels of pleasure and low levels of pain, as monitored by experiential beepers that buzz randomly throughout a day. Life-satisfaction and experiential definitions widely overlap in reference, although not entirely. For example, parents might report stronger happiness about having children when they make cognitive appraisals of their lives than they do according to experiential studies that more closely monitor the challenges in everyday child care.

I favor hybrid definitions that integrate experiential measures with life satisfaction, and many positive psychologists are moving in this direction.[11] In my formulation, to be happy is to love one's life, valuing it in ways manifested in predominant tendencies to experience enjoyment and a sense of meaning. Nevertheless, exactly how the ideas of life satisfaction and enjoyments are operationalized—that is, given descriptors to make them empirically testable—is open to refinement as research proceeds. Most likely there will never be complete consensus among researchers on which operational definition is best, and certainly there will always be controversy about definitions of happiness in everyday discourse. This lack of consensus is not an insurmountable obstacle to a politics of happiness, and the same problem surrounds other core concepts in public policy, for example health and justice. Nevertheless, it reminds us that caution is needed in applying studies about the sources and ingredients of happiness. As members of the public we need to be aware of the definitions scientists are using, and be able to relate them to their way of understanding of happiness.

Confusion can result from additional sources, some of a more practical nature. Relatively minor challenges center on the general dangers in interactions between science and politics. For example, there is the danger that a single attention-grabbing study will be touted by the mass media before there is time for rigorous scientific confirmation or disconfirmation.[12] Here we can agree that scientific studies need to be applied cautiously, allowing time for a rough consensus about policy goals to emerge.

A second issue concerns political ideology—the "politics" in a politics of happiness. Bok, Halpern, and Layard are left leaning in politics, and some critics worry that a politics of happiness will carry a liberal agenda. To the contrary, Arthur C. Brooks contends that happiness studies strongly support a politically conservative agenda, for they underscore that personal responsibility, marriage, and religious faith strongly advance happiness.[13] It is too early to conclude whether happiness studies favor a left-wing or right-wing political agenda or neither, but most likely they will have mixed implications. To repeat an earlier example, Ed Diener and Martin E. P. Seligman observe that happiness studies indicate the need to support stable personal relationships, but that "could mean offering tax breaks to married couples (a conservative proposal), and it could mean adopting marriage for gay and lesbian couples (a liberal position)."[14] Diener and Seligman rightly insist that happiness studies will only be useful if they are conducted with scientific rigor so as to yield facts that are themselves politically neutral. Those facts will then be open to the usual democratic practices of interpretation, evaluation, and debate in light of competing political visions of a good society. And even if it turns out that happiness studies promote one political ideology, they do not show that ideology to be preferable overall. Again, happiness is one important value, but justice is another, and political ideologies often disagree about fundamental issues of justice.

A third set of issues concern coercion, manipulation, and injustice, especially when the focus is on the happiness of majorities. Bhutan is a much-publicized cautionary tale. In 1972, Bhutan's king adopted the goal of increasing his country's Gross National Happiness, as distinct from its Gross Domestic Product.[15] On the surface, his concrete proposals about how to increase happiness were not radical: increase democracy, economic growth, sustainable environmental policies, and preservation of culture. In practice, focusing on the happiness of the majority yields mixed results, sometimes moving the country forward and other times supporting injustice. An example of the latter is the advancement of the majority of citizens who are Buddhist (90 percent) and oppression of the ethnic minority of Nepalese (10 percent), all in the name of preserving the culture and promoting the most good for the most people.[16]

Maximizing overall happiness is not the same as increasing opportunities for all people to pursue happiness. Democratic values affirm equal rights, as well as majority rule, and equal rights limit majority rule. To take a relatively clear-cut example, spirituality and participation in religious communities rank high as happiness promoters, and happiness studies might bolster the case for allowing contributions to religions to be tax deductible. They should not be used, as in Bhutan, to favor any majority religion. And if happiness studies happened to reveal that one particular religion tended to be especially effective in promoting happiness that would not justify giving any special government recognition to it. In a democratic setting, happiness studies provide one source of information relevant to social policy, but they do not constitute a basis for dictating social policy.

Happiness studies typically report statistical generalizations about what makes most people happy or unhappy. If they begin to take on the ubiquitous role that Halpern foresees, they are likely to influence policy matters on drugs, gambling, pornography, prostitution, guns, abortion, and vesting many other issues involving important moral and social values. I agree they should, for happiness is an important value and psychologists deepen our understanding of how to pursue it. But to repeat, happiness is only one dimension of good lives, and it is both limited and guided by other moral values such as human rights. It is one thing to support gay marriage by applying studies revealing that most gay couples are happier by having the option to marry. It is another thing to oppose gay marriage by invoking studies revealing that the majority of the population is unhappy with accepting gay marriage. The supportive stance already presupposes the validity of gay rights; the oppositional stance reflects their denial and (in my view) homophobia. In general, happiness studies need to be applied within an enlightened version of human rights and justice.

In *Brave New World* Aldous Huxley warns against governments manipulating majorities by indulging natural human tendencies. Making freely available drugs (*soma*) that bring instant bliss without side effects creates happiness by pandering to the masses in order to exercise deeper forms of power. In a preface written decades before the emergence of positive psychology, Huxley wrote that "the most important Manhattan Projects of the future will be vast government-sponsored enquiries into what the politicians and the participating scientists will call 'the problem of happiness'—in other words, the problem of making people love their servitude."[17] Bok and Halpern are confident that democracies grounded in human rights will prevent majority views of happiness from suppressing minority views, at least in the long run. Within the framework of human rights, they see happiness as a limited but useful way to integrate other important values. They are aware, however, that freedom is always at risk and can be infringed in more subtle ways than through outright injustice, including through some forms of paternalism.

A fourth concern, then, is paternalism—interfering with individuals' freedom with the aim of increasing their good or preventing them from harming themselves. In my view, not all paternalism is objectionable; laws requiring seat belts and Social Security taxes, and prohibiting dueling and cocaine, are examples.[18] But there are worries about government's encroachment into ever-widening areas of our freedom in the name of promoting happiness—as distinct from preventing harm. To be sure, at first glance applying the results of positive psychology does not seem paternalistic. It simply extends and refines the ubiquitous use of pollster's satisfaction surveys, and thereby respects people's wishes. In fact, satisfaction surveys and happiness studies can differ significantly, especially owing to widespread illusions about what makes us happy. As we have seen, illusion is the most familiar theme in happiness studies by psychologists. Biases constantly distort our estimates of what does, did, or will make us happy. For example, nostalgically looking to the past, we tend to gloss over many things that once made us unhappy. Again, optimistically looking to the future, we believe that winning the lottery will vastly increase our happiness because we focus only on the moment of winning, ignoring our tendencies to adapt and return to our pre-winning levels of happiness. Using these studies as a basis for public policy might encourage paternalistic prohibitions on gambling, an activity that thrives on illusions that winning the jackpot increases happiness. In contrast, satisfaction surveys express people's conscious beliefs about what makes them happy, and about how happy they are, including their happiness concerning public policy matters.

Many citizens welcome selective paternalism that has a scientific foundation and broadly benefits the community. The world has become exceedingly complex, and government promises to make some aspects of our lives simpler and more secure. Programs like Social Security and Medicare are hugely popular in the United States, and European social democracies favor a much broader safety net. Other citizens, however, are hostile to what they regard as "big government" and the "nanny state." In particular, libertarians want to dismantle government welfare programs and see the extensive application of happiness studies as a rationale for extending the nanny state that violates individual freedom and responsibility. The two sides agree that information about happiness tendencies should be widely disseminated to citizens in making personal choices. Even here, however, there are disagreements about using taxpayer money to fund research on happiness. If consensus is to emerge, it will probably be around values other than happiness.

More moderate approaches to advancing economic security and health make happiness a supportive rather than a primary consideration. Of special interest is the "nudge" approach argued for by Richard Thaler and Cass Sunstein, and endorsed by Halpern.[19] Governments, corporations, and other powerful groups influence conduct no matter what they do, including doing nothing, so they might as well nudge their citizens in beneficial directions. To nudge is to arrange options, especially default options, in a manner that preserves freedom of choice while moving groups in a desirable direction. Thaler and Sunstein call their view "libertarian paternalism," using an oxymoron to elicit appreciation of areas of reasonable compromise: seek nudges that preserve liberty by allowing opting out and also developed with full participation by group members (hence "libertarian") while promoting the good of individuals (hence "paternalism").

To cite a familiar example, most people do not save enough for retirement, resulting in unhappiness-making financial insecurity during retirement and possibly making them a burden on others. Even when employers offer matching contributions only 10 percent of people fill out the paperwork to take full advantage of that extra money. Employers should change the default option: Everyone is enrolled automatically in the retirement plan so as to take advantage of the matching funds, and perhaps also enrolled in a program that increases their retirement contributions when they get raises. The individuals are free to opt out of the plans by filling out a form, and hence their freedom is preserved. Moreover, such policies need to be developed openly and with full cooperation by employees, again preserving freedom. In fact, most people do not opt out, and hence great good is done for them paternalistically but without undermining liberty. Thaler and Sunstein apply this approach to a wide variety of value-based choices, including everything from protecting the environment (e.g., making recycling choices more straightforward) to donating organs (e.g., the default choice is to donate one's organs at death). Although happiness has not been their primary focus, all the values they apply bear directly or indirectly on happiness.

Although their books appeared in 2010, in the aftermath of the worst economic crisis since the Great Depression of the 1930s, Halpern and Bok seem exceedingly optimistic about the prospects for community action in moving beyond reducing bad and toward promoting good, centered on happiness. For example, services for mental disorders are dramatically underfunded and often support less expensive pharmaceutical therapies over more expensive psychotherapy. Noting this underfunding and emphasizing that mental disorders are a major source of unhappiness, Halpern and Bok believe a positive focus on health promises to attract greater resources. The relevant nudges encourage people to get help by making services readily available.

Their optimism might not be widely shared for some time, however, given the economic turmoil that opened the twenty-first century. Indeed, such optimism might invite a backlash. Most contemporary definitions of health are holistic and accent positive well-being, in tune with the World Health Organization's definition of health as complete physical, mental, and social well-being, and not merely the absence of mental disorders. Essentially these definitions build in a strong disposition to happiness (if not happiness itself). Employing such definitions opens the floodgate to the heavy funding of health, at the expense of other important goods such as education and environmental protection. In a time of limited funding, the backlash against excesses and imbalance might result in even more limited funding. But then again, the very depth of economic insecurity confronting us might force reasonable compromises of the sort envisioned by all the advocates of a politics of happiness.

Finally, happiness skeptics object to a politics of happiness on the grounds that we are already far too preoccupied with happiness. Saturating politics with happiness studies that report statistical trends will just further increase mediocrity and decrease concern with matters far more serious than happiness, in particular with striving for excellence in all its forms. This line of thought resonates more widely, as we envision the possibility of government overreach in areas better left to individuals, and government failures to aspire to ideals more inclusive than happiness. Nietzsche expressed this skepticism in one of his barbs against British culture: "People don't strive for happiness, only the English do."[20] But happiness skeptics are not alone in worrying about how excessive government involvement in happiness might promote mediocrity. Mill was anything but a happiness pessimist, and his utilitarianism would have both governments and individuals maximize happiness as a moral mandate. Nevertheless, he was deeply worried about both government and mass culture becoming a "tyranny of majority" that promotes mediocrity and threatens individuality and authenticity. In On Liberty he renounced paternalism and limited the role of government to controlling harm to other people, giving his utilitarianism an emphatic libertarian cast. His argument depended in part on optimism about each of us being the best judge about what makes us happy, a view called into question by positive psychologists. But it depended far more on his emphasis on individuality and the claim that authenticity requires us to pursue our happiness through exercising personal choice and judgment, even when we make errors about what is best for us. And even at the individual level, he took seriously the paradox that we do best to pursue happiness indirectly, as a by-product of pursuing other important values.

The paradoxes of happiness remind us that happiness is most effectively pursued by concentrating on valuable activities and relationships that bring meaning and enjoyment.

I suspect that many of these paradoxes can be extended to public policy goals, in ways paralleling personal pursuits of happiness. Furthermore, there is much room for experimentation in seeing whether governments can fruitfully apply happiness studies. But it might turn out that governments do well to focus on increasing the opportunities for individuals to secure goods and services that tend most to yield happiness, taking into account scientific inquiries. Happiness, in short, might not prove to be a sound direct focus for public policy—only time and experimentation will tell. Certainly happiness studies need to be applied intelligently and morally, in limited ways guided by additional democratic values. Still, we should welcome the broad dissemination to the public of information uncovered by positive psychologists and other researchers. This information will help inform citizens in voting and making choices about positive directions of societies, not by themselves, but as part of responsible judgments about how happiness enters into good communities and good lives.

PERSONAL HAPPINESS IN GOOD LIVES

Government should provide a supportive framework for pursuits of happiness in good lives, but these pursuits will always remain highly personal. This is because happiness and good lives take myriad forms, and it is because good lives have multiple dimensions, each of which is complex and interacts with happiness in complicated ways. In concluding, I highlight a few of these complexities by drawing on Johann Wolfgang von Goethe. Goethe's reflections on happiness integrated his personal and political life, and his insights resonate with many of my themes.

Goethe came from a wealthy family and acquired literary fame in his twenties, primarily from *The Sorrows of Young Werther*. Yet he chose to continue working as a civil servant at Weimar, steadily increasing his wealth and power while experiencing mounting tension between the demands of creative writing and government work. An unrequited love precipitated a full-blown midlife crisis and sent him fleeing on an extended vacation to study art in Italy, the land of his childhood dreams. There he was equally charmed by the beauty of the countryside and the happy temperament of the people, especially the Neapolitans who seemed satisfied with simple daily pleasures and quickly resigned to misfortunes.[21] He hoped to learn from them, knowing that he lacked their happy temperament but convinced that happiness is vital to the good life he sought.

Goethe sometimes uses a normative concept of happiness that builds in additional aspects of good lives, in particular authenticity and self-fulfillment. Other times he thinks of happiness as what today we call subjective well-being, which he depicts as "unconsciously rejoicing" in one's life.[22] For the most part, what he says is in tune with my conception of happiness as loving one's life, valuing it in ways manifested by predominant patterns of enjoyment and a sense of meaning. As such, happiness is one vital dimension of good lives, interwoven with other vital dimensions. He says, for example, that intelligent people derive their happiness from valuable activities and relationships: the mark and privilege of "reasonable beings" is to behave so that their lives contain "the greatest possible sum of reasonable and happy moments."[23]

Accordingly, people could be exceptionally happy and yet have lives that are not good in other respects. That is what he comes to believe about the Neapolitans. Although they "have a great desire for culture and a thirst for knowledge," "they are too happy-go-lucky to set about it in the right way."[24] Conversely, individuals could lead admirable lives in many respects but not be very happy. That was true of a talented and fortunate painter Goethe encountered in Rome, a woman who had great talent and exceptional good fortune but who lacked the happiness she desired. This led Goethe to one of his periodically melancholy reflections about "people who have enough of everything [but] do not know how to use it or enjoy it."[25] The goal should be to cherish happiness while integrating it into a life that has value in multiple additional dimensions.

Even if a politics of happiness succeeds in advancing general happiness, it might neglect other important aspects of good lives and good societies. Goethe appreciates that good societies will promote, or at least make possible, good lives in all their major dimensions. Each of these dimensions is complex and interacts with other dimensions, sometimes by way of confluence but at times in tension. Still drawing on Goethe, I conclude by highlighting a few creative tensions between happiness and other aspects of good lives that I have emphasized: morality, authenticity, meaningfulness, mental health, and self-fulfillment.

Happiness and Morality. Happiness is both a moral and personal good. Furthermore, the right to liberty implies a right to pursue happiness, and the virtue and duty of self-respect implies a responsibility to take our happiness seriously—to create and sustain a life we can love and value as enjoyable and meaningful. Both the right and responsibility to pursue happiness are limited by numerous additional rights and responsibilities, with which they need to be balanced.

Goethe agrees that happiness is a moral as well as a self-interested value, and he sets himself against intellectuals who denigrate it as a trivial concern.[26] He also opposes religious thinkers who postpone happiness to a life after death. Our lives in this world are sacred, and it is in these lives where we must seek happiness. Goethe renounces Kant's separation of morality (concerned with duty) and prudence (concerned with happiness). His renunciation came after a long struggle; it took him ten years to understand Kant and another ten years to rid himself of his influence.[27] Nevertheless he acknowledges that the value of happiness increases insofar as it interweaves with additional values characterizing good lives, an idea compatible with one theme in Kant. At times Goethe seems to regard happiness as the supreme value, but he is then employing a normative definition of happiness as including authenticity and a host of rational (valuable) enjoyments and activities; he is not saying that happiness is more important than moral decency and justice.

In addition to happiness being a moral good, which we have rights and responsibilities to pursue, happiness extensively interacts with the virtues. At times a particular virtue is in tension with happiness, as for example with the stern demands of justice or love. Overall, however, the virtues tend to support happiness; they are a good bet in pursuing it. Believing we are virtuous, of course, tends to elevate self-esteem and thereby happiness, but the primary contribution of the virtues to happiness comes in the form of psychological strengths. Conversely, happiness itself is a psychological strength that contributes to virtues in good lives.

Goethe explores many ways in which virtue and happiness are connected, as well as sometimes in tension. For example, he highlights gratitude, self-mastery, and courage as moral strengths that promote happiness, and vice versa. Gratitude, which includes both appreciation of what we have been given by others and appreciation of the good in the world, is a typical and essential feature of lives we love. Most of us have everything we need to be happy, but we often have difficulty appreciating it and applying it to sustain the enjoyments and meaning that characterize happiness.[28] For Goethe the most important goods include the beauty of art and nature, excellence and skill in earning a living and influencing events, and friendship and love. Contact with all these goods must be first-hand, rather than merely read about in books, and unfolded in receptiveness to the good that is continually before us.

Self-mastery includes the willingness to forego some goods in order to obtain greater goods. It implies an acceptance of limits and a creative resignation, which Goethe celebrates in Spinoza and the Stoics. Creative resignation is integral to self-respect and not to be confused with pessimism or self-denigration. Resignation includes as well the willingness to face the world as it is, with hope but without gross illusion. It includes accepting our limitations while remaining committed to the good we can accomplish. And it implies accepting that we are complex and ultimately contradictory beings, who nevertheless must make peace with ourselves.[29]

Courage is needed to confront the fears and dangers that erode happiness, including fears of taking difficult steps sometimes needed in pursuing happiness in good lives. In *Wilhelm Meister's Apprenticeship*, the abbot challenges Wilhelm: "Dare to be happy."[30] In the context, Wilhelm has sought confirmation from the abbot that young Felix is his son, the offspring of an affair with Mariane, who in his absence died shortly after giving birth. The happiness enjoined is a happiness bathed in love and responsibility for his son. In general, adventurous, creative courage is needed in learning how to be happy as part of a good life, not just in the pursuit of pleasure.

Happiness and Authenticity. Authenticity is a moral virtue, but it warrants emphasis as a distinct dimension of good lives. Authenticity requires using that self-knowledge

182 HAPPINESS AND THE GOOD LIFE

as the basis for pursuing self-development. As such, authenticity precludes passive social conformity driven by anxiety to fit in. It also precludes eccentric rebellion whereby we merely want to be different, an impulse that ironically retains a focus on social expectations.[31]

When Goethe worked with a normative definition of happiness he would build in authenticity. As T. J. Reed summarizes, "Goethe's happiness was not facile in the sense of being mere hedonistic enjoyment. It lay in responding to diversity, harmonizing what seemed disharmonious, meeting the challenge of the world about him and ultimately of the potential within him."[32] As we have seen, despite his privileged upbringing and great talent, Goethe lacks a naturally happy temperament and hence must struggle to achieve happiness. This struggle is more like learning an art than trying to get something, and happiness itself is a dynamic process rather than a static state.

In response to Goethe (and Rousseau), I am more cautious about authenticity as a guide to happiness. Authenticity plays a vital role in putting us in touch with our deepest desires, thereby tapping wellsprings of enjoyment and meaning. Yet authenticity has multiple aspects that can pull in different directions: wholehearted caring, self-honesty, self-acceptance, self-creation, self-realization, and self-expression. Equally important, authenticity is not an independent guide to happiness, for what makes us happy partly reveals our authentic selves in the first place. In addition, authenticity is linked to other values that define growth and self-realization, and that sometimes conflict with happiness. Orienting ourselves to these other values is important in pursuing authenticity and happiness in tandem.

Authentic lives take innumerable forms. Goethe embraces ethical pluralism long before it became fashionable to be so. Lives can embody moral and other goods in myriad ways, no one of which should be paraded as best or "the only way" for everyone.[33] He adds that there is a point in recognizing many saints so that each of us can emulate the virtues we find most engaging.[34] He is aware of the tensions between happiness and other dimensions of good lives, but he identifies natural tendencies toward confluence along all these dimensions so as to create coherent good lives. Goethe also celebrates the honesty and courage involved in authenticity, even as they reveal a world of both horror and beauty. Yet he knows that other important virtues can be in tension with honesty, including love and hope. There is a legitimate role for limited self-deception in facilitating happiness and sustaining the self-esteem and confidence needed to pursue excellence. With his characteristic realism, he writes that "if a man is to accomplish all that is demanded of him, he must deem himself greater than he is. So long as he does not carry this to an absurd length, we readily put up with it."[35] Again, happiness depends on sustaining a certain emphasis on faith in achieving good, and even a creative imagination that brings enchantment to the world.[36]

Happiness and Meaningfulness. Good lives typically embody sound values from categories beyond morality, for example artistic expression and aesthetic appreciation, athletic achievement and appreciation of physical excellence, business acumen, spiritual responsiveness, a sense of humor, a sense of tragedy, humanistic and historical understanding, scientific understanding, and creativity in many forms. The pursuit of any of these values, including moral values, contributes to happiness by sustaining a (subjective) sense of meaning and by providing a multitude of enjoyments, both of which enter into my definition of happiness. The same pursuits, however, can also generate suffering in the forms of frustrated expectations, envious rivalries, anxiety and exhaustion, and tragedy. Happiness in good lives typically involves commitments and responsibilities that can be onerous, for example creative endeavors. In general, happiness and (justified) meaning stand in tension, often a healthy and mutually enriching tension, although sometimes pulling in opposing directions.

Myriad additional values provide meaning and enjoyment directly, and thereby promote happiness. This indirectness bears on the paradoxes of happiness. We naturally assume that important goods need to be pursued directly and mindfully. Paradoxically, that mind-set is frequently self-defeating in the pursuit of happiness. Most of the time happiness is best pursued by focusing on other goods, especially by immersing ourselves in activities and relationships that we value intrinsically, not for their payoff in terms of happiness. Goethe explores the character distortions that occur when our own happiness becomes a preoccupation that subverts attention to goods beyond ourselves. In particular, Werther's self-absorption resulting from unhappy love leads to suicide, although he avoids the petty egotism that precludes friendship, love, and joyous pursuits in the arts, sciences, business, government, and other meaningful endeavors.

Happiness and Mental Health. Happiness is compatible with a variety of mental disorders, given our remarkable powers to adjust to difficulties and challenges. Nevertheless, severe mental disorders can kill happiness by eroding both enjoyment and a sense of meaning; so can neuroticism, which is excessive and chronic anxiety, depression, and rage. Writing long before Freud, Goethe does not employ the jargon of neurotic perfectionism, narcissistic personality disorder, a sense of inferiority, and masochism, but he brilliantly portrays all these phenomena in depicting Werther.[37] In that novel and elsewhere, Goethe critiques self-indulgent excesses he saw in Romanticism (as did Mary Shelley, who has her monster read *The Sufferings of Young Werther*), and he would no doubt see the same excesses in our therapeutic culture.

Some, even much, suffering is compatible with living good lives, even though incompatible with episodic happiness. Other instances of suffering are at odds with happiness, and some of it is self-induced and irrational, especially among those of us "who have enough of everything [but] do not know how to use it or enjoy it."[38] Despite all the suffering the world contains, Faust is saved because he is able to sustain his conviction that the world is good. Goethe celebrates how happiness helps us be open to beauty and meaning, whereas unhappiness closes these things off from us: "Just as a happy mind will invest even crumbling walls and scattered masonry with new life, like a fresh, perennial vegetation, so a melancholy [i.e., depressed] mind robs a living creature of its most beautiful adornment and reduces it, in our eyes, to a bare skeleton."[39]

The capacity for happiness is generally taken to be one of the criteria for mental health, at least when mental health is understood holistically as the psychological well-functioning of a human being. Mental health does not imply actually being happy, for the handicaps and tragedies of life might preclude happiness in varying degrees. And even psychotherapy, when realistic about its goals, usually only alleviates unhappiness and nudges in the direction of happiness, without by any means ensuring it. Indeed, the self-understanding achieved through psychotherapy sometimes adds miseries of its own, as it undermines illusions on which we have based what happiness we have.[40] Yet the capacity for happiness under "normal" conditions is one mark of mental well-functioning.

The virtues, at least in minimal degrees, are also embedded in contemporary concepts of mental health. Typically they are concealed: for example, the virtue of self-respect appears as self-esteem; self-control as opposing harmful addictions; honesty as rationality and as part of "the reality principle" as Freud called it; and responsibility as underlying capacities for social relatedness.[41]

Happiness and Self-Fulfillment. A fulfilling life usually is grounded in authenticity, genuine meaning, and morality, but the idea of self-fulfillment also highlights development of talents in a balanced way. Self-fulfillment tends to promote happiness by unfolding an array of talents in ways that are enjoyable and deepen a sense of meaning. Self-fulfillment requires knowing what we desire most strongly and value most highly, and where our primary talents lie. As with authenticity, happiness is one indicator of self-fulfillment, as well as in part promoted by self-fulfillment. In this way, the ideas are distinct but interwoven.

As a focus in thinking about balance, I discussed balance between work and leisure. I suggested that even the most balanced life contains conflicts and tensions, including among the pursuit of happiness in various domains. Nevertheless, happiness is one of the defining criteria, along with morality and health, for determining when our lives are balanced. Work enters into happy lives in many ways, providing self-esteem and a sense of excellence as well as economic security. Goethe says he lives in order to work, but much of his work often looks more like passionate hobbies.[42] He is often said to be the last Renaissance person who made contributions in law, government, business, the arts, and even original contributions to science. During his Italian journey he came to realize that his primary vocation was as a poet, but he returned to the wealth-producing and influence-exercising work that he also valued. Balance, proportion, and inner harmony remained a struggle throughout his life. But the ideal of continuous and balanced growth is always clear and central.[43] So is the ideal of simplicity, in the sense of keeping central what is most important, rather than being continually distracted by what is less important.

Finally, happiness skeptics have been eager to highlight the junctures where happiness and morality diverge and form crosscurrents, and where happiness and authenticity, self-fulfillment, mental health, and justified meaning are in tension. That emphasis is appropriate insofar as these dimensions of good life are distinct and sometimes pull in different directions. ("Everything is what it is, and not another thing," as Joseph Butler reminds us.[44]) Yet the confluence of happiness with the other dimensions of good lives deserves equal emphasis, not only in ethics and in applying positive psychology to social policy, but also in personal pursuits of happiness in good lives.

NOTES

Chapter 1

1. Jean-Jacques Rousseau, *Confessions*, Angela Scholar, trans. (New York: Oxford University Press, 2000), p. 86.

2. Roger Ebert, review of *Happy-Go-Lucky*, www.rogerebert.com, October 23, 2008. In his next film, *Another Year* (2010), Mike Leigh revisits happiness, this time studying a long and happy marriage.

3. Other definitions that combine meaning, enjoyment, and affirmative attitudes toward one's life include Roy F. Baumeister, *Meanings of Life* (New York: Guilford Press, 1991); David G. Myers, *The Pursuit of Happiness* (New York: Quill, 1992); and Tal Ben-Shahar, *Happier* (New York: McGraw-Hill, 2007).

4. Overemphasis on evaluating to the neglect of valuing mars the otherwise illuminating discussions by L. W. Sumner in *Welfare, Happiness, and Ethics* (Oxford: Clarendon Press, 1996), p. 146; and Daniel M. Haybron in "Life Satisfaction, Ethical Reflection, and the Science of Happiness," *Journal of Happiness Studies*, vol. 8 (2006): 99–138.

5. Loving persons, of course, is a major source of happiness, and hence it provides something like a synecdoche for happiness as loving our lives. Irving Singer clarifies the distinction between evaluating and valuing in *The Nature of Love*, Vol. 1: *Plato to Luther*, 2nd ed. (Chicago: University of Chicago Press, 1984), pp. 3–22.

6. Robert Nozick, *The Examined Life* (New York: Simon and Schuster, 1989), p. 76.

7. Daniel M. Haybron, *The Pursuit of Unhappiness* (New York: Oxford University Press, 2008), pp. 111–121.

8. Ibid., p. 147.

9. Fred Feldman, *What Is This Thing Called Happiness?* (New York: Oxford University Press, 2010), p. 109.

10. Ed Diener and Robert Biswas-Diener, *Happiness* (Malden, MA: Blackwell Publishing, 2008), p. 4. According to Ed Diener, "subjective well-being" has a scientific ring that helps them obtain funding for research. Comment reported by Robert H. Frank, *Falling Behind: How Rising Inequality Harms the Middle Class* (Berkeley: University of California Press, 2007), p. 15.

11. Quoted by David Michaelis, *Schulz and Peanuts: A Biography* (New York: HarperCollins, 2007), p. 343.

12. Definitions and sources of happiness are repeatedly confused by the narrator/protagonist in Lisa Grunwald, *Whatever Makes You Happy* (New York: Random House, 2005).

13. Wladyslaw Tatarkiewicz, *Analysis of Happiness*, trans. Edward Rothert and Danuta Zielinskn (The Hague: Martinus Nijhoff, 1976), p. 223. See also Mike W. Martin, "Of Mottos and Morals," *International Journal of Applied Philosophy* 25:1 (2011): 49–60.

14. John Kekes explores the importance of enjoyment in different styles of life in *Enjoyment: The Moral Significance of Styles of Life* (Oxford: Clarendon Press, 2008).

15. Daniel M. Haybron, *The Pursuit of Unhappiness*, p. 110.

16. Julia Child, with Alex Prud'homme, *My Life in France* (New York: Anchor Books, 2006); Noel Riley Fitch, *Appetite for Life: The Biography of Julia Child* (New York: Anchor Books, 1999); and Nora Ephron's film *Julie and Julia* (2009).

17. Joshua Wolf Shenk, "What Makes Us Happy?," *The Atlantic Online (Psychology)*, June 2009. http://www.theatlantic.com/doc/print/200906/happiness. And see Ben Bradlee, *A Good Life: Newspapering and Other Adventures* (New York: Simon and Schuster, 1995).

18. P. D. James, *Time to Be in Earnest* (New York: Ballantine Books, 1999), p. 240.

19. Ibid., p. 179.

20. Ibid., p. xiii.

21. P. Brickman, D. Coates, and R. Janoff-Bulman, "Lottery Winners and Accident Victims: Is Happiness Relative?" *Journal of Personality and Social Psychology*, vol. 36, no. 8 (1978): 917–927.

22. Sonja Lyubomirsky, *The How of Happiness* (New York: Penguin, 2007), p. 20.

23. Liz Hoggard, *How to Be Happy* (London: BBC Books, 2005), p. 16.

24. Robert Nozick, *The Examined Life*, p. 102.

25. John Dewey, *Human Nature and Conduct* (New York: Modern Library, 1922), p. 47.

26. Jill Ker Conway, *True North* (New York: Alfred A. Knopf, 1994), p. 93.

27. Martha C. Nussbaum, "Who Is the Happy Warrior? Philosophy Poses Questions to Psychology," in Eric A. Posner and Cass R. Sunstein, eds., *Law and Happiness* (Chicago: University of Chicago Press, 2010), p. 86.

28. Richard Layard, *Happiness* (New York: Penguin, 2005), pp. 12, 17.

29. Robert Nozick, *The Examined Life*, p. 104.

30. Valerie Tiberius and Alexandra Plakias develop a definition of well-being that might be interpreted as a partly normative life satisfaction definition of happiness: "satisfaction with how one's life is going overall with respect to one's values," where those values are not "ill informed or ill suited" to one's nature, and where satisfaction is "a positive cognitive/affective attitude toward one's life as a whole." "Well-Being," in John M. Doris and the Moral Psychology Research Group, eds., *The Moral Psychology Handbook* (New York: Oxford University Press, 2010), pp. 402–432, at pp. 421–423.

31. Martha C. Nussbaum suggests there is a crucial ambiguity surrounding the idea of satisfaction with one's life as a whole. The satisfaction might refer to (1) "a subjective state of satisfaction, which is at least closely akin to the feeling of pleasure," or (2) "a reflective judgment about one's life, which judgment might or might not be accompanied by feelings of satisfaction, contentment, or pleasure." "Who Is the Happy Warrior? Philosophy Poses Questions to Psychology," in Eric A. Posner and Cass R. Sunstein, eds., *Law and Happiness* (Chicago: University of Chicago Press, 2010), pp. 81–113, at pp. 86–87. Here I have the second, judgment (evaluative), sense in mind.

32. More careful psychologists, however, combine life satisfaction with experiential sampling techniques that measure levels of enjoyment. For example, Daniel Kahneman, "Objective Happiness," in Daniel Kahneman, Ed Diener, Norbert Schwarz, eds., *Well-Being* (New York: Russell Sage Foundation, 1999), pp. 3–25.

33. E. Diener, R. Emmons, R. Larsen, and S. Griffin, "The Satisfaction with Life Scale," *Journal of Personality Assessment* 49 (1985): 71–75.

34. Elizabeth Telfer, *Happiness* (New York: St. Martin's Press, 1980), p. 16; see also p. 8.

35. Cf. Roy F. Baumeister, *Meanings of Life* (New York: Guilford Press, 1991), p. 214.

36. Norman Malcolm, *Ludwig Wittgenstein, A Memoir* (New York: Oxford University Press, 1958), p. 100.

37. Martin E. P. Seligman, *Authentic Happiness* (New York: Free Press, 2002), p. 7; and Daniel Nettle, *Happiness* (New York: Oxford University Press, 2005), pp. 47, 173.
38. Albert Camus, *The Myth of Sisyphus and Other Essays* (New York: Vintage Books, 1955), p. 91.
39. Julia Annas, "Happiness as Achievement," *Daedalus*, 133:2 (Spring 2004): 44.
40. Ibid., p. 46.
41. Cf. Irwin Goldstein, "Happiness: The Role of Non-Hedonic Criteria in Its Evaluation," *International Philosophical Quarterly* 13 (1973): 523–534.
42. Aristotle, *Nicomachean Ethics*, Sarah Broadie and Christopher Rowe, trans. (New York: Oxford University Press, 2002), p. 97 (1094a19–1095a20).
43. For example, see Josef Pieper, *Happiness and Contemplation*, Richard and Clara Winston, trans.(South Bend, IN: St. Augustine's Press, 1998); The Dalai Lama and Howard C. Cutler, *The Art of Happiness* (New York: Riverhead Books, 1998). A useful resource is Richard Schoch, *The Secrets of Happiness* (New York: Scribner, 2006).
44. John Rawls, *A Theory of Justice* (Cambridge, MA: Harvard University Press, 1971), p. 548.
45. If I were forced to offer a normative definition of "true happiness," I would say it is loving our lives, valuing them as shown in ample enjoyments and a robust sense of meaning, where our lives are morally decent and good, authentic, meaningful in terms of justified values, healthy, and fulfilling. Such a definition would be unwieldy and not very useful. What is important is how happiness interweaves with and sometimes is in tension with the other aspects of good lives, and to understand that we need philosophical and psychological exploration rather than a normative definition.

Chapter 2

1. Robert Nozick, *The Examined Life* (New York: Simon and Schuster, 1989), p. 99. See also Daniel M. Haybron, *The Pursuit of Unhappiness* (New York: Oxford University Press, 2008), p. 123.
2. Darrin M. McMahon, *Happiness: A History* (New York: Atlantic Monthly Press, 2006), pp. 331–332.
3. Thomas Jefferson, cited in Charles B. Sanford, *The Religious Life of Thomas Jefferson* (Charlottesville: University of Virginia Press, 1984), p. 36.
4. Darrin M. McMahon, *Happiness: A History*, p. 325.
5. Ibid., p. 330.
6. Perhaps this subjectivity explains why the right to pursue happiness appears in U.S. court rulings more rarely than one might expect, given its prominence in the Declaration of Independence.
7. William James, *The Varieties of Religious Experience* (New York: Modern Library, 1902), p. 77. Some positive psychologists share James's view, for example Sonja Lyubomirsky, *The How of Happiness* (New York: Penguin Press, 2007), p. 1.
8. This is only part of Roy F. Baumeister's list in *The Cultural Animal: Human Nature, Meaning, and Social Life* (New York: Oxford University Press, 2005), pp. 82–168.
9. Charles Darwin, *Autobiography*, Nora Barlow, ed. (New York: W. W. Norton, 1958), p. 88.
10. Roy F. Baumeister, *The Cultural Animal: Human Nature, Meaning, and Social Life*, p. 86.
11. P. Brickman and D. T. Campbell, "Hedonic Relativism and Planning the Good Society," in M. H. Appley, ed., *Adaptation Level Theory: A Symposium* (New York: Academic, 1971), pp. 287–302.
12. John Kekes, *The Examined Life* (Lewisburg, PA: Bucknell University Press, 1988), pp. 161–173.

13. Barbara L. Fredrickson, "What Good Are Positive Emotions?" *Review of General Psychology* 2 (1998): 300–319; and Barbara L. Fredrickson, *Positivity* (New York: Crown Publishers, 2009).

14. James Griffin, *Well-Being* (Oxford: Clarendon Press, 1986), p. 88.

15. The World Health Organization set forth the most famous definition of positive health: "Health is a state of complete physical, mental and social well-being, not merely the absence of disease or infirmity." Preamble to the Constitution of the World Health Organization, *Official Record of the World Health Organization*, 1946, vol. 2, p. 100.

16. Shelley E. Taylor, *Positive Illusions: Creative Self-Deception and the Healthy Mind* (New York: Basic Books, 1989), p. 47.

17. Marie Jahoda, *Current Concepts of Positive Mental Health* (New York: Basic Books, 1958), pp. 20–21.

18. Alan Gewirth, *Self-Fulfillment* (Princeton: Princeton University Press, 1998), p. 62.

19. Ibid., pp. 14–15.

20. Robert Nozick, *The Examined Life*, p. 104.

21. Ibid., p. 106.

22. James Griffin, *Well-Being* (Oxford: Clarendon Press, 1986), p. 132.

23. John Dewey, *Reconstruction in Philosophy* (Boston: Beacon Press, 1957), p. 179.

24. John Dewey, *Theory of the Moral Life* (New York: Holt, Rinehart and Winston, 1960), pp. 45–46.

25. Gregory S. Kavka uses this expression in "The Reconciliation Project," in David Zimmerman and David Copp, eds., *Morality, Reason, and Truth* (Totowa, NJ: Rowman and Allanheld, 1985), pp. 297–319.

26. John Rawls, *A Theory of Justice* (Cambridge, MA: Harvard University Press, 1971), p. 426. The principle is only rough and open to counterexamples. See John Kekes, *Enjoyment: The Moral Significance of Styles of Life* (Oxford: Clarendon Press, 2008), pp. 40–42.

27. Immanuel Kant, *Practical Philosophy*, p. 49, italics removed.

28. Alain, *Alain on Happiness*, Jane E. Cottrell, trans. (New York: Frederick Ungar Publishing, 1973), p. 241.

29. Dennis Prager, *Happiness Is a Serious Problem* (New York: Regan Books, 1998), p. 3. See also Alain, *Alain on Happiness*, pp. 247–249.

30. This error occurs, for example, in Arthur C. Brooks, *Gross National Happiness: Why Happiness Matters for America—and How We Can Get More of It* (New York: Basic Books, 2008).

31. Elizabeth Telfer, *Happiness* (New York: St. Martin's Press, 1980), pp. 121, 120.

32. Ibid., p. 119. See also pp. 98–99.

33. Immanuel Kant, *Practical Philosophy*, Mary J. Gregor, trans. and ed. (New York: Cambridge University Press, 1996), pp. 214–215.

34. Cf. Joseph Butler, Preface to *Fifteen Sermons* (London: G. Bell and Sons, 1964), p. 24.

35. Kant, *Practical Philosophy*, p. 49.

36. Ibid., p. 282.

37. Ibid.

38. Thomas E. Hill argues that a duty of self-beneficence to pursue our own happiness is "conceptually impossible." Just as other people have the right to consent to or refuse our help, we would have the right to refuse to pursue such a duty of self-beneficence, which means it could not be a genuine duty. Hill provides little textual evidence that Kant used such an argument, and the argument seems implausible to me because it is based on a dubious analogy with interpersonal beneficence. And if the analogy worked here, it would seem to

undermine other duties to ourselves. *Human Welfare and Moral Worth: Kantian Perspectives* (Oxford: Clarendon Press, 2002), pp. 164–200, especially p. 189.

39. Wladyslaw Tatarkiewicz, *Analysis of Happiness*, Edward Rothert and Danuta Zielinskn, trans. (The Hague: Martinus Nijhoff, 1976), p. 351. Cf. Robert Nozick, *The Examined Life*, p. 115.

40. E.g., Sonja Lyubomirsky, *The How of Happiness* (New York: Penguin Press, 2007), p. 2.

41. Eric G. Wilson, *Against Happiness* (New York: Farrar, Straus and Giroux, 2008), pp. 9, 6.

42. Ibid., p. 8.

43. Deal W. Hudson, *Happiness and the Limits of Satisfaction* (Lanham, MD: Rowman and Littlefield, 1996). For related views see Eva S. Moskowitz, *In Therapy We Trust* (Baltimore: Johns Hopkins University Press, 2001); Robert N. Bellah, Richard Madsen, William M. Sullivan, Ann Swidler, and Steven M. Tipton, *Habits of the Heart* (Berkeley: University of California Press, 1985); and C. S. Lewis, "We Have No 'Right to Happiness,'" in Louis P. Pojman and Lewis Vaughn, eds. *The Moral Life*, 4th ed. (New York: Oxford University Press, 2011), pp. 714–719.

44. Deal W. Hudson, *Happiness and the Limits of Satisfaction*, p. 6.

45. Alan Wolfe offers a more upbeat assessment of Americans in *One Nation, After All* (New York: Penguin, 1999).

46. Raymond Angelo Belliotti, *Happiness Is Overrated* (Lanham, MD: Rowman and Littlefield, 2004), p. 93.

47. Ibid., p. xi.

48. Ibid., p. 122. See also pp. 84–85, 92–93, 120, 123.

49. Ibid., pp. 48–50, 71–72.

50. Arthur Schopenhauer, *The World as Will and Representation*, Vol. II, E. F. J. Payne, trans. (New York: Dover, 1958), pp. 573, 574.

51. *Ecclesiastes*, King James translation, 1:14.

52. Bertrand Russell, *The Conquest of Happiness* (New York: Liveright, 1996 [1930]), p. 27.

53. Daniel Nettle, *Happiness: The Science Behind Your Smile* (New York: Oxford University Press, 2005), pp. 7–64.

54. Ibid., p. 51. For recent figures, see Carol Graham, *Happiness Around the World* (New York: Oxford University Press, 2009).

55. David Lykken, *Happiness* (New York: St. Martin's Griffin, 1999).

Chapter 3

1. Rosalind Hursthouse, *On Virtue Ethics* (New York: Oxford University Press, 1999), p. 172. Regarding faith in morality, see Annette Baier, *Postures of the Mind: Essays on Mind and Morals* (Minneapolis: University of Minnesota Press, 1985), pp. 292–308.

2. Jonathan Haidt, *The Happiness Hypothesis: Finding Modern Truth in Ancient Wisdom* (New York: Basic Books, 2006), p. 158.

3. Robert C. Roberts, "The Blessings of Gratitude: A Conceptual Analysis," in Robert A. Emmons and Michael E. McCullough, eds., *The Psychology of Gratitude* (New York: Oxford University Press, 2004), pp. 58–78.

4. Philip C. Watkins, "Gratitude and Subjective Well-Being," in Robert A. Emmons and Michael E. McCullough, eds., *The Psychology of Gratitude*, pp. 167–192. See also Robert A. Emmons, *Thanks: How Practicing Gratitude Can Make You Happier* (New York: Houghton Mifflin Company, 2007).

5. Paul F. Camenisch, "Gift and Gratitude in Ethics," *The Journal of Religious Ethics* 9 (1981), p. 23.

6. Henry David Thoreau, *Walden* (Princeton: Princeton University Press, 2004), p. 78.

7. Robert C. Solomon, *Spirituality for the Skeptic: The Thoughtful Love of Life* (New York: Oxford University Press, 2002), p. 104.

8. Albert Schweitzer, *Reverence for Life: Sermons 1909–1919*, Reginald H. Fuller, trans. (New York: Irvington Publishers, 1993), p. 141. See also Mike W. Martin, *Albert Schweitzer's Reverence for Life: Ethical Idealism and Self-Realization* (Burlington, VT: Ashgate Publishing, 2007), pp. 65–73.

9. Daniel C. Dennett, "Thank Goodness!" in Louise M. Antony, ed., *Philosophers Without Gods* (New York: Oxford University Press, 2007), pp. 113–117.

10. Stephen Darwall, "Two Kinds of Respect," in Robin S. Dillon, ed., *Dignity, Character and Self-Respect* (New York: Routledge, 1995), pp. 181–197. See also Robin S. Dillon, "Toward a Feminist Conception of Self-Respect," in Robin S. Dillon, ed., *Dignity, Character, and Self-Respect*, pp. 290–310.

11. Shelley E. Taylor, *Positive Illusions* (New York: Basic Books, 1989), pp. 48, 227. Self-esteem and happiness are so closely linked that researchers have had to struggle to pull them apart. See Sonja Lyubomirsky, Chris Tkach, and M. Robin Dimatteo, "What Are the Differences Between Happiness and Self-Esteem?" *Social Indicators Research* 78 (2006): 363–404.

12. David G. Myers, *The Pursuit of Happiness* (New York: HarperCollins, 2002), p. 108.

13. Robert C. Solomon, *The Passions* (New York: Anchor Books, 1977), p. 294.

14. Pathological depression takes many forms. American Psychiatric Association, *Diagnostic and Statistical Manual of Mental Disorders*, 4th ed., text revision (Washington, DC: American Psychiatric Association, 2000), pp. 345–428.

15. John Rawls, *A Theory of Justice* (Cambridge, MA: Harvard University Press, 1971), p. 551.

16. Harry G. Frankfurt, *The Importance of What We Care About* (New York: Cambridge University Press, 1988), pp. 80–94; and *The Reasons of Love* (Princeton: Princeton University Press, 2004).

17. Robert Nozick, *Philosophical Explanations* (Cambridge, MA: Harvard University Press, 1981), pp. 594–619.

18. George Eliot, *Middlemarch* (New York: Penguin, 1994), p. 838.

19. Christopher Peterson and Martin E. P. Seligman, *Character Strengths and Virtues* (New York: Oxford University Press, 2004), pp. 325–335.

20. Daniel Putman, "Psychological Courage," *Philosophy, Psychiatry, and Psychology* 4:1 (1997): 1–11 at p. 1.

21. T. S. Eliot, "The Love Song of J. Alfred Prufrock," in T. S. Eliot, *The Complete Poems and Plays, 1909–1950* (New York: Harcourt, Brace and World, 1952), pp. 3–7. Rushworth M. Kidder uses this example in *Moral Courage* (New York: HarperCollins, 2005), pp. 133–135.

22. Michael Slote speaks of "dependent virtues" in this connection. *Goods and Virtues* (Oxford: Clarendon Press, 1983), p. 62.

23. Epictetus, *The Handbook*, Nicholas P. White, trans. (Indianapolis, IN: Hackett Publishing, 1983), Remark 1, p. 11.

24. Alfred R. Mele, *Irrationality* (New York: Oxford University Press, 1987), p. 26.

25. See, for example, Albert Ellis and Irving Becker, *A Guide to Personal Happiness* (Chatsworth, CA: Wilshire Book Company, 1982).

26. This version of the Serenity Prayer is used by Alcoholics Anonymous. Reinhold Niebuhr offered an earlier formulation: "God, give us grace to accept with serenity the things that cannot be changed, courage to change the things that should be changed, and the wisdom to distinguish the one from the other." Elisabeth Sifton, *The Serenity Prayer* (New York: W. W. Norton,

2003); and Laurie Goodstein, "Once in Doubt, Credit for Prayer Won't Change," *New York Times*, Nov. 28, 2009, pp. A1, A11.

27. Steven Luper, *Invulnerability: On Securing Happiness* (Chicago: Open Court, 1996), pp. 81, 87.

28. Epictetus, *The Handbook*, Remark 8, p. 13.

29. Sonja Lyubomirsky, *The How of Happiness* (New York: Penguin, 2007), pp. 20, 52.

30. "Ac-Cent-Tchu-Ate the Positive," lyrics by Johnny Mercer, music by Harold Arlen (1944).

31. Melvin Rader, *The Right to Hope: Crisis and Community* (Seattle: University of Washington Press, 1981), p. 6.

32. Martin E. P. Seligman, *Learned Optimism* (New York: Alfred A. Knopf, 1991), pp. 5–6. Barbara Ehrenreich insightfully critiques the excesses of optimism in *Bright-Sided: How the Relentless Promotion of Positive Thinking Has Undermined America* (New York: Metropolitan Books, 2009).

33. Martin E. P. Seligman, *Authentic Happiness* (New York: Free Press, 2002), p. 96.

34. Words inscribed at the Greek Temple of Apollo at Delphi.

35. John Dewey, *Human Nature and Conduct* [1922] (New York: Modern Library, 1957), p. 183.

36. Robert Sternberg, *Wisdom, Intelligence, and Creativity Synthesized* (New York: Cambridge University Press, 2003), p. 152. See also Barry Schwartz and Kenneth Sharpe, *Practical Wisdom: The Right Way to do the Right Thing* (New York: Riverhead Books, 2010).

37. Valerie Tiberius, *The Reflective Life: Living Wisely with Our Limits* (New York: Oxford University Press, 2008), p. 79.

38. Norvin Richards, *Humility* (Philadelphia: Temple University Press, 1992), p. xii.

39. Robert C. Roberts and W. Jay Wood, "Humility and Epistemic Goods," in Michael DePaul and Linda Zagzebski, eds., *Intellectual Virtue* (Oxford: Clarendon Press, 2003), p. 258.

40. Janet Landman, *Regret: The Persistence of the Possible* (New York: Oxford University Press, 1993).

41. Michael E. McCullough, Kenneth I. Pargament, and Carl E. Thoresen, eds., *Forgiveness: Theory, Research, and Practice* (New York: Guilford Press, 2000).

42. Cf. Charles L. Griswold, *Forgiveness* (New York: Cambridge University Press, 2007).

43. William James, *Psychology: Briefer Course* (New York: Collier Books, 1962), p. 199.

44. Benjamin Franklin, *Autobiography of Benjamin Franklin*, 2nd ed., Leonard W. Labaree, Ralph L. Ketcham, Helen C. Boatfield, and Helene H. Fineman, eds. (New Haven: Yale University Press, 1964), p. 207.

45. On Nietzsche's conception of health see Mike W. Martin, *From Morality to Mental Health: Virtue and Vice in a Therapeutic Culture* (New York: Oxford University Press, 2006), pp. 42–45.

46. Christopher Peterson and Martin E. P. Seligman, eds., *Character Strengths and Virtues*, p. 274.

47. Bertrand Russell, *The Conquest of Happiness* (New York: Liveright, 1930), p. 124. See also Kay Redfield Jamison, *Exuberance: The Passion for Life* (New York: Alfred A. Knopf, 2004).

48. Mihaly Csikszentmihalyi, *Flow* (New York: Harper and Row, 1990).

49. My comments summarize what I say in "Happiness and Virtue in Positive Psychology," *Journal for the Theory of Social Behaviour* 37:1 (2007): 89–103. See also Kristjan Kristjansson, "Positive Psychology, Happiness, and Virtue: The Troublesome Conceptual Issues," *Review of General Psychology* 14:4 (2010): 296–310.

50. Martin E. P. Seligman, *Authentic Happiness*, p. xiii.

51. Martin E. P. Seligman, *Authentic Happiness*, p. 246.

52. Barbara Ehrenreich, *Bright-Sided: How the Relentless Promotion of Positive Thinking Has Undermined America* (New York: Metropolitan Books, 2009), pp. 147–176.

53. Christopher Peterson and Martin E. P. Seligman, eds., *Character Strengths and Virtues: A Handbook and Classification* (New York: Oxford University Press, 2004).

54. Martin E. P. Seligman, *Authentic Happiness*, p. 129.

55. Ibid., p. 125.

56. Ibid., p. 121.

57. Ibid., pp. 112, 102.

58. Ibid., p. 15.

59. Martin E. P. Seligman, *Authentic Happiness*, p. 8.

60. Ibid., p. 261.

61. Christopher Peterson and Martin E. P. Seligman, eds., *Character Strengths and Virtues*, p. 13. Although they seem sensitive to the difference between having one virtue and being virtuous overall (p. 88), they leave unclear how they intend to deal with it.

62. John M. Doris, *Lack of Character: Personality and Moral Behavior* (New York: Cambridge University Press, 2002).

63. On this "slide to subjectivity," see Charles Taylor, *The Ethics of Authenticity* (Cambridge, MA: Harvard University Press, 1991).

64. E.g., Sonja Lyubomirsky, *The How of Happiness*, p. 2.

65. Woody Allen, *Without Feathers*. Quoted in Kevin Jackson, ed., *The Oxford Book of Money* (New York: Oxford University Press, 1996), p. 17.

66. Martin E. P. Seligman, *Flourish: A Visionary New Understanding of Happiness and Well-Being* (New York: Free Press, 2011), pp. 9–10.

67. Ibid., p. 17.

Chapter 4

1. James Dickey, in an interview with Bruce Joel Hillman, in Bill Strickland, ed., *On Being a Writer* (Cincinnati, OH: Writer's Digest Books, 1989), p. 180.

2. And earlier, the Oracle at Delphi.

3. Friedrich Nietzsche, "The Challenge of Every Great Philosophy," in *Existentialism from Dostoevsky to Sartre*, Walter Kaufmann, ed., rev. ed. (New York: New American Library, 1975), p. 123.

4. Friedrich Nietzsche, *The Gay Science*, Richard Polt, trans. (Indianapolis: Hackett Publishing, 1995), Remark 270.

5. Soren Kierkegaard, *Either/Or*, vol. II, Walter Lowrie, trans. (Princeton: Princeton University Press, 1959), p. 263.

6. Ralph Waldo Emerson, "Self-Reliance," *Selected Writings of Ralph Waldo Emerson*, Brooks Atkinson, ed. (New York: Modern Library, 1959), p. 146.

7. Shakespeare, *Hamlet*, I.iii.

8. "My Way," lyrics by Paul Anka, melody by Claude Francois and Jacques Revaux, and popularized by Frank Sinatra.

9. J. L. Austin, *Sense and Sensibilia* (London: Oxford University Press, 1962), p. 69.

10. J. D. Salinger, *The Catcher in the Rye* (New York: Bantam Books, 1951).

11. Harry G. Frankfurt, *The Importance of What We Care About* (New York: Cambridge University Press, 1988), pp. 80–94.

12. The distinction between human and individual nature is drawn by Joel Feinberg, *Freedom and Fulfillment* (Princeton: Princeton University Press, 1992), p. 317.

13. Friedrich Nietzsche, *The Gay Science*, Josefine Nauckhoff, trans. (New York: Cambridge University Press, 2001), pp. 163–164.

14. Charles Taylor, *The Ethics of Authenticity* (Cambridge, MA: Harvard University Press, 1992), pp. 28–29.

15. Jean-Paul Sartre, "Existentialism Is a Humanism," Philip Mairet, trans., in Walter Kaufmann, ed., *Existentialism from Dostoevsky to Sartre* (New York: New American Library, 1975), pp. 345–369.

16. Cheshire Calhoun, "Standing for Something," *The Journal of Philosophy* 92 (May 1995): 235–260; and Charles Guignon, *On Being Authentic* (New York: Routledge, 2004), pp. 155–158.

17. Joseph Campbell, with Bill Moyers, *The Power of Myth,* Betty Sue Flowers, ed. (New York: Anchor Books, 1988), p. 113.

18. Jean-Jacques Rousseau, *Discourse on the Origin of Inequality,* Donald A. Cress, trans. (Indianapolis, IN: Hackett Publishing Company, 1992), p. 70.

19. Jean-Jacques Rousseau, *Lettres Morales,* in *Oeuvres Completes,* Bernard Gagnebin and Marcel Raymond, eds., 5 vols. (Paris: Gallimard, 1969), 4:1112 (Letter 6); cited and translated by Darrin M. McMahon in *Happiness: A History* (New York: Atlantic Monthly Press, 2006), p. 239.

20. Jean-Jacques Rousseau, *The Reveries of the Solitary Walker,* Charles E. Butterworth, trans. (Indianapolis, IN: Hackett Publishing Company, 1992), p. 69.

21. Ibid., p. 71.

22. See David Gauthier, *Rousseau: The Sentiment of Existence* (New York: Cambridge University Press, 2006), p. 9.

23. Phillip C. McGraw, *Self Matters: Creating Your Life from the Inside Out* (New York: Simon and Schuster, 2001), p. 30.

24. Alain de Botton, *Status Anxiety* (New York: Pantheon Books, 2004), pp. vii–viii.

25. Ibid., pp. 181–182.

26. Ibid., p. 293.

27. Annette Baier, *Postures of the Mind* (Minneapolis: University of Minnesota Press, 1985), p. 94.

28. Charles Taylor, *The Ethics of Authenticity* (Cambridge, MA: Harvard University Press, 1992), p. 66.

29. Ibid., pp. 40–41.

30. Ziyad Marar, *The Happiness Paradox* (London: Reaktion Books, 2003), p. 76.

31. Jean-Paul Sartre, *Being and Nothingness,* Hazel E. Barnes, trans. (New York: Washington Square Press, 1966), p. 76.

32. John Stuart Mill, *Utilitarianism* (Indianapolis, IN: Hackett Publishing Company, 1979), pp. 11–13.

33. John Stuart Mill, *On Liberty* (Indianapolis, IN: Hackett Publishing Company, 1978), p. 56.

34. Ibid., p. 54.

35. Ibid., p. 64.

36. Robert Nozick, *The Examined Life* (New York: Simon and Schuster, 1989), p. 102.

37. E.g., Erik Parens, ed., *Enhancing Human Traits* (Washington, DC: Georgetown University Press, 1998); and L. L. E. Bolt, "True to Oneself? Broad and Narrow Ideas on Authenticity in the Enhancement Debate," *Theoretical Medicine and Bioethics* 28 (2007): 285–300.

38. Kirsten Scharnberg, "Undo-plasties Swell in a Nip-Tuck World," *Los Angeles Times,* February 3, 2008, p. B7.

39. Sonja Lyubomirsky, *The How of Happiness* (New York: Penguin Press, 2007), p. 45.

40. Susan Bordo, "Braveheart, Babe, and the Contemporary Body," in Erik Parens, ed., *Enhancing Human Traits* (Washington, DC: Georgetown University Press, 1998), pp. 189–221.

41. Carl Elliott, *Better than Well* (New York: W. W. Norton, 2003), pp. 189–193.

42. Erik Parens, "Authenticity and Ambivalence: Toward Understanding the Enhancement Debate," *Hastings Center Report* 35:3 (2005): 34–41 at p. 38.

43. Peter Kramer, *Listening to Prozac* (New York: Penguin Books, 1997), pp. 1–21.

44. President's Council on Bioethics, *Beyond Therapy: Biotechnology and the Pursuit of Happiness* (New York: Dana Press, 2003), p. 160.

45. Ibid., p. 170. Michael J. Sandel was influential in shaping the Council's thinking. See also his book, *The Case Against Perfection: Ethics in the Age of Genetic Engineering* (Cambridge, MA: Harvard University Press, 2007).

46. President's Council on Bioethics, *Beyond Therapy: Biotechnology and the Pursuit of Happiness*, p. 300.

47. Ibid., pp. 230–231, 238–239.

48. Ibid., p. 331.

Chapter 5

1. Henrik Ibsen, *The Wild Duck*, in *Four Major Plays*, Rolf Fjelde, trans. (New York: New American Library, 1965), p. 202.

2. I discuss these and other views in *Self-Deception and Morality* (Lawrence: University Press of Kansas, 1986).

3. Roy Schafer, *A New Language for Psychoanalysis* (New Haven: Yale University Press, 1976).

4. Roy F. Baumeister, *Meanings of Life* (New York: Guilford Press, 1991), p. 229. See also Joan S. Lockard and Delroy L. Paulhus, eds., *Self-Deception: An Adaptive Mechanism?* (Englewood Cliffs, NJ: Prentice Hall, 1988).

5. Jonathan Swift, *A Tale of a Tub*, in *The Portable Swift*, Carl Van Doren, ed. (New York: Viking Press, 1958), p. 66.

6. Two discussions stand out in the voluminous philosophical literature on what self-deception is and how it is possible: Herbert Fingarette, *Self-Deception*, new edition (Berkeley: University of California Press, 2000), and Alfred R. Mele, *Self-Deception Unmasked* (Princeton: Princeton University Press, 2001).

7. E.g., Shelley E. Taylor, *Positive Illusions* (New York: Basic Books, 1989), p. 49; Ed Diener, "Subjective Well-Being," *Psychological Bulletin* 895 (1984): 542–575.

8. Wladyslaw Tatarkiewicz, *Analysis of Happiness*, Edward Rothert and Danuta Zielinskn, trans. (The Hague: Martinus Nijhoff, 1976), pp. 13–14. See also Robert Nozick, *The Examined Life* (New York: Simon and Schuster, 1989), p. 111.

9. Richard Kraut, "Two Conceptions of Happiness," in Steven M. Cahn and Christine Vitrano, eds., *Happiness: Classic and Contemporary Readings in Philosophy* (New York: Oxford University Press, 2008), pp. 206–207.

10. E.g., Richard Layard, *Happiness* (New York: Penguin Press, 2005), pp. 12–13, 17.

11. Daniel Nettle, *Happiness* (New York: Oxford University Press, 2005), pp. 47, 173.

12. Leo Tolstoy, *Anna Karenina*, David Magarshack, trans. (New York: Signet, 1961), part 6, ch. 24, p. 658.

13. Daniel M. Haybron, "Do We Know How Happy We Are? On Some Limits of Affective Introspection and Recall," *Nous* 41:3 (2007): 394–428, at p. 400. Haybron criticizes a hedonistic definition of happiness (as pleasure), but he implies the same holds for life-satisfaction definitions.

14. Anne Giardini, *The Sad Truth About Happiness* (New York: HarperPerennial, 2005), p. 269.

15. Virginia Woolf, *To the Lighthouse* (San Diego: Harcourt Brace Jovanovich, 1955), p. 70; see also p. 177.

16. Ibid., p. 70.

17. Daniel Nettle, *Happiness*, pp. 65–68.

18. Sonja Lyubomirsky, *The How of Happiness* (New York: Penguin Press, 2007), pp. 41–47.

19. Joan S. Lockard and Delroy L. Paulhus, "General Introduction," *Self-Deception: An Adaptive Mechanism?* (Englewood Cliffs, NJ: Prentice Hall, 1988), p. 2.

20. Shelley E. Taylor, *Positive Illusions*, p. 7.

21. Mike W. Martin, *From Morality to Mental Health* (New York: Oxford University Press, 2006), pp. 154–156.

22. Shelley E. Taylor, *Positive Illusions*, p. 198. See also pp. 44, 126.

23. Sigmund Freud, *The Future of an Illusion*, James Strachey, trans. (New York: W. W. Norton, 1961), p. 39. Cf. Mike W. Martin, *From Morality to Mental Health*, p. 156.

24. Shelley E. Taylor, *Positive Illusions*, pp. 200, 209.

25. Mike W. Martin, *From Morality to Mental Health*, pp. 154–156.

26. Daniel Gilbert, *Stumbling on Happiness* (New York: Alfred A. Knopf, 2006), especially pp. 113, 224–230.

27. Ibid., pp. 161 and 162.

28. Ibid., p. 162.

29. Ibid., p. 174. The last phrase alludes to Timothy Wilson, *Strangers to Ourselves: Discovering the Adaptive Unconscious* (Cambridge, MA: Harvard University Press, 2002).

30. Daniel Gilbert, *Stumbling on Happiness*, p. 167; and see pp. 20–23.

31. Ibid., p. 32.

32. Ibid., pp. 33–34.

33. Gilbert and Joel Cooper earlier discussed self-deception in "Social Psychological Strategies of Self-Deception," in Mike W. Martin, ed., *Self-Deception and Self-Understanding: New Essays in Philosophy and Psychology* (Lawrence: University Press of Kansas, 1985), pp. 75–94.

34. Normative concepts of happiness tend to collapse these two aspects of good lives.

35. Leo Tolstoy, *The Death of Ivan Ilych*, Aylmer Maude, trans., in Randall Jarrell, ed., *Six Russian Short Novels* (New York: Anchor Books, 1963), p. 291. See also Ilham Dilman and D. Z. Phillips, *Sense and Delusion* (New York: Humanities Press, 1971).

36. Tolstoy, *The Death of Ivan Ilych*, p. 296.

37. Ibid.

38. Valerie Tiberius, *The Reflective Life* (New York: Oxford University Press, 2008).

39. Robert Nozick, *The Examined Life*, pp. 104–106.

40. Philip Kitcher, "A Pragmatist's Progress: The Varieties of James's Strategies for Defending Religion," in Wayne Proudfoot, ed., *William James and a Science of Religions* (New York: Columbia University Press, 2004), pp. 98–138.

41. L. W. Sumner, *Welfare, Happiness, and Ethics* (Oxford: Clarendon Press, 1996), p. 167.

42. Ibid., p. 157.

43. Henrik Ibsen, *The Wild Duck*, pp. 202, 203. See also Jerome Neu, "Life-Lies and Pipe Dreams: Self-Deception in Ibsen's *The Wild Duck* and O'Neill's *The Iceman Cometh*," *The Philosophical Forum* 19:4 (1988): 241–269.

44. Cf. Fyodor Dostoyevsky, *The Brothers Karamazov*, Constance Garnett, trans. (New York: New American Library, 1957), p. 49.

45. Eugene O'Neill, *The Iceman Cometh*, (New York: Vintage Books, 1957), p. 239.

46. Ibid., p. 10.

47. Ibid., p. 258.

Chapter 6

1. Wladyslaw Tatarkiewicz, *Analysis of Happiness*, Edward Rothert and Danuta Zielinskn, trans. (The Hague: Martinus Nijhoff, 1976), p. 356, modifying the translation from "man" to "a person."

2. Eric J. Cassell defines suffering as perceiving the "impending destruction of the person" in *The Nature of Suffering and the Goals of Medicine*, 2nd ed. (New York: Oxford University Press, 2004), p. 32. That is too strong as a general definition, but it captures part of what Radner experiences.

3. Gilda Radner, *It's Always Something* (New York: Avon Books, 1989), p. 232.

4. Ibid., p. 263.

5. Ibid., p. 200.

6. Ibid., p. 268.

7. John D. Arras, "Nice Story, But So What?: Narrative and Justification in Ethics," in Hilde Lindemann Nelson, ed., *Stories and Their Limits* (New York: Routledge, 1997), pp. 65–88.

8. Elaine Scarry, *The Body in Pain* (New York: Oxford University Press, 1985).

9. Arthur W. Frank, *The Wounded Storyteller: Body, Illness, and Ethics* (Chicago: University of Chicago Press, 1995), p. 115.

10. Roy F. Baumeister, *Meanings of Life* (New York: Guilford Press, 1991), p. 232.

11. Reynolds Price, *A Whole New Life: An Illness and a Healing* (New York: Plume, 1995), p. 192, italics removed.

12. Ibid., p. 157.

13. Daniel Gilbert, *Stumbling on Happiness* (New York: Alfred A. Knopf, 2006), p. 153.

14. Daniel Nettle, *Happiness* (New York: Oxford University Press, 2005), p. 113. In moving away from Freudian ideas, American psychiatrists dropped the term "neurosis" from the *Diagnostic and Statistical Manual of Mental Disorders* (DSM), 4th ed., text revision (Washington, DC: American Psychiatric Association, 2000).

15. Michael Miller, "Foreword" to Jacques Hassoun, *The Cruelty of Depression* (Reading, MA: Addison-Wesley, 1997), p. vii.

16. Robert C. Solomon, *The Passions* (Notre Dame, IN: University of Notre Dame Press, 1983), p. 294.

17. Andrew Solomon, *The Noonday Demon* (New York: Scribner, 2001), p. 19.

18. Ibid., p. 443.

19. Elfriede Jelinek, cited by Allen Shawn, *Wish I Could Be There: Notes from a Phobic Life* (New York: Viking Press, 2007), p. 223.

20. Allen Shawn, *Wish I Could Be There: Notes from a Phobic Life*, p. 249.

21. Caroline Knapp, *Drinking: A Love Story* (New York: Dell Publishing, 1996), pp. 5–6.

22. Ibid., p. 75.

23. Cited by Marie Jahoda, *Current Concepts of Mental Health* (New York: Basic Books, 1958), p. 19.

24. Preamble to the Constitution of the World Health Organization, *Official Record of the World Health Organization* (Geneva: World Health Organization, 1946), vol. 2, p. 100.

25. Marie Jahoda, *Current Concepts of Mental Health*, p. 20.

26. David Lykken, *Happiness* (New York: St. Martin's Griffin, 1999); Martin E. P. Seligman, *Authentic Happiness* (New York: Free Press, 2002).

27. Wladyslaw Tatarkiewicz, *Analysis of Happiness*, p. 216.

28. See also Darrin M. McMahon, in *Happiness: A History* (New York: Atlantic Monthly Press, 2006), p. 273.

29. Jonathan Haidt, *The Happiness Hypothesis* (New York: Basic Books, 2006), p. 153.

30. Interview with Peter Matthiessen and George Plimpton in Malcolm Cowley, ed., *Writers at Work*, First Series (New York: Penguin Books, 1958), pp. 272, 273.

31. Ralph Keyes, *The Courage to Write* (New York: Henry Holt and Company, 1995), p. 198.

32. Daniel Gilbert, *Stumbling on Happiness*, p. 221.

33. Susan Nolen-Hoessema and Christopher G. Davis, "Positive Responses to Loss: Perceiving Benefits and Growth," in C. R. Snyder and Shane J. Lopez, eds., *Handbook of Positive Psychology* (New York: Oxford University Press, 2002), p. 598.

34. Troy Jollimore, "Meaningless Happiness and Meaningful Suffering," *Southern Journal of Philosophy* 47 (2004): 333–347.

35. John Dewey, *Theory of the Moral Life* (New York: Holt, Rinehart and Winston, 1960), pp. 45–46.

36. Ibid., p. 47.

37. William James, *The Varieties of Religious Experience* (New York: Modern Library, 1902), p. 162.

38. Ibid., pp. 147–148, 242.

39. Bentham's view was recently embraced by economist Richard Layard, *Happiness* (New York: Penguin Press, 2005). Epicurus set forth a related view, although he thought of pleasure primarily as the absence of suffering: "When, therefore, we maintain that pleasure is the end [of life], we do not mean the pleasures of profligates and those that consist in sensuality . . . but freedom from pain in the body and from trouble in the mind." Epicurus, "Letter to Menoeceus," Cyril Bailey, trans., in Steven M. Cahn and Christine Vitrano, eds., *Happiness* (New York: Oxford University Press, 2008), p. 36.

40. Cf. Robert Nozick, *The Examined Life* (New York: Simon and Schuster, 1989), p. 104.

41. Arthur Schopenhauer, *The World as Will and Representation*, E. F. J. Payne, trans., Vol. I (New York: Dover Publications, 1969), p. 318.

42. *Ecclesiastes*, 1:18, King James translation.

43. Friedrich Nietzsche, *The Anti-Christ*, Remark 2, in *The Anti-Christ, Ecce Homo, Twilight of the Idols, and Other Writings*, Aaron Ridley and Judith Norman, eds., Judith Norman, trans. (New York: Cambridge University Press, 2005), p. 4.

44. Friedrich Nietzsche, *Thus Spoke Zarathustra*, Walter Kaufmann, trans. (New York: Penguin Books, 1978), p. 87.

45. Friedrich Nietzsche, *The Gay Science*, Josefine Nauckhoff, trans. (New York: Cambridge University Press, 2001), p. 192.

46. Friedrich Nietzsche, *On the Genealogy of Morality*, Maudemarie Clark and Alan J. Swensen, trans. (Indianapolis, IN: Hackett Publishing Company, 1998), p. 44.

47. Bernard Reginster, *The Affirmation of Life: Nietzsche on Overcoming Nihilism* (Cambridge, MA: Harvard University Press, 2006), p. 234.

48. Friedrich Nietzsche, *The Will to Power*, Walter Kaufmann and R. J. Hollingdale, trans. (New York: Vintage Books, 1968), Remark 910, p. 481.

49. Deal W. Hudson, *Happiness and the Limits of Satisfaction* (Lanham, MD: Rowman & Littlefield Publishers, 1996), p. 152.

50. Ibid., p. 162.

51. Ibid., p. 136.

52. Epictetus, *Handbook of Epictetus*, Nicholas While, trans. (Indianapolis, IN: Hackett Publishing, 1983), p. 13, Remark 5.

53. Ibid., p. 13, Remark 8.

54. Ibid., p. 11, Remark 1.

55. The formula inspired the serenity prayer of Alcoholics Anonymous, via Reinhold Neibuhr. Elisabeth Sifton, *The Serenity Prayer* (New York: W. W. Norton, 2003), p. 292.
56. The Stoics' influence is acknowledged by Albert Ellis and W. Dryden, *The Practice of Rational Emotive Behavioural Therapy* (New York: Springer, 1997).
57. Steven Luper, *Invulnerability: On Securing Happiness* (Chicago: Open Court, 1996).

Chapter 7

1. Alain (pseudonym of Emile Chartier), *Alain on Happiness*, Robert D. and Jane E. Cottrell, trans. (New York: Frederick Ungar Publishing, 1973), p. 236.
2. Jerome Lawrence, "The Joys of Menschhood," in Philip L. Berman, ed., *The Courage to Grow Old* (New York: Ballantine Books, 1989), pp. 91–95, at p. 92.
3. John Stuart Mill, *Autobiography* (New York: Penguin, 1989), p. 117.
4. John Stuart Mill, *Utilitarianism* (Indianapolis, IN: Hackett Publishing, 1979), pp. 7, 11.
5. John Stuart Mill, *Autobiography*, p. 118.
6. John Stuart Mill, *Utilitarianism*, p. 16.
7. Joel Feinberg, "Psychological Egoism," in Joel Feinberg and R. Shafer-Landau, eds., *Reason and Responsibility* (Belmont, CA: Wadsworth, 2002), p. 551.
8. Henry Sidgwick, *Methods of Ethics*, 7th ed. (Chicago: University of Chicago Press, 1907), p. 120.
9. Ibid., p. 405.
10. Joseph Butler, *Fifteen Sermons* (London: G. Bell and Sons, 1964), p. 171.
11. George Orwell, "Arthur Koestler," in Sonia Orwell and Ian Angus, eds., *As I Please* (New York: Harcourt, Brace and World, 1968), 234–244, at p. 244.
12. Bertrand Russell, *The Conquest of Happiness* (New York: Liveright, 1996), p. 123.
13. Robert H. Frank, *Passions Within Reason* (New York: W. W. Norton and Company, 1988), p. ix.
14. Abraham H. Maslow, "Comments on Dr. Frankl's Paper," in Anthony J. Sutich and Miles A. Vich, eds., *Readings in Humanistic Psychology* (New York: Free Press, 1969), pp. 128–129.
15. Raymond Angelo Belliotti, *Happiness Is Overrated* (Lanham, MD: Rowman and Littlefield Publishers, 2004), p. xi.
16. W. Randall Jones, *The Richest Man in Town* (New York: Business Plus, 2009), pp. 25–39.
17. John Dewey, *Human Nature and Conduct* (New York: Modern Library, 1957), pp. 8–9.
18. Immanuel Kant, *Practical Philosophy*, Mary J. Gregor, trans. (New York: Cambridge University Press, 1996), p. 51.
19. Ibid., p. 54.
20. Victoria S. Wike, *Kant on Happiness in Ethics* (Albany: State University of New York Press, 1994); Thomas E. Hill, Jr., *Human Welfare and Moral Worth: Kantian Perspectives* (Oxford: Clarendon Press, 2002).
21. Immanuel Kant, *Practical Philosophy*, pp. 70–71.
22. R. Biswas-Diener, E. Diener, and M. Tamir, "The Psychology of Subjective Well-being," *Daedalus* 133:2 (2004): 18–25, at p. 21.
23. Nicholas White, *A Brief History of Happiness* (New York: Blackwell Publishing, 2006), pp. vii, 162, 166.
24. Ibid., pp. vii–viii.
25. Elizabeth Telfer, *Happiness* (New York: St. Martin's Press, 1980), p. 30.
26. Ibid., pp. 32–33.
27. John R. O'Neil, *The Paradox of Success* (New York: G. P. Putnam's Sons, 1993).

28. Jonathan Haidt, *The Happiness Hypothesis* (New York: Basic Books, 2006), p. 84.

29. Robert Nozick, *The Examined Life* (New York: Simon and Schuster, 1989), p. 116.

30. Mihaly Csikszentmihalyi, *Finding Flow* (New York: Basic Books, 1997).

31. Friedrich Nietzsche, *Thus Spoke Zarathustra*, Walter Kaufmann, trans. (New York: Penguin Books, 1978), p. 115. See also Bernard Reginster, "Happiness as a Faustian Bargain," *Daedalus* (Spring 2004): 52–59, at p. 56.

32. P. Brickman, and D. T. Campbell, "Hedonic Relativism and Planning the Good Society," in M. H. Apley, ed., *Adaptation-Level Theory: A Symposium* (New York: Academic Press, 1971), pp. 287–302.

33. Robert Lane, *The Loss of Happiness in Market Democracies* (New Haven: Yale University Press, 2000); Michael Argyle, *The Psychology of Happiness*, 2nd ed. (New York: Routledge, 2001); Gregg Easterbrook, *The Progress Paradox* (New York: Random House, 2003). The paradox of economic progress is also called the Easterlin paradox, after Richard A. Easterlin who first identified it: "Does Economic Growth Improve the Human Lot? Some Empirical Evidence," in Paul A. David and Melvin W. Reder, eds., *Nations and Households in Economic Growth* (New York: Academic Press, 1974), pp. 89–125.

34. It is also worth noting that there are reasons other than happiness for earning money, including the good we can do with it for ourselves and others.

35. Robert H. Frank, *Luxury Fever* (New York: Free Press, 1999), and Robert H. Frank, "How Not to Buy Happiness," *Daedalus* 36 (2004): 69–79.

36. S. J. Solnick and D. Hemenway, "Is More Always Better?: A Survey on Positional Concerns," *Journal of Economic Behavior and Organization* 37 (1998): 373–383.

37. Richard Layard, *Happiness* (New York: Penguin Press, 2005), pp. 41–45.

38. Alain de Botton, *Status Anxiety* (New York: Pantheon, 2004).

39. Mike W. Martin, *Virtuous Giving: Philanthropy, Voluntary Service, and Caring* (Bloomington: Indiana University Press, 1994), pp. 156–160.

40. Harry G. Frankfurt, *The Importance of What We Care About* (New York: Cambridge University Press, 1989), p. 89.

41. William James, *The Varieties of Religious Experience* (New York: Modern Library, 1902), p. 108.

42. Willa Cather, *My Antonia* (Boston: Houghton Mifflin Company, 1977), p. 18. Cather puts the words in the voice of the narrator of the novel, but the last sentence in the passage also appears on her tombstone.

43. Alan Gewirth, *Self-Fulfillment* (Princeton: Princeton University Press, 1998), p. 50.

44. Barry Schwartz, *The Paradox of Choice* (New York: HarperPerennial, 2005), p. 32.

45. Ibid., pp. 77–116.

46. Ziyad Marar, *The Happiness Paradox* (London: Reaktion Books, 2003), p. 32.

47. Ibid., p. 187.

48. See Maurice Maeterlinck, *The Blue Bird: A Fairy Play in Six Acts*, Alexander Teixeira De Mattos, trans. (Middlesex, England: Echo Library, 2006).

49. Stephen M. Pollan, and Mark Levine, *It's All in Your Head: Thinking Your Way to Happiness* (New York: HarperCollins, 2005).

50. Epictetus, *The Handbook of Epictetus*, Nicholas P. White, trans. (Indianapolis, IN: Hackett Publishing, 1983), p. 13.

51. Ibid.

52. Norman Vincent Peale, *The Power of Positive Thinking* (New York: Simon and Schuster, 2003), pp. 60–61.

53. Martin E. P. Seligman, *Learned Optimism* (New York: Alfred A. Knopf, 1991), p. 221, and Martin E. P. Seligman, *Authentic Happiness* (New York: Free Press, 2002), p. 96.

54. David Lykken, *Happiness* (New York: St. Martin's Griffin, 1999), p. 56.
55. P. Brickman, D. Coates, and R. Janoff-Bulman, "Lottery Winners and Accident Victims: Is Happiness Relative?" *Journal of Personality and Social Psychology* 36 (1978): 917–927.
56. Jonathan Haidt, *The Happiness Hypothesis*, p. 86.
57. R. A. Easterlin, "The Economics of Happiness," *Daedalus* 133:2 (2004): 26–33.
58. Nicholas White, *A Brief History of Happiness*, pp. 109–115.

Chapter 8

1. Aristotle, *Nicomachean Ethics*, Terence Irwin, trans. (Indianapolis, IN: Hackett Publishing Company, 1985), p. 87.
2. Quoted by Robert H. Bremner, *American Philanthropy*, 2nd ed. (Chicago: University of Chicago Press, 1988), p. 12.
3. Mike W. Martin, *Virtuous Giving: Philanthropy, Voluntary Service, and Caring* (Bloomington: Indiana University Press, 1994), p. 1. Bill Clinton distinguishes varieties of philanthropy in *Giving: How Each of Us Can Change the World* (New York: Alfred A. Knopf, 2007).
4. Jonathan Haidt, *The Happiness Hypothesis* (New York: Basic Books, 2006), pp. 172–175.
5. David G. Myers, *The Pursuit of Happiness* (New York: Quill, 1992), pp. 20–21; Jonathan Haidt, *The Hypothesis* (New York: Basic Books, 2006), p. 173.
6. A. M. Isen and P. F. Levin, "Effect of Feeling Good on Helping: Cookies and Kindness," *Journal of Personality and Social Psychology* 21 (1972): 384–388.
7. Peggy A. Thoits and Lyndi N. Hewitt, "Volunteer Work and Well-Being," *Journal of Health and Social Behavior* 42 (2001): 115–131.
8. Graham Greene, *A Burnt-Out Case* (New York: Penguin Books, 1960).
9. Gregory S. Kavka dubs this view "predominant egoism": "Self-interested motives tend to take precedence over non-self-interested motives in determining human actions." *Hobbesian Moral and Political Theory* (Princeton: Princeton University Press, 1986), pp. 64–65.
10. Jane A. Piliavin and P. L. Callero, *Giving Blood: The Development of an Altruistic Identity* (Baltimore: Johns Hopkins University Press, 1991).
11. Ibid., p. 243. See also Carolyn Schwartz, "Altruism and Subjective Well-Being," and Elizabeth Midlarsky and Eva Kahana, "Altruism, Well-Being, and Mental Health in Late Life," both in Stephen G. Post, ed., *Altruism and Health* (New York: Oxford University Press, 2007), pp. 32–42 and 56–69, respectively.
12. P. A. Thoits and L. N. Hewitt, "Volunteer Work and Well-Being," *Journal of Health and Social Behavior* 42 (2001): 115–131.
13. Sonja Lyubomirsky, *The How of Happiness: A Scientific Approach to Getting the Life You Want* (New York: Penguin Press, 2007), pp. 129–130.
14. John O'Connor, "Philanthropy and Selfishness," *Social Philosophy and Policy* 4:2 (1987): 113–127.
15. Quoted by Joseph P. Lash, *Eleanor and Franklin* (New York: Signet, 1973), p. 554.
16. Robert A. Stebbins, "Serious Leisure, Volunteerism, and Quality of Life," in John T. Haworth and A. J. Veal, eds., *Work and Leisure* (New York: Routledge, 2004), pp. 200–201.
17. Robert A. Stebbins, *Between Work and Leisure: The Common Ground of Two Separate Worlds* (New Brunswick, NJ: Transaction Publishers, 2004), pp. 6–7, 52–53.
18. Ibid., pp. 8–9.
19. M. Snyder and A. M. Omoto, "Who Helps and Why? The Psychology of AIDS Volunteerism," in S. Spacapan and S. Oskamp, eds., *Helping and Being Helped* (Newbury Park, CA: Sage, 1991), pp. 213–239.

20. Philanthropic professionals are also at risk for burnout. See Laura Horn and Howard Gardner, "The Lonely Profession," in William Damon and Susan Verducci, eds., *Taking Philanthropy Seriously* (Bloomington: Indiana University Press, 2006), p. 77.

21. Robert Wuthnow, *Acts of Compassion* (Princeton: Princeton University Press, 1991), pp. 97–98. Also see p. 290.

22. David Hume, *An Enquiry Concerning the Principles of Morals*, Section II, Part I, italics removed. I discuss a fuller range of philanthropic virtues in *Virtuous Giving*, pp. 29–61.

23. Mary Midgley, *Beast and Man: The Roots of Human Nature*, rev. ed. (London: Routledge, 1995), p. 331.

24. Immanuel Kant, *Foundations of the Metaphysics of Morals*, Lewis White Beck, trans., reprinted in *Foundations of the Metaphysics of Morals*, Robert Paul Wolff, ed., (Indianapolis: Bobbs-Merrill, 1969), p. 17. Unusual for a sociologist, James Davison Hunter also calls (implausibly) for purity of motivation in *The Death of Character* (New York: Basic Books, 2000), p. 127.

25. Aristotle, *Nicomachean Ethics*, p. 87.

26. Iris Murdoch, *The Sovereignty of Good* (London: Ark Paperbacks, 1985), p. 62.

27. John Dewey, *Human Nature and Conduct* (New York: Modern Library, 1957), pp. 8–9. See also John Kekes, *Moral Tradition and Individuality* (Princeton: Princeton University Press, 1989), pp. 222–235.

28. Robert N. Bellah, Richard Madsen, William M. Sullivan, Ann Swidler, Steven M. Tipton, *Habits of the Heart* (Berkeley: University of California Press, 1985).

29. Robert Wuthnow, *Acts of Compassion*, p. 290.

30. Albert Schweitzer, *Out of My Life and Thought*, A. B. Lemke, trans. (New York: Henry Holt and Company, 1990), p. 82. See also Mike W. Martin, *Albert Schweitzer's Reverence for Life: Ethical Idealism and Self-Realization* (Burlington, VT: Ashgate Publishing Company, 2007).

31. Peter Singer, *The Life You Can Save* (New York: Random House, 2009), pp. 15–16.

32. Ibid., pp. 164–5.

33. Ibid., p. 169.

34. This view strikes me as one plausible interpretation of John Arthur, "Rights and the Duty to Bring Aid," in William Aiken and Hugh La Follette, eds., *World Hunger and Moral Obligation* (Englewood Cliffs, NJ: Prentice Hall, 1977), pp. 37–48.

Chapter 9

1. Robert A. Heinlein, *Stranger in a Strange Land* (New York: G. P. Putnam's Sons, 1961), p. 340.

2. Andrew J. Cherlin, *The Marriage-Go-Round: The State of Marriage and the Family in America Today* (New York: Alfred A. Knopf, 2009), p. 136.

3. Stephanie Coontz, *Marriage, A History* (New York: Viking, 2005), p. 247.

4. Sonja Lyubomirsky, *The How of Happiness* (New York: Penguin, 2007), pp. 141–146.

5. Ibid., p. 146.

6. Arthur C. Brooks, *Gross National Happiness: Why Happiness Matters for America—and How We Can Get More of It* (New York: Basic Books, 2008), p. 61. Brooks cites the 2004 *General Social Surveys, 1972–2004*, James A. Davis Tom W. Smith, and Peter V. Marsden, principal investigators (Chicago: National Opinion Research Center, 2004).

7. Ibid., p. xiv.

8. June Bingham, *Braided Lives: A 20th Century Pursuit of Happiness* (Straus Historical Society [Syracuse, NY], distributed by Syracuse University Press, 2008), p. 429.

9. Ibid., pp. 175, 259.

10. Ibid., p. 383.

11. Plato, *Symposium*, Alexander Nehamas and Paul Woodruff, trans. (Indianapolis, IN: Hackett Publishing Company, 1989), p. 27.

12. Ibid., p. 28.

13. Ibid., p. 30.

14. Robert C. Solomon, *About Love: Reinventing Romance for Our Times* (New York: Simon and Schuster, 1988), p. 199.

15. Ibid., p. 239.

16. Irving Singer, *The Pursuit of Love* (Baltimore: Johns Hopkins University Press, 1994), pp. 25–26. Cf. Irving Singer, *The Nature of Love*, 2nd ed., Vol. 3 (Chicago: University of Chicago Press, 1987), pp. 406–416. Cf. David G. Myers, *The Pursuit of Happiness* (New York: Quill, 1992), p. 157.

17. Robert Nozick, *The Examined Life* (New York: Simon and Schuster, 1989), p. 71.

18. Ibid., p. 68.

19. Neera Kapur Badhwar, "Altruism Versus Self-Interest: Sometimes a False Dichotomy," in Ellen Frankel Paul, Fred D. Miller, Jr., and Jeffrey Paul, eds., *Altruism* (New York: Cambridge University Press, 1993), pp. 90–117.

20. Robert A. Heinlein, *Stranger in a Strange Land*, p. 340.

21. Martha C. Nussbaum, *The Fragility of Goodness: Luck and Ethics in Greek Tragedy and Philosophy* (New York: Cambridge University Press, 1986), p. 359. See also Harry G. Frankfurt, *The Reasons of Love* (Princeton: Princeton University Press, 2004).

22. Mike W. Martin, *Love's Virtues* (Lawrence: University Press of Kansas, 1996).

23. Hazel E. Barnes, *The Story I Tell Myself* (Chicago: University of Chicago Press, 1997), p. 275.

24. Judith S. Wallerstein and Sandra Blakeslee, *The Good Marriage* (New York: Houghton Mifflin Company, 1995), pp. 331–332.

25. Leo Tolstoy, *Anna Karenina*, Richard Pevear and Larissa Volokhonsky, trans. (New York: Penguin Books, 2001), p. 1.

26. John Gottman and Nan Silver, *The Seven Principles for Making Marriage Work* (London: Orion Books, 2000), pp. 25–46.

27. Andrew J. Cherlin, *The Marriage-Go-Round: The State of Marriage and the Family in America Today* (New York: Alfred A. Knopf, 2009), p. 183.

28. Ben Bradlee, *A Good Life: Newspapering and Other Adventures* (New York: Simon and Schuster, 1996), p. 175.

29. Sandra Tsing Loh, "Let's Call the Whole Thing Off," *The Atlantic*, July/August 2009, p. 126.

30. Rafael Yglesias, *A Happy Marriage* (New York: Scribner, 2009). See Malena Watrous's review, "Terminal Bliss," *New York Times*, July 19, 2009, p. 9.

31. Ibid., p. 264.

32. Rafael Yglesias, *A Happy Marriage*, p. 295.

Chapter 10

1. Joanne B. Ciulla, *The Working Life* (New York: Random House, 2000), p. xi.

2. John Haworth, "Work, Leisure and Well-Being in Changing Social Conditions," in John Haworth and Graham Hart, eds., *Well-Being* (New York: Palgrave, 2007), pp. 241–255; and Al Gini, *The Importance of Being Lazy* (New York: Routledge, 2003).

3. Arthur C. Brooks, *Gross National Happiness* (New York: Basic Books, 2008), pp. 153–174.

4. The situation roughly parallels what was said in chapter 4 about the relation between authenticity and happiness: authenticity is not a fully independent guide to happiness because what makes us happy is one of the indicators of authenticity.

5. John T. Haworth and A. J. Veal, "Introduction," in John T. Haworth and A. J. Veal, eds., *Work and Leisure* (New York: Routledge, 2004), p. 1.

6. Michael Argyle, *Social Psychology of Leisure* (New York: Penguin, 1996), p. 3.

7. Valerie Tiberius provides an illuminating discussion from this subjective perspective in "Value Commitments and the Balanced Life," *Utilitas*, 17:1 (2005): 24–45.

8. Mike W. Martin, *Creativity: Ethics and Excellence in Science* (Lanham, MD: Lexington Books, 2007), pp. 105–112.

9. Robert J. Sternberg, *Wisdom, Intelligence, and Creativity Synthesized* (New York: Cambridge University Press, 2003), p. 158.

10. Robert Nozick, *The Examined Life* (New York: Simon and Schuster, 1989), p. 278.

11. Peter Warr, *Work, Happiness, and Unhappiness* (Mahwah, NJ: Lawrence Erlbaum Associates, Publishers, 2007), pp. 9–10.

12. Ibid., pp. 83–89.

13. Mihaly Csikszentmihalyi, *Flow* (New York: HarperPerennial, 1990).

14. Daniel Nettle, *Happiness: The Science Behind Your Smile* (New York: Oxford University Press, 2005), pp. 26–27.

15. Mihaly Csikszentmihalyi, *Finding Flow* (New York: Basic Books, 1997), p. 32.

16. Russell Muirhead, *Just Work* (Cambridge, MA: Harvard University Press, 2004), p. 2.

17. Ibid., p. 162.

18. Alan Gewirth, *Self-Fulfillment* (Princeton: Princeton University Press, 1998), p. 62.

19. Robert A. Stebbins, "Serious Leisure, Volunteerism, and Quality of Life," in John T. Haworth and A. J. Veal, eds., *Work and Leisure*, pp. 200–201.

20. Robert A. Stebbins, *Between Work and Leisure: The Common Ground of Two Separate Worlds* (New Brunswick, NJ: Transaction Publishers, 2004), pp. 6–7, 52–53.

21. Robert A. Stebbins, *Between Work and Leisure*, pp. 8–9.

22. For additional examples of balancing work activities, see Jeffrey Solomon, "A Balancing Act: How Physicians and Teachers Manage Time Pressures and Responsibilities," in Howard Gardner, ed., *Responsibility at Work* (San Francisco: John Wiley and Sons, 2007), pp. 107–132.

23. Martin E. P. Seligman, *Authentic Happiness* (New York: Free Press, 2002), pp. 177–184.

24. Robert A. Stebbins, *Serious Leisure* (New Brunswick, NJ: Transaction Publishers, 2007), p. 58.

25. Daniel Gilbert, *Stumbling on Happiness* (New York: Alfred A. Knopf, 2006), p. 221.

26. Stephanie Coontz, "Till Children Do Us Part," *New York Times*, February 5, 2009, p. A-27, reporting the research of Philip and Carolyn Cowan.

27. Jiri Zuzanek, "Work, Leisure, Time-Pressure and Stress," in John T. Haworth and A. J. Veal, eds., *Work and Leisure*, p. 131.

28. John De Graaf, David Wann, and Thomas H. Naylor, *Affluenza: The All-Consuming Epidemic* (San Francisco: Berrett-Koehler Publishers, 2002), p. 2.

29. Ilene Philipson, *Married to the Job* (New York: Free Press, 2002), pp. 1, 34–35.

30. Mike W. Martin, *From Morality to Mental Health* (New York: Oxford University Press, 2006).

31. Preamble to the Constitution of the World Health Organization, *Official Record of the World Health Organization* (Geneva: World Health Organization, 1947), vol. 2, p. 100.

32. Lewis Mumford, *The Conduct of Life* (New York: Harcourt Brace Jovanovich, 1951), p. 184.

33. Ibid., p. 185.

34. John Dewey, *Reconstruction in Philosophy* (Boston: Beacon Press, 1957 [1920]), p. 167.

35. Gilbert C. Meilaender, *Friendship* (Notre Dame, IN: University of Notre Dame Press, 1981), p. 97.

36. Cited in Deborah J. Swiss and Judith P. Walker, *Women and the Work/Family Dilemma* (New York: Wiley, 1993), p. 63.

37. Mike W. Martin, *Albert Schweitzer's Reverence for Life* (Aldershot, England: Ashgate Publishing, 2007), pp. 45–51.

38. Quoted from Wilhelm von Humboldt by John Stuart Mill, *On Liberty* (Indianapolis, IN: Hackett Publishing Company, 1978), p. 55.

39. Albert Schweitzer, *Philosophy of Civilization*, C. T. Campion, trans. (New York: Prometheus Books, 1987), p. 12.

40. Adam Smith, *An Inquiry Into the Nature and Causes of the Wealth of Nations*, vol. 2, R. H. Campbell and A. S. Skinner, eds. (Indianapolis, IN: Liberty Fund, 1981), p. 782.

41. Also, whereas MacIntyre thinks of corporations as aimed at external goods primarily, I would say that many corporations aim at internal goods, including moral goods. See Mike W. Martin, *Meaningful Work: Rethinking Professional Ethics* (New York: Oxford University Press, 2000), pp. 125–128.

42. Alasdair MacIntyre, *After Virtue*, 2nd ed. (Notre Dame, IN: University of Notre Dame Press, 1984), p. 188.

43. Mike W. Martin, *Virtuous Giving: Philanthropy, Voluntary Service, and Caring* (Bloomington: Indiana University Press, 1994).

44. Deirdre N. McCloskey, *The Bourgeois Virtues: Ethics for an Age of Commerce* (Chicago: University of Chicago Press, 2006).

45. Owen Flanagan, *Varieties of Moral Personality* (Cambridge, MA: Harvard University Press, 1991); John M. Doris, *Lack of Character: Personality and Moral Behavior* (New York: Cambridge, 2002).

46. For this criticism, see John D. Arras, "Nice Story, But So What? Narrative and Justification in Ethics," and Tom Tomlinson, "Perplexed about Narrative Ethics," in Hilde Lindemann Nelson, ed., *Stories and Their Limits* (New York: Routledge, 1997), pp. 65–88 and 123–133, respectively.

47. Ibid., pp. 160, 190.

48. John Kekes, "Attitudinal and Episodic Happiness," in Steven M. Cahn and Christine Vitrano, eds., *Happiness* (New York: Oxford University Press, 2008), pp. 184–186.

49. Suzan Lewis and Christina Purcell, "Well-Being, Paid Work and Personal Life," in John Haworth and Graham Hart, eds., *Well-Being* (New York: Palgrave, 2007), pp. 225–240.

50. John Dewey, *Human Nature and Conduct* (New York: Modern Library, 1957), p. 181.

51. Ibid., p. 183. Jeffrey Stout reworks pragmatic ethics and applies it to the professions, although not to work-leisure balance, in *Ethics After Babel* (Princeton: Princeton University Press, 2001), especially pp. 243–292.

52. Mary Catherine Bateson, *Composing a Life* (New York: Plume, 1990), p. 1.

53. Nicholas White, *A Brief History of Happiness* (Malden, MA: Blackwell, 2006), pp. 163–173.

54. Enlightened employers help employees to "manage boundaries" between work and leisure with an array of family-friendly work options. See Boris B. Baltes, Malissa A. Clark, and Madhura Chakrabarti, "Work-Life Balance: The Roles of Work-Family Conflict and Work-Family Facilitation," in P. Alex Linley, Susan Harrington, and Nicola Garcea, eds., *Oxford Handbook of Positive Psychology and Work* (New York: Oxford University Press, 2010), pp. 201–212.

Chapter 11

1. Henry David Thoreau, *The Journal of Henry D. Thoreau*, Bradford Torrey and Francis H. Allen, eds., Vol. 5 (Boston: Houghton Mifflin Company, 1949), p. 411 (September 1, 1853), omitting a comma after "simplicity."

2. Henry D. Thoreau, *Walden* (Princeton: Princeton University Press, 2004), pp. 91, 8, 78. See also pp. 16, 328.

3. Amitai Etzioni, "Voluntary Simplicity: Characterization, Select Psychological Implications, and Societal Consequences", *Journal of Economic Psychology* 19 (1998): 619–643; and Amitai Etzioni, "Introduction" to Daniel Doherty and Amitai Etzioni, eds., *Voluntary Simplicity: Responding to Consumer Culture* (Lanham, MD: Rowman and Littlefield Publishers, 2003), pp. 1–25, especially pp. 8–12.

4. For some variations on voluntary simplicity, see David E. Shi, *The Simple Life* (New York: Oxford University Press, 1985); David E. Shi, ed., *In Search of the Simple Life* (Salt Lake City, UT: Gibbs M. Smith, Inc., 1986); Jerome M. Segal, *Graceful Simplicity: The Philosophy and Politics of the Alternative American Dream* (Berkeley: University of California Press, 2003); and Cecile Andrews and Wanda Urbanska, eds., *Less Is More* (British Columbia, Canada: New Society Publishers, 2009).

5. Thomas J. Stanley and William D. Danko, *The Millionaire Next Door* (New York: Pocket Books, 1996).

6. Tim Kasser, *The High Price of Materialism* (Cambridge, MA: MIT Press, 2002); Tim Kasser, "Materialism and Its Alternatives," in Mihaly Csikszentmihalyi and Isabella Selega Csikszentmihalyi, eds., *A Life Worth Living: Contributions to Positive Psychology* (New York: Oxford University Press, 2006), pp. 200–214.

7. K. W. Brown and T. Kasser, "Are Psychological and Ecological Well-Being Compatible? The Role of Values, Mindfulness, and Lifestyle," in *Social Indicators Research* 74 (2005): 349–368.

8. Tim Kasser and Kirk Warren Brown, "A Scientific Approach to Voluntary Simplicity," in Cecile Andrews and Wanda Urbanska, *Less Is More*, pp. 35–40, at p. 39; and Kirk Warren Brown and Tim Kasser, "Are Psychological and Ecological Well-Being Compatible? The Role of Values, Mindfulness, and Lifestyle," *Social Indicators Research* 74 (2005): 349–368.

9. Fred B. Bryant and Joseph Veroff, *Savoring: A New Model of Positive Experience* (Mahwah, NJ: Lawrence Erlbaum Associates, Publishers, 2007), pp. xi, 187.

10. Ibid., pp. 65–66.

11. James B. Twitchell, *Lead Us into Temptation: The Triumph of American Materialism* (New York: Columbia University Press, 1999).

12. Leo Tolstoy, *The Death of Ivan Ilyich*, Lynn Solotaroff, trans. (New York: Bantam, 1981), p. 43.

13. Duane Elgin, *Voluntary Simplicity*, 2nd rev. ed. (New York: Harper, 2010), p. 93.

14. Ibid., pp. 90, 95.

15. As noted by David E. Shi, *The Simple Life*, p. 279.

16. Lewis Mumford, *The Conduct of Life* (New York: Harcourt Brace Jovanovich, 1970), p. 272.

17. Ibid., p. 270.

18. Donald A. Norman, *Living With Complexity* (Cambridge, MA: MIT Press, 2011), p. 4. Norman is unhelpful, however, when he says simplicity is entirely "in the mind" and complexity is "a fact of the world" (p. 53), for both the world and theories (in human minds) about the world can be both simple and complex, in different respects.

19. Mike W. Martin, *From Morality to Mental Health: Virtue and Vice in a Therapeutic Culture* (New York: Oxford University Press, 2006).

20. C. R. Snyder, ed., *Coping with Stress: Effective People and Processes* (New York: Oxford University Press, 2001).

21. Erica Frydenberg, ed., *Beyond Coping: Meeting Goals, Visions, and Challenges* (New York: Oxford University Press, 2002).

22. Amitai Etzioni, "Introduction" to Daniel Doherty and Amitai Etzioni, eds., *Voluntary Simplicity: Responding to Consumer Culture*, p. 24, italics removed.

Chapter 12

1. Bernard Williams, *Ethics and the Limits of Philosophy* (Cambridge, MA: Harvard University Press, 1985), p. 45.

2. Clive James, "Happiness Writes White," *The Monthly*, December 2006–January 2007, No. 19. Http://www.themonthly.com. Accessed 1/10/2010.

3. For example, in *One Writer's Beginnings*, Eudora Welty charmingly celebrates her life as a writer, but that very charm leads Carolyn Heilbrun to charge Welty with dishonest nostalgia that masks unacknowledged anger. Carolyn G. Heilbrun, *Writing a Woman's Life* (New York: W. W. Norton, 1988), pp. 13–15. For a reply, see Suzanne Marrs, *Eudora Welty* (New York: Harcourt, 2004), p. xiv.

4. The novel has been reinterpreted with every wave of literary criticism. See, e.g., Mary Shelley, *Frankenstein, Case Studies in Contemporary Criticism*, 2nd ed., Johanna M. Smith, ed. (Boston: Bedford/St. Martin's, 2000), and Graham Allen, *Shelley's Frankenstein* (London: Continuum, 2008).

5. On historical backgrounds, see Robert Anderson, "'Misery Made Me a Fiend': Social Reproduction in Mary Shelley's *Frankenstein* and Robert Owen's Early Writings," *Nineteenth-Century Contexts* 24:4 (2002): 417–438.

6. Parenthetical page references are to Mary Shelley, *Frankenstein*, Maurice Hindle, ed., rev. ed. (New York: Penguin Books, 2003). This book contains the 1831 edition, but what I say also applies to the 1818 edition. On the debate about which edition is preferable, see Anne K. Mellor, "Choosing a Text of *Frankenstein* to Teach," in J. Paul Hunter, ed., Mary Shelley, *Frankenstein* (New York: W. W. Norton and Company, 1996), pp. 160–166.

7. E.g., Anne K. Mellor, "Making a Monster," in Harold Bloom, ed., *Mary Shelley's Frankenstein*, updated edition (New York: Chelsea House, 2007).

8. Harriet Hustis, "Responsible Creativity and the 'Modernity' of Mary Shelley's Prometheus," *SEL, Studies in English Literature 1500–1900* 43:4 (2003): 845–858.

9. Lawrence Lipking, "*Frankenstein*, the True Story; or, Rousseau Judges Jean-Jacques," in J. Paul Hunter, ed., Mary Shelley, *Frankenstein*, pp. 313–331, at p. 316.

10. John Dewey, *Human Nature and Conduct* (New York: Modern Library, 1957), p. 8.

11. James O'Rourke, "'Nothing More Unnatural': Mary Shelley's Revision of Rousseau," *ELH* 56(3) (1989), pp. 543–69. Quoted by Berthold Schoene-Harwood, Mary Shelley, *Frankenstein* (New York: Columbia University Press, 2000), p. 50.

12. Ibid.

13. Immanuel Kant, *Practical Philosophy*, Mary J. Gregor, trans. (New York: Cambridge University Press, 1996), pp. 214–215. Chris McCord insightfully explores Kantian themes in "Frankenstein Meets Kant (and the Problem of Wide Duties)," *Teaching Philosophy* 27:2 (June 2004): 127–141.

14. Sonja Lyubomirsky, *The How of Happiness* (New York: Penguin Press, 2007), pp. 125–149.

15. Jonathan Haidt, *The Happiness Hypothesis* (New York: Basic Books, 2006), p. 158.

16. Martin E. P. Seligman, *Authentic Happiness* (New York: Free Press, 2002).

Chapter 13

1. Johann Wolfgang von Goethe, *Wilhelm Meister's Apprenticeship*, Eric A. Blackall, trans. (New York: Suhrkamp Publishers, 1989), p. 304.
2. Benjamin Franklin, *Autobiography of Benjamin Franklin*, 2nd ed. (New Haven: Yale University Press, 2003), p. 207.
3. E.g., Helen Johns and Paul Ormerod, *Happiness, Economics and Public Policy* (London: Institute of Economic Affairs, 2007).
4. Ed Diener and Martin E. P. Seligman, "Beyond Money: Toward an Economy of Well-Being," *Psychological Science in the Public Interest* 5:1 (2004): 1–31; Richard Layard, *Happiness: Lessons from a New Science* (New York: Penguin Press, 2005); David Halpern, *The Hidden Wealth of Nations* (Cambridge, UK: Polity Press, 2010); Arthur C. Brooks, *Gross National Happiness* (New York: Basic Books, 2008); Derek Bok, *The Politics of Happiness* (Princeton: Princeton University Press, 2010). On President Sarkozy and Prime Minister David Cameron, see Bok, *Politics of Happiness*, p. 4. For additional sources, see Eric A. Posner and Cass R. Sunstein, eds., *Law and Happiness* (Chicago: University of Chicago Press, 2010).
5. David Halpern, *The Hidden Wealth of Nations*, p. 41.
6. Richard A. Easterlin, "Does Economic Growth Improve the Human Lot? Some Empirical Evidence," in Paul A. David and Melvin W. Reder, eds., *Nations and Households in Economic Growth* (New York: Academic Press, 1974), pp. 89–125.
7. Richard Layard, *Happiness: Lessons from a New Science*, pp. 224–225.
8. Ibid., p. 224.
9. Ibid., p. 12. R. Veenhoven also advances a utilitarian politics of happiness in "Happiness as a Public Policy Aim: The Greatest Happiness Principle," in P. A. Linley and S. Joseph, eds. *Positive Psychology in Practice* (Hoboken: Wiley, 2004), pp. 658–678. For a critique of utilitarian proposals, see Grant Duncan, "Should Happiness-Maximization Be the Goal of Government?" *Journal of Happiness Studies* 11 (2010): 163–178.
10. Derek Bok, *The Politics of Happiness*, p. 60; David Halpern, *The Hidden Wealth of Nations*, p. 32.
11. David Halpern, *The Hidden Wealth of Nations*, p. 14.
12. Alan Wolfe, "Joy to the World," (review of Derek Bok's *Politics of Happiness*), *New York Times Book Review*, February 21, 2010, p. 16.
13. Arthur C. Brooks, *Gross National Happiness*, p. 27.
14. Ed Diener and Martin E. P. Seligman, "Beyond Money: Toward an Economy of Well-Being," p. 24.
15. Vijay K. Shrotryia, "Happiness and Development: Public Policy Initiatives in the Kingdom of Bhutan," in Yew-Kwang Ng and Lok Sang Ho, eds., *Happiness and Public Policy: Theory, Case Studies and Implications* (New York: Palgrave/Macmillan, 2006), pp. 193–208.
16. Tessa Piper, "The Exodus of Ethnic Nepalis from Southern Bhutan," *Refugee Survey Quarterly* 14 (1995): 52. Cited by Derek Bok, *The Politics of Happiness*, p. 212, n4.
17. Aldous Huxley, *Brave New World* and *Brave New World Revisited* (New York: HarperPerennial, 2005), pp. 11–12.
18. Gerald Dworkin, *The Theory and Practice of Autonomy* (New York: Cambridge University Press, 1988).
19. Richard H. Thaler and Cass R. Sunstein, *Nudge: Improving Decisions About Health, Wealth, and Happiness* (New Haven: Yale University Press, 2008). David Halpern sympathetically discusses Thaler and Sunstein's approach, *The Hidden Wealth of Nations*, pp. 231–253.

20. Friedrich Nietzsche, *Twilight of the Idols*, Judith Norman, trans., in *Friedrich Nietzsche, The Anti-Christ, Ecce Homo, Twilight of the Idols, and Other Writings*, Aaron Ridley and Judith Norman, eds. (New York: Cambridge University Press, 2005), p. 157.

21. Johann Wolfgang von Goethe, *Italian Journey*, W. H. Auden and Elizabeth Mayer, trans. (New York: Penguin Books, 1970), pp. 199.

22. Quoted and translated by Julie D. Prandi, *"Dare To Be Happy!": A Study of Goethe's Ethics* (Lanham, MD: University Press of America, 1993), p. 4.

23. Goethe, *Italian Journey*, p. 405.

24. Ibid., p. 221.

25. Ibid., p. 376; cf. p. 309.

26. T. J. Reed, "Goethe and Happiness," in Elizabeth M. Wilkinson, ed., *Goethe Revisited: A Collection of Essays* (New York: Riverrun Press, 1984), pp. 111–131.

27. Cited and translated by Julie D. Prandi, *"Dare To Be Happy!": A Study of Goethe's Ethics*, p. 2.

28. Goethe, *Italian Journey*, p. 376.

29. Ibid., pp. 339, 403.

30. Johann Wolfgang von Goethe, *Wilhelm Meister's Apprenticeship*, Eric A. Blackall, trans. (New York: Suhrkamp Publishers, 1989), p. 304. The words are voiced by the abbot, a character in the novel, but the attitude is Goethe's. See Julie D. Prandi, *"Dare To Be Happy!": A Study of Goethe's Ethics*.

31. John Armstrong, *Love, Life, Goethe* (New York: Farrar, Straus and Giroux, 2006), p. 330.

32. T. J. Reed, "Goethe and Happiness," p. 118.

33. Goethe, *Italian Journey*, p. 398.

34. Ibid., p. 313.

35. *Reflections and Maxims*, W. B. Ronnfeldt, trans., in Stephen Spender, ed., *Great Writings of Goethe* (New York: New American Library, 1958), p. 272.

36. Goethe, *Italian Journey*, pp. 435–436.

37. Harry Steinhauer, Afterword, in Johann Wolfgang von Goethe, *The Sufferings of Young Werther*, Harry Steinhauer, trans. (New York: W. W. Norton and Company, 1970), p. 113.

38. Goethe, *Italian Journey*, p. 376.

39. Ibid., pp. 435–436.

40. Richard A. Friedman, "When Self-Knowledge Is Only the Beginning," *New York Times*, January 18, 2011, p. D-5.

41. Mike W. Martin, *From Morality to Mental Health: Virtue and Vice in a Therapeutic Culture* (New York: Oxford University Press, 2006).

42. Goethe, *Italian Journey*, p. 386.

43. John Armstrong, *Love, Life, Goethe*, p. 5.

44. Joseph Butler, *Fifteen Sermons*, W. R. Matthews, ed. (London: G. Bell and Sons, 1964), p. 23.

BIBLIOGRAPHY

Alain (pseudonym of Emile Chartier). *Alain on Happiness*. Robert D. and Jane E. Cottrell, trans. New York: Frederick Ungar Publishing, 1973.

Allen, Graham. *Shelley's Frankenstein*. London: Continuum, 2008.

American Psychiatric Association. *Diagnostic and Statistical Manual of Mental Disorders*, Fourth Edition, Text Revision. Washington, DC: American Psychiatric Association, 2000.

Anderson, Robert. "'Misery Made Me a Fiend': Social Reproduction in Mary Shelley's *Frankenstein* and Robert Owen's Early Writings." *Nineteenth-Century Contexts* 24:4 (2002): 417–438.

Andrews, Cecile, and Wanda Urbanska, eds. *Less Is More*. British Columbia, Canada: New Society Publishers, 2009.

Annas, Julia, 2004. "Happiness as Achievement." *Daedalus* 133:2 (Spring 2004): 44–51.

———. *The Morality of Happiness*. New York: Oxford University Press, 1993.

Argyle, Michael. *The Psychology of Happiness*. 2nd ed. New York: Routledge, 2001.

———. *Social Psychology of Leisure*. New York: Penguin, 1996.

Aristotle. *Nicomachean Ethics*. Sarah Broadie and Christopher Rowe, trans. New York: Oxford University Press, 2002.

———. *Nicomachean Ethics*. Terence Irwin, trans. Indianapolis, IN: Hackett Publishing Company, 1985.

Armstrong, John. *Love, Life, Goethe*. New York: Farrar, Straus and Giroux, 2006.

Arras, John D. "Nice Story, But So What?: Narrative and Justification in Ethics." In Hilde Lindemann Nelson, ed., *Stories and Their Limits*. New York: Routledge, 1997. Pp. 65–88.

Arthur, John. "Rights and the Duty to Bring Aid." In William Aiken and Hugh La Follette, eds., *World Hunger and Moral Obligation*. Englewood Cliffs, NJ: Prentice-Hall, 1977. Pp. 37–48.

Austin, J. L. *Sense and Sensibilia*. London: Oxford University Press, 1962.

Badhwar, Neera Kapur. "Altruism Versus Self-Interest: Sometimes a False Dichotomy." In Ellen Frankel Paul, Fred D. Miller, Jr., and Jeffrey Paul, eds., *Altruism*. New York: Cambridge University Press, 1993. Pp. 90–117.

Baier, Annette. *Postures of the Mind: Essays on Mind and Morals*. Minneapolis: University of Minnesota Press, 1985.

Baltes, Boris B., Malissa A. Clark, and Madhura Chakrabarti. "Work-Life Balance: The Roles of Work-Family Conflict and Work-Family Facilitation." In P. Alex Linley, Susan Harrington, and Nicola Garcea, eds., *Oxford Handbook of Positive Psychology and Work*. New York: Oxford University Press, 2010. Pp. 201–212.

Barnes, Hazel E. *The Story I Tell Myself*. Chicago: University of Chicago Press, 1997.

Bateson, Mary Catherine. *Composing a Life*. New York: Plume, 1990.

Baumeister, Roy F. *The Cultural Animal: Human Nature, Meaning, and Social Life*. New York: Oxford University Press, 2005.

———. *Meanings of Life*. New York: Guilford Press, 1991.

Bellah, Robert N., Richard Madsen, William M. Sullivan, Ann Swidler, and Steven M. Tipton. *Habits of the Heart*. Berkeley: University of California Press, 1985.

Belliotti, Raymond Angelo. *Happiness Is Overrated*. Lanham, MD: Rowman and Littlefield, 2004.

Ben-Shahar, Tal. *Happier*. New York: McGraw-Hill, 2007.

Bingham, June. *Braided Lives: A 20th Century Pursuit of Happiness*. Straus Historical Society (Syracuse, NY), distributed by Syracuse University Press, 2008.

Biswas-Diener, R., E. Diener, and M. Tamir. "The Psychology of Subjective Well-being." *Daedalus* 133:2 (2004): 18–25.

Bok, Derek. *The Politics of Happiness*. Princeton: Princeton University Press, 2010.

Bok, Sissela. *Exploring Happiness: From Aristotle to Brain Science*. New Haven: Yale University Press, 2010.

Bolt, L. L. W. "True to Oneself? Broad and Narrow Ideas on Authenticity in the Enhancement Debate." *Theoretical Medicine and Bioethics* 28 (2007): 285–300.

Bordo, Susan. "Braveheart, Babe, and the Contemporary Body." In Erik Parens, ed., *Enhancing Human Traits*. Washington, DC: Georgetown University Press, 1998. Pp. 189–221.

Bortolotti, Lisa, ed. *Philosophy and Happiness*. Hampshire, UK: Palgrave, 2009.

Botton, Alain de. *Status Anxiety*. New York: Pantheon Books, 2004.

Bradlee, Ben. *A Good Life: Newspapering and Other Adventures*. New York: Simon and Schuster, 1995.

Bremner, Robert. *American Philanthropy*, 2nd ed. Chicago: University of Chicago Press, 1988.

Brickman, P., and D. T. Campbell. "Hedonic Relativism and Planning the Good Society." In M. H. Appley, ed., *Adaptation Level Theory: A Symposium*. New York: Academic, 1971. Pp. 287–302.

Brickman, P., D. Coates, and R. Janoff-Bulman. "Lottery Winners and Accident Victims: Is Happiness Relative?" *Journal of Personality and Social Psychology* 36:8 (1978): 917–927.

Brooks, Arthur C. *Gross National Happiness: Why Happiness Matters for America—and How We Can Get More of It*. New York: Basic Books, 2008.

Brown, K. W., and T. Kasser. "Are Psychological and Ecological Well-Being Compatible? The Role of Values, Mindfulness, and Lifestyle." In *Social Indicators Research* 74 (2005): 349–368.

Brulde, Bengt. "Happiness and the Good Life, Introduction and Conceptual Framework," *Journal of Happiness Studies* 8 (2007): 1–14.

Bruni, Luigino, and Pier Luigi Porta, eds. *Economics and Happiness*. New York: Oxford University Press, 2005.

Bryant, Fred B., and Joseph Veroff. *Savoring: A New Model of Positive Experience*. Mahwah, NJ: Lawrence Erlbaum Associates, 2007.

Butler, Joseph. *Fifteen Sermons*. London: G. Bell and Sons, 1964.

Cahn, Steven M., and Christine Vitrano, eds. *Happiness: Classic and Contemporary Readings in Philosophy*. New York: Oxford University Press, 2008.

Calhoun, Cheshire. "Standing for Something." *The Journal of Philosophy* 92 (May 1995): 235–260.

Camenisch, Paul F. "Gift and Gratitude in Ethics." *The Journal of Religious Ethics* 9 (1981): 1–34.

Campbell, Joseph, with Bill Moyers. *The Power of Myth*. Betty Sue Flowers, ed. New York: Anchor Books, 1988.

Camus, Albert. *The Myth of Sisyphus and Other Essays*. New York: Vintage Books, 1955.

Cassell, Eric J. *The Nature of Suffering and the Goals of Medicine*, 2nd ed. New York: Oxford University Press, 2004.

Cather, Willa. *My Antonia*. Boston: Houghton Mifflin Company, 1977.

Cavell, Stanley. *Pursuits of Happiness: The Hollywood Comedy of Remarriage*. Cambridge, MA: Harvard University Press, 1981.

Cherlin, Andrew J. *The Marriage-Go-Round: The State of Marriage and the Family in America Today*. New York: Alfred A. Knopf, 2009.

Child, Julia, with Alex Prud'homme. *My Life in France*. New York: Anchor Books, 2006.

Ciulla, Joanne B. *The Working Life*. New York: Random House, 2000.

Clinton, Bill. *Giving: How Each of Us Can Change the World*. New York: Alfred A. Knopf, 2007.

Conway, Jill Ker. *True North*. New York: Alfred A. Knopf, 1994.

Coontz, Stephanie. *Marriage, A History*. New York: Viking, 2005.

———. "Till Children Do Us Part." *New York Times*, Feb. 5, 2009, p. A-27.

Csikszentmihalyi, Mihaly. *Finding Flow*. New York: Basic Books, 1997.

———. *Flow*. New York: Harper and Row, 1990.

Dalai Lama, and Howard C. Cutler. *The Art of Happiness*. New York: Riverhead Books, 1998.

Darwall, Stephen. "Two Kinds of Respect." In Robin S. Dillon, ed., *Dignity, Character and Self-Respect*. New York: Routledge, 1995. Pp. 181–197.

Darwin, Charles. *Autobiography*. Nora Barlow, ed. New York: W. W. Norton, 1958.

Davis, James A., Tom W. Smith, and Peter V. Marsden. *2004 General Social Surveys, 1972–2004*. Chicago: National Opinion Research Center, 2004.

De Graaf, John, David Wann, and Thomas H. Naylor. *Affluenza: The All-Consuming Epidemic*. San Francisco: Berrett-Koehler Publishers, 2002.

Dennett, Daniel C. "Thank Goodness!" In Louise M. Antony, ed. *Philosophers Without Gods*. New York: Oxford University Press, 2007. Pp. 113–117.

Dewey, John. *Human Nature and Conduct*. New York: Modern Library, 1957 [1922].

———. *Reconstruction in Philosophy*. Boston: Beacon Press, 1957.

———. *Theory of the Moral Life*. New York: Holt, Rinehart and Winston, 1960.

Diener, Ed. "Subjective Well-Being." *Psychological Bulletin* 895 (1984): 542–575.

Diener, Ed, and Martin E. P. Seligman. "Beyond Money: Toward an Economy of Well-Being." *Psychological Science in the Public Interest* 5:1 (2004): 1–31.

Diener, Ed., and Eunkook M. Suh, eds. *Culture and Subjective Well-Being*. Cambridge, MA: MIT Press, 2000.

Diener, Ed, and Robert Biswas-Diener. *Happiness*. Malden, MA: Blackwell Publishing, 2008.

Diener, E., R. Emmons, R. Larsen, and S. Griffin. "The Satisfaction with Life Scale." *Journal of Personality Assessment* 49 (1985): 71–75.

Dillon, Robin S. "Toward a Feminist Conception of Self-Respect." In Robin S. Dillon, ed., *Dignity, Character, and Self-Respect*. New York: Routledge, 1995. Pp. 290–310.

Dilman, Ilham, and D. Z. Phillips. *Sense and Delusion*. New York: Humanities Press, 1971.

Doris, John M. *Lack of Character: Personality and Moral Behavior*. New York: Cambridge University Press, 2002.

Doris, John M., and the Moral Psychology Research Group, eds. *The Moral Psychology Handbook*. New York: Oxford University Press, 2010.

Dostoyevsky, Fyodor. *The Brothers Karamazov*. Constance Garnett, trans. New York: New American Library, 1957.

Duncan, Grant. "Should Happiness-Maximization Be the Goal of Government?" *Journal of Happiness Studies* 11 (2010):163–178.

Dworkin, Gerald. *The Theory and Practice of Autonomy*. New York: Cambridge University Press, 1988.

Easterbrook, Gregg. *The Progress Paradox*. New York: Random House, 2003.

Easterlin, Richard A. "Does Economic Growth Improve the Human Lot? Some Empirical Evidence." In Paul A. David and Melvin W. Reder, eds., *Nations and Households in Economic Growth*. New York: Academic Press, 1974.

———. "The Economics of Happiness." *Daedalus* 133:2 (2004): 26–33.

Ebert, Robert. Review of *Happy-Go-Lucky*, www.rogerebert.com. October 23, 2008.

Ehrenreich, Barbara. *Bright-Sided: How the Relentless Promotion of Positive Thinking Has Undermined America*. New York: Metropolitan Books, 2009.

Elgin, Duane. *Voluntary Simplicity*. Second Revised Edition. New York: HarperCollins, 2010.

Eliot, George. *Middlemarch*. New York: Penguin, 1994.

Eliot, T. S. "The Love Song of J. Alfred Prufrock." In T. S. Eliot, *The Complete Poems and Plays, 1909–1950*. New York: Harcourt, Brace and World, 1952. Pp. 3–7.

Elliott, Carl. *Better than Well*. New York: W. W. Norton, 2003.

Ellis, Albert, and Irving Becker. *A Guide to Personal Happiness*. Chatsworth, CA: Wilshire Book Company, 1982.

Ellis, Albert, and W. Dryden. *The Practice of Rational Emotive Behavior Therapy*. New York: Springer, 1997.

Emerson, Ralph Waldo. "Self-Reliance." In Brooks Atkinson, ed., *Selected Writings of Ralph Waldo Emerson*. New York: Modern Library, 1959.

Emmons, Robert A. *Thanks: How Practicing Gratitude Can Make You Happier*. New York: Houghton Mifflin Company, 2007.

Emmons, Robert A., and Michael E. McCullough, eds. *The Psychology of Gratitude*. New York: Oxford University Press, 2004.

Epictetus. *The Handbook*. Nicholas P. White, trans. Indianapolis, IN: Hackett Publishing, 1983.

Epicurus. "Letter to Menoeceus." Cyril Bailey, trans. In Steven M. Cahn and Christine Vitrano, eds., *Happiness*. New York: Oxford University Press, 2008. Pp. 34–37.

Etzioni, Amitai. "Introduction" to Daniel Doherty and Amitai Etzioni, eds., *Voluntary Simplicity: Responding to Consumer Culture*. Lanham, MD: Rowman and Littlefield Publishers, 2003. Pp. 1–25.

———. "Voluntary Simplicity: Characterization, Select Psychological Implications, and Societal Consequences," *Journal of Economic Psychology* 19 (1998): 619–643.

Feinberg, Joel. *Freedom and Fulfillment*. Princeton: Princeton University Press, 1992.

———. "Psychological Egoism." In Joel Feinberg and R. Shafer-Landau, eds., *Reason and Responsibility*. Belmont, CA: Wadsworth, 2002.

Feldman, Fred. *What Is This Thing Called Happiness?* New York: Oxford University Press, 2010.

Fingarette, Herbert. *Self-Deception*, new edition. Berkeley: University of California Press, 2000.

Fitch, Noel Riley. *Appetite for Life: The Biography of Julia Child*. New York: Anchor Books, 1999.

Flanagan, Owen. *Varieties of Moral Personality*. Cambridge, MA: Harvard University Press, 1991.

Frank, Arthur W. *The Wounded Storyteller: Body, Illness, and Ethics*. Chicago: University of Chicago Press, 1995.

Frank, Robert H. *Falling Behind: How Rising Inequality Harms the Middle Class*. Berkeley: University of California Press, 2007.

———. "How Not to Buy Happiness." *Daedalus* 36 (2004): 69–79.

———. *Luxury Fever*. New York: Free Press, 1999.

———. *Passions Within Reason*. New York: W. W. Norton and Company, 1988.

Frankfurt, Harry G. *The Importance of What We Care About*. New York: Cambridge University Press, 1988.

———. *The Reasons of Love*. Princeton: Princeton University Press, 2004.

Franklin, Benjamin. *Autobiography of Benjamin Franklin*, 2nd ed. Leonard W. Labaree, Ralph L. Ketcham, Helen C. Boatfield, and Helene H. Fineman, eds. New Haven: Yale University Press, 1964.

Fredrickson, Barbara L. *Positivity*. New York: Crown Publishers, 2009.

———. "What Good Are Positive Emotions?" *Review of General Psychology* 2 (1998): 300–319.

Freud, Sigmund. *The Future of an Illusion*. James Strachey, trans. New York: W. W. Norton, 1961.

Frey, Bruno S. *Happiness: A Revolution in Economics*. Cambridge, MA: MIT Press, 2008.

Friedman, Richard A. "When Self-Knowledge Is Only the Beginning." *New York Times,* January 18, 2011, p. D-5.

Frydenberg, Erica. ed. *Beyond Coping: Meeting Goals, Visions, and Challenges*. New York: Oxford University Press, 2002.

Gauthier, David. *Rousseau: The Sentiment of Existence*. New York: Cambridge University Press, 2006.

Gewirth, Alan. *Self-Fulfillment*. Princeton: Princeton University Press, 1998.

Giardini, Anne. *The Sad Truth About Happiness*. New York: Harper Perennial, 2005.

Gilbert, Daniel. *Stumbling on Happiness*. New York: Alfred A. Knopf, 2006.

Gilbert, Daniel, and Joel Cooper. "Social Psychological Strategies of Self-Deception." In Mike W. Martin, ed., *Self-Deception and Self-Understanding: New Essays in Philosophy and Psychology*. Lawrence: University Press of Kansas, 1985. Pp. 75–94.

Gini, Al. *The Importance of Being Lazy*. New York: Routledge, 2003.

Goethe, Johann Wolfgang von. *Italian Journey*. W. H. Auden and Elizabeth Mayer, trans. New York: Penguin Books, 1970.

———. *Reflections and Maxims*. W. B. Ronnfeldt, trans. In Stephen Spender, ed., *Great Writings of Goethe*. New York: New American Library, 1958. Pp. 271–277.

———. *Wilhelm Meister's Apprenticeship*. Eric A. Blackall, trans. New York: Suhrkamp Publishers, 1989.

Goldstein, Irwin. "Happiness: The Role of Non-Hedonic Criteria in Its Evaluation." *International Philosophical Quarterly* 13 (1973): 523–534.

Goodstein, Laurie. "Once in Doubt, Credit for Prayer Won't Change." *New York Times,* November 28, 2009, pp. A1, A11.

Gottman, John, and Nan Silver. *The Seven Principles for Making Marriage Work*. London: Orion Books, 2000.

Graham, Carol. *Happiness Around the World*. New York: Oxford University Press, 2009.

Greene, Graham. *A Burnt-Out Case*. New York: Penguin Books, 1960.

Griffin, James. *Well-Being*. Oxford: Clarendon Press, 1986.

———. "What Do Happiness Studies Study?" *Journal of Happiness Studies* 8 (2007): 139–148.

Griswold, Charles L. *Forgiveness*. New York: Cambridge University Press, 2007.

Grunwald, Lisa. *Whatever Makes You Happy*. New York: Random House, 2005.

Guignon, Charles. *On Being Authentic*. New York: Routledge, 2004.

Haidt, Jonathan. *The Happiness Hypothesis: Finding Modern Truth in Ancient Wisdom*. New York: Basic Books, 2006.

Halpern, David. *The Hidden Wealth of Nations*. Cambridge, UK: Polity Press, 2010.

Haney, Mitchell R., and A. David Kline, eds. *The Value of Time and Leisure in a World of Work*. Lanham, MD: Rowman and Littlefield, 2010.

Haworth, John. "Work, Leisure and Well-Being in Changing Social Conditions." In John Haworth and Graham Hart, eds., *Well-Being*. New York: Palgrave, 2007. Pp. 241–255.

Haworth, John T., and A. J. Veal, eds. *Work and Leisure*. New York: Routledge, 2004.

Haybron, Daniel M. "Do We Know How Happy We Are? On Some Limits of Affective Introspection and Recall." *Nous* 41:3 (2007): 394–428.

———. "Life Satisfaction, Ethical Reflection, and the Science of Happiness." *Journal of Happiness Studies* 8 (2006): 99–138.

———. *The Pursuit of Unhappiness*. New York: Oxford University Press, 2008.

Headey, Bruce, Ruud Muffels, and Mark Wooden. "Money Does Not Buy Happiness: Or Does
It? A Reassessment Based on the Combined Effects of Wealth, Income and Consumption." *Social Indicators Research* 87 (2008): 65–82.

Hecht, Jennifer Michael. *The Happiness Myth*. New York: HarperCollins, 2007.

Heilbrun, Carolyn G. *Writing a Woman's Life*. New York: W. W. Norton, 1988.

Heinlein, Robert A. *Stranger in a Strange Land*. New York: G. P. Putnam's Sons, 1961.

Hill, Thomas E. *Human Welfare and Moral Worth: Kantian Perspectives*. Oxford: Clarendon
Press, 2002.

Hillman, Bruce Joel. "James Dickey." In Bill Strickland, ed., *On Being a Writer*. Cincinnati, OH:
Writer's Digest Books, 1989. Pp. 181–186.

Hoggard, Liz. *How to Be Happy*. London: BBC Books, 2005.

Horn, Laura, and Howard Gardner. "The Lonely Profession." In William Damon and Susan
Verducci, eds., *Taking Philanthropy Seriously*. Bloomington: Indiana University Press,
2006. Pp. 77–93.

Hudson, Deal W. *Happiness and the Limits of Satisfaction*. Lanham, MD: Rowman and Littlefield, 1996.

Hume, David. *An Enquiry Concerning the Principles of Morals*. New York: C. W. Hendel, 1957.

Hunter, James Davison. *The Death of Character*. New York: Basic Books, 2000.

Hunter, J. Paul, ed. *Mary Shelley, Frankenstein*. New York: W. W. Norton, 1996.

Huppert, Felicia A., Nick Baylis, and Barry Keverne. eds. *The Science of Well-Being*. New York:
Oxford University Press, 2005.

Hursthouse, Rosalind. *On Virtue Ethics*. New York: Oxford University Press, 1999.

Hustis, Harriet. "Responsible Creativity and the 'Modernity' of Mary Shelley's Prometheus."
SEL, Studies in English Literature 1500–1900 43:4 (2003): 845–858.

Huxley, Aldous. *Brave New World and Brave New World Revisited*. New York: HarperPerennial, 2005.

Ibsen, Henrik. *Four Major Plays*. Rolf Fjelde, trans. New York: New American Library, 1965.

Irvine, William B. *A Guide to the Good Life*. New York: Oxford University Press, 2009.

Isen, A. M., and P. F. Levin. "Effect of Feeling Good on Helping: Cookies and Kindness," *Journal of Personality and Social Psychology* 21 (1972): 384–388.

Jackson, Kevin, ed. *The Oxford Book of Money*. New York: Oxford University, 1996.

Jahoda, Marie. *Current Concepts of Positive Mental Health*. New York: Basic Books, 1958.

James, Clive. "Happiness Writes White." *The Monthly* (December 2006–January 2007), No. 19.
Http://www.themonthly.com. Accessed 1/10/2010.

James, P. D. *Time to Be in Earnest*. New York: Ballantine Books, 1999.

James, William. *Psychology: Briefer Course*. New York: Collier Books, 1962.

———. *The Varieties of Religious Experience*. New York: Modern Library, 1902.

Jamison, Kay Redfield. *Exuberance: The Passion for Life*. New York: Alfred A. Knopf, 2004.

Johns, Helen, and Paul Ormerod. *Happiness, Economics and Public Policy*. London: Institute of
Economic Affairs, 2007.

Jollimore, Troy. "Meaningless Happiness and Meaningful Suffering." *Southern Journal of Philosophy* 47 (2004): 333–347.

Jones, W. Randall. *The Richest Man in Town*. New York: Business Plus, 2009.

Kahneman, Daniel. "Objective Happiness." In Daniel Kahneman, Ed Diener, Norbert Schwarz, eds., *Well-Being*. New York: Russell Sage Foundation, 1999. Pp. 3–25.

Kant, Immanuel. *Foundations of the Metaphysics of Morals*. Lewis White Beck, trans. Robert Paul Wolff, ed. Indianapolis, IN: Bobbs-Merrill, 1969.

———. *Practical Philosophy*. Mary J. Gregor, trans. and ed. New York: Cambridge University Press, 1996.

Kasser, Tim. *The High Price of Materialism*. Cambridge, MA: MIT Press, 2002.

———. "Materialism and Its Alternatives." In Mihaly Csikszentmihalyi and Isabella Selega Csikszentmihalyi, eds., *A Life Worth Living: Contributions to Positive Psychology*. New York: Oxford University Press, 2006. Pp. 200–214.

Kasser, Tim, and Kirk Warren Brown. "A Scientific Approach to Voluntary Simplicity." In Cecile Andrews and Wanda Urbanska, *Less Is More*, pp. 35–40.

Kasser, Tim, and Allen D. Kanner, eds. *Psychology and Consumer Culture*. Washington, DC: American Psychological Association, 2004.

Kavka, Gregory S. *Hobbesian Moral and Political Theory*. Princeton: Princeton University Press, 1986.

———. "The Reconciliation Project." In David Zimmerman and David Copp, eds., *Morality, Reason, and Truth*. Totowa, NJ: Rowman and Allanheld, 1985. Pp. 297–319.

Kekes, John. "Attitudinal and Episodic Happiness." In Steven M. Cahn and Christine Vitrano, eds., *Happiness*. New York: Oxford University Press, 2008. Pp. 184–186.

———. *Enjoyment: The Moral Significance of Styles of Life*. Oxford: Clarendon Press, 2008.

———. *The Examined Life*. Lewisburg, PA: Bucknell University Press, 1988.

———. *Moral Tradition and Individuality*. Princeton: Princeton University Press, 1989.

Keyes, Corey L., and Jonathan Haidt, eds. *Flourishing: Positive Psychology and the Life Well-Lived*. Washington, DC: American Psychological Association, 2003.

Keyes, Ralph. *The Courage to Write*. New York: Henry Holt and Company, 1995.

Kidder, Rushworth. *Moral Courage*. New York: HarperCollins, 2005.

Kierkegaard, Søren. *Either/Or*. Vol. II. Walter Lowrie, trans. Princeton: Princeton University Press, 1959.

Kingwell, Mark. *In Pursuit of Happiness*. New York: Crown Publishers, 1998.

Kitcher, Philip. "A Pragmatist's Progress: The Varieties of James's Strategies for Defending Religion." In Wayne Proudfoot, ed., *William James and a Science of Religions*. New York: Columbia University Press, 2004. Pp. 98–138.

Knapp, Caroline. *Drinking: A Love Story*. New York: Dell Publishing, 1996.

Kramer, Peter. *Listening to Prozac*. New York: Penguin Books, 1997.

Kraut, Richard. "Two Conceptions of Happiness." In Steven M. Cahn and Christine Vitrano, eds., *Happiness: Classic and Contemporary Readings in Philosophy*. New York: Oxford University Press, 2008. Pp. 201–222.

Kristjansson, Kristjan. "Positive Psychology, Happiness, and Virtue: The Troublesome Conceptual Issues." *Review of General Psychology* 14:4 (2010): 296–310.

Landman, Janet. *Regret: The Persistence of the Possible*. New York: Oxford University Press, 1993.

Lane, Robert. *The Loss of Happiness in Market Democracies*. New Haven: Yale University Press, 2000.

Lash, Joseph P. *Eleanor and Franklin*. New York: Signet, 1973.

Lawrence, Jerome. "The Joys of Menschhood." In Philip L. Berman, ed., *The Courage to Grow Old*. New York: Ballantine Books, 1989.

Layard, Richard. *Happiness*. New York: Penguin, 2005.

Lewis, C. S. "We Have No 'Right to Happiness.'" In Louis P. Pojman and Lewis Vaughn, eds., *The Moral Life*, 4th ed. New York: Oxford University Press, 2011.

Lewis, Suzan, and Christina Purcell. "Well-Being, Paid Work and Personal Life." In John Haworth and Graham Hart, eds., *Well-Being*. New York: Palgrave, 2007. Pp. 225–240.

Lipking, Lawrence. "Frankenstein, the True Story; or, Rousseau Judges Jean-Jacques." In J. Paul Hunter, ed., *Mary Shelley, Frankenstein*. New York: W. W. Norton, 1996. Pp. 313–331.

Lockard, Joan S., and Delroy L. Paulhus, eds. *Self-Deception: An Adaptive Mechanism?* Englewood Cliffs, NJ: Prentice Hall, 1988.

Loh, Sandra Tsing. "Let's Call the Whole Thing Off." *The Atlantic* (July/August 2009): 116–126.

Luper, Steven. *Invulnerability: On Securing Happiness*. Chicago: Open Court, 1996.

Lykken, David. *Happiness*. New York: St. Martin's Griffin, 1999.

Lyubomirsky, Sonja. *The How of Happiness*. New York: Penguin, 2007.

Lyubomirsky, Sonja, Chris Tkach, and M. Robin Dimatteo. "What Are the Differences Between Happiness and Self-Esteem?" *Social Indicators Research* 78 (2006): 363–404.

McCloskey, Deirdre N. *The Bourgeois Virtues: Ethics for an Age of Commerce*. Chicago: University of Chicago Press, 2006.

McCord, Chris. "Frankenstein Meets Kant (and the Problem of Wide Duties)." *Teaching Philosophy* 27:2 (June 2004): 127–141.

McCullough, Michael E., Kenneth I. Pargament, and Carl E. Thoresen, eds. *Forgiveness: Theory, Research, and Practice*. New York: Guilford Press, 2000.

McFall, Lynne. *Happiness*. New York: Peter Lang, 1989.

McGraw, Phillip C. *Self Matters: Creating Your Life from the Inside Out*. New York: Simon and Schuster, 2001.

MacIntyre, Alasdair. *After Virtue*, 2nd ed. Notre Dame, IN: University of Notre Dame Press, 1984.

McMahon, Darrin M. *Happiness: A History*. New York: Atlantic Monthly Press, 2006.

Maeterlinck, Maurice. *The Blue Bird: A Fairy Play in Six Acts*. Alexander Teixeira De Mattos, trans. Middlesex, England: Echo Library, 2006.

Malcolm, Norman. *Ludwig Wittgenstein, A Memoir*. New York: Oxford University Press, 1958.

Marar, Ziyad. *The Happiness Paradox*. London: Reaktion Books, 2003.

Marrs, Suzanne. *Eudora Welty*. New York: Harcourt, 2004.

Martin, Mike W. *Albert Schweitzer's Reverence for Life: Ethical Idealism and Self-Realization*. Burlington, VT: Ashgate Publishing, 2007.

———. "Balancing Work and Leisure." In *The Value of Time and Leisure in a World of Work*. Mitchell Haney and David Kline, eds. Lanham, MD: Lexington Books, 2010. Pp. 7–24.

———. *Creativity: Ethics and Excellence in Science*. Lanham, MD: Lexington Books, 2007.

———. *Everyday Morality*, 4th ed. Belmont, CA: Thomson/Wadsworth, 2007.

———. *From Morality to Mental Health: Virtue and Vice in a Therapeutic Culture*. New York: Oxford University Press, 2006.

———. "Happily Self-Deceived." *Social Theory and Practice* 35:1 (2009): 29–44.

———. "Happiness and Virtue in Positive Psychology." *Journal for the Theory of Social Behaviour* 37:1 (2007): 89–103.

———. *Love's Virtues*. Lawrence: University Press of Kansas, 1996.

———. *Meaningful Work: Rethinking Professional Ethics*. New York: Oxford University Press, 2000.

———. "Of Mottos and Morals." *International Journal of Applied Philosophy*, 25:1 (2011): 49–60.

———. "Paradoxes of Happiness." *Journal of Happiness Studies* 9:2 (2008): 171–184.

———. *Self-Deception and Morality*. Lawrence: University Press of Kansas, 1986.

────── Ed., *Self-Deception and Self-Understanding: New Essays in Philosophy and Psychology.* Lawrence: University Press of Kansas, 1985.

──────. "Suffering in Happy Lives." In Lisa Bortolotti, ed., *Philosophy and Happiness.* New York: Palgrave Macmillan, 2009. Pp. 100–115.

──────. *Virtuous Giving: Philanthropy, Voluntary Service, and Caring.* Bloomington: Indiana University Press, 1994.

Maslow, Abraham H. "Comments on Dr. Frankl's Paper." In Anthony J. Sutich and Miles A. Vich, eds., *Readings in Humanistic Psychology.* New York: Free Press, 1969.

Meilaender, Gilbert C. *Friendship.* Notre Dame, IN: University of Notre Dame Press, 1981.

Mele, Alfred R. *Irrationality.* New York: Oxford University Press, 1987.

──────. *Self-Deception Unmasked.* Princeton: Princeton University Press, 2001.

Mellor, Anne K. "Choosing a Text of *Frankenstein* to Teach." In J. Paul Hunter, ed., *Mary Shelley, Frankenstein.* New York: W. W. Norton and Company, 1996. Pp. 160–166.

──────. "Making a Monster." In Harold Bloom, ed., *Mary Shelley's Frankenstein,* updated edition. New York: Chelsea House, 2007.

Michaelis, David. *Schulz and Peanuts: A Biography.* New York: HarperCollins, 2007.

Midgley, Mary. *Beast and Man: The Roots of Human Nature.* Rev. ed. London: Routledge, 1995.

Midlarsky, Elizabeth, and Eva Kahana. "Altruism, Well-Being, and Mental Health in Late Life." In Stephen G. Post, ed., *Altruism and Health.* New York: Oxford University Press, 2007. Pp. 56–69.

Mill, John Stuart. *Autobiography.* New York: Penguin, 1989.

──────. *On Liberty.* Indianapolis, IN: Hackett Publishing Company, 1978.

──────. *Utilitarianism.* Indianapolis, IN: Hackett Publishing Company, 1979.

Miller, Michael. "Foreword" to Jacques Hassoun, *The Cruelty of Depression.* Reading, MA: Addison-Wesley, 1997. Pp. vii–xxix.

Moskowitz, Eva S. *In Therapy We Trust.* Baltimore: Johns Hopkins University Press, 2001.

Muirhead, Russell. *Just Work.* Cambridge, MA: Harvard University Press, 2004.

Mumford, Lewis. *The Conduct of Life.* New York: Harcourt Brace Jovanovich, 1951.

Murdoch, Iris. *The Sovereignty of Good.* London: Ark Paperbacks, 1985.

Myers, David G. *The American Paradox.* New Haven, Conn.: Yale University Press, 2000.

──────. *The Pursuit of Happiness.* New York: Quill, 1992.

Nettle, Daniel. *Happiness.* New York: Oxford University Press, 2005.

Neu, Jerome. "Life-Lies and Pipe Dreams: Self-Deception in Ibsen's *The Wild Duck* and O'Neill's *The Iceman Cometh.*" *The Philosophical Forum* 19:4 (1988): 241–269.

Nietzsche, Friedrich. *The Anti-Christ, Ecce Homo, Twilight of the Idols, and Other Writings.* Aaron Ridley and Judith Norman, eds. Judith Norman, trans. New York: Cambridge University Press, 2005.

──────. "The Challenge of Every Great Philosophy." In Walter Kaufmann, ed., *Existentialism from Dostoevsky to Sartre.* Rev. ed. New York: New American Library, 1975. Pp. 122–125.

──────. *The Gay Science,* Josefine Nauckhoff, trans. New York: Cambridge University Press, 2001.

──────. *The Gay Science.* Richard Polt, trans. Indianapolis, IN: Hackett Publishing, 1995.

──────. *On the Genealogy of Morality.* Maudemarie Clark and Alan J. Swensen, trans. Indianapolis, IN: Hackett Publishing Company, 1998.

──────. *Thus Spoke Zarathustra.* Walter Kaufmann, trans. New York: Penguin Books, 1978.

──────. *The Will to Power.* Walter Kaufmann and R. J. Hollingdale, trans. New York: Vintage Books, 1968.

Nolen-Hoessema, Susan, and Christopher G. Davis. "Positive Responses to Loss: Perceiving Benefits and Growth." In C. R. Snyder and Shane J. Lopez, eds., *Handbook of Positive Psychology.* New York: Oxford University Press, 2002. Pp. 598–607.

Norman, Donald A. *Living with Complexity.* Cambridge, MA: MIT Press, 2011.

Nozick, Robert. *The Examined Life.* New York: Simon and Schuster, 1989.

———. *Philosophical Explanations.* Cambridge, MA: Harvard University Press, 1981.

Nussbaum, Martha C. *The Fragility of Goodness: Luck and Ethics in Greek Tragedy and Philosophy.* New York: Cambridge University Press, 1986.

———. "Who Is the Happy Warrior? Philosophy Poses Questions to Psychology." In Eric A. Posner and Cass R. Sunstein, eds., *Law and Happiness.* Chicago: University of Chicago Press, 2010. Pp. 81–113.

O'Connor, John. "Philanthropy and Selfishness." *Social Philosophy and Policy* 4:2 (1987): 113–127.

O'Neil, John R. *The Paradox of Success.* New York: G. P. Putnam's Sons, 1993.

O'Neill, Eugene. *The Iceman Cometh.* New York: Vintage Books, 1957.

O'Rourke, James. "'Nothing More Unnatural': Mary Shelley's Revision of Rousseau." *ELH* 56:3 (1989): 543–69.

Orwell, George. "Arthur Koestler." In Sonia Orwell and Ian Angus, eds., *As I Please.* New York: Harcourt, Brace and World, 1968.

Parens, Erik, ed., *Enhancing Human Traits.* Washington, DC: Georgetown University Press, 1998.

Parens, Erik. "Authenticity and Ambivalence: Toward Understanding the Enhancement Debate." *Hastings Center Report* 35, no. 3 (2005): 34–41.

Peale, Norman Vincent. *Power of Positive Thinking.* New York: Simon and Schuster, 2003.

Peterson, Christopher, and Martin E. P. Seligman. *Character Strengths and Virtues.* New York: Oxford University Press, 2004.

Philipson, Ilene. *Married to the Job.* New York: Free Press, 2002.

Pieper, Josef. *Happiness and Contemplation.* Richard and Clara Winston, trans. South Bend, IN: St. Augustine's Press, 1998.

Piliavin, Jane A., and P. L. Callero. *Giving Blood: The Development of an Altruistic Identity.* Baltimore: Johns Hopkins University Press, 1991.

Piper, Tessa. "The Exodus of Ethnic Nepalis from Southern Bhutan." *Refugee Survey Quarterly* 14 (1995), p. 52.

Plato. *Symposium.* Alexander Nehamas and Paul Woodruff, trans. Indianapolis, IN: Hackett Publishing Company, 1989.

Pollan, Stephen M., and Mark Levine. *It's All in Your Head: Thinking Your Way to Happiness.* New York: HarperCollins, 2005.

Posner, Eric A., and Cass R. Sunstein, eds. *Law and Happiness.* Chicago: University of Chicago Press, 2010.

Prager, Dennis. *Happiness Is a Serious Problem.* New York: Regan Books, 1998.

Prandi, Julie D. *"Dare To Be Happy!": A Study of Goethe's Ethics.* Lanham, MD: University Press of America, 1993.

President's Council on Bioethics. *Beyond Therapy: Biotechnology and the Pursuit of Happiness.* New York: Dana Press, 2003.

Price, Reynolds. *A Whole New Life: An Illness and a Healing.* New York: Plume, 1995.

Putman, Daniel. "Psychological Courage." *Philosophy, Psychiatry, and Psychology* 4:1 (1997): 1–11.

Rader, Melvin. *The Right to Hope: Crisis and Community.* Seattle: University of Washington Press, 1981.

Radner, Gilda. *It's Always Something.* New York: Avon Books, 1989.

Rawls, John. *A Theory of Justice*. Cambridge, MA: Harvard University Press, 1971.

Reed, T. J. "Goethe and Happiness." In Elizabeth M. Wilkinson, ed., *Goethe Revisited: A Collection of Essays*. New York: Riverrun Press, 1984. Pp. 111–131.

Reginster, Bernard. *The Affirmation of Life: Nietzsche on Overcoming Nihilism*. Cambridge, MA: Harvard University Press, 2006.

———. "Happiness as a Faustian Bargain." *Daedalus* (Spring 2004): 52–59.

Richards, Norvin. *Humility*. Philadelphia: Temple University Press, 1992.

Roberts, Robert C. "The Blessings of Gratitude: A Conceptual Analysis." In Robert A. Emmons and Michael E. McCullough, eds., *The Psychology of Gratitude*. New York: Oxford University Press, 2004. Pp. 58–78.

Roberts, Robert C., and W. Jay Wood. "Humility and Epistemic Goods." In Michael DePaul and Linda Zagzebski, eds., *Intellectual Virtue*. Oxford: Clarendon Press, 2003. Pp. 257–279.

Rousseau, Jean-Jacques. *Confessions*. Angela Scholar, trans. New York: Oxford University Press, 2000.

———. *Discourse on the Origin of Inequality*. Donald A. Cress, trans. Indianapolis, IN: Hackett Publishing Company, 1992.

———. *Lettres Morales*, in *Oeuvres Completes*. Bernard Gagnebin and Marcel Raymond, eds. 5 vols. Paris: Gallimard, 1969.

———. *The Reveries of the Solitary Walker*. Charles E. Butterworth, trans. Indianapolis, IN: Hackett Publishing Company, 1992.

Russell, Bertrand. *The Conquest of Happiness*. New York: Liveright, 1996 [1930].

Salinger, J. D. *The Catcher in the Rye*. New York: Bantam Books, 1951.

Sandel, Michael J. *The Case Against Perfection: Ethics in the Age of Genetic Engineering*. Cambridge, MA: Harvard University Press, 2007.

Sanford, Charles B. *The Religious Life of Thomas Jefferson*. Charlottesville: University of Virginia Press, 1984.

Sartre, Jean-Paul. *Being and Nothingness*. Hazel E. Barnes, trans. New York: Washington Square Press, 1966.

———. "Existentialism Is a Humanism." Philip Mairet, trans. In Walter Kaufmann, ed., *Existentialism from Dostoevsky to Sartre*. New York: New American Library, 1975. Pp. 345–369.

Scarry, Elaine. *The Body in Pain*. New York: Oxford University Press, 1985.

Schafer, Roy. *A New Language for Psychoanalysis*. New Haven: Yale University Press, 1976.

Scharnberg, Kirsten. "Undo-plasties Swell in a Nip-Tuck World." *Los Angeles Times*, February 3, 2008, p. B7.

Schoch, Richard. *The Secrets of Happiness*. New York: Scribner, 2006.

Schoene-Harwood, Berthold. Mary Shelley, *Frankenstein*. New York: Columbia University Press, 2000.

Schopenhauer, Arthur. *The World as Will and Representation*. 2 vols. E. F. J. Payne, trans. New York: Dover, 1958.

Schumaker, John F. *In Search of Happiness*. Westport, CT: Praeger, 2007.

Schwartz, Barry. *The Paradox of Choice*. New York: HarperPerennial, 2005.

Schwartz, Barry, and Kenneth Sharpe. *Practical Wisdom: The Right Way to do the Right Thing*. New York: Riverhead Books, 2010.

Schwartz, Carolyn. "Altruism and Subjective Well-Being." In Stephen G. Post, ed., *Altruism and Health*. New York: Oxford University Press, 2007. Pp. 32–42.

Schweitzer, Albert. *Out of My Life and Thought*. A. B. Lemke, trans. New York: Henry Holt and Company, 1990.

———. *Philosophy of Civilization*. C. T. Campion, trans. New York: Prometheus Books, 1987.

———. *Reverence for Life: Sermons 1909–1919*. Reginald H. Fuller, trans. New York: Irvington Publishers, 1993.

Segal, Jerome M. *Graceful Simplicity: The Philosophy and Politics of the Alternative American Dream*. Berkeley: University of California Press, 2003.

Seligman, Martin E. P. *Flourish: A Visionary New Understanding of Happiness and Well-Being*. New York: Free Press, 2011.

———. *Authentic Happiness*. New York: Free Press, 2002.

———. *Learned Optimism*. New York: Alfred A. Knopf, 1991.

Shawn, Allen. *Wish I Could Be There: Notes from a Phobic Life*. New York: Viking Press, 2007.

Shelley, Mary. *Frankenstein*. Maurice Hindle, ed. Rev. ed. New York: Penguin Books, 2003.

Shenk, Joshua Wolf. "What Makes Us Happy?" *The Atlantic Online (Psychology)*, June 2009. http://www.theatlantic.com/doc/print/200906/happiness.

Shi, David E., ed. *In Search of the Simple Life*. Salt Lake City, UT: Gibbs M. Smith, Inc., 1986.

———. *The Simple Life*. New York: Oxford University Press, 1985.

Shrotryia, Vijay K. "Happiness and Development: Public Policy Initiatives in the Kingdom of Bhutan." In Yew-Kwang Ng and Lok Sang Ho, eds., *Happiness and Public Policy: Theory, Case Studies and Implications*. New York: Palgrave/Macmillan, 2006. Pp. 193–208.

Sidgwick, Henry. *Methods of Ethics*. 7th ed. Chicago: University of Chicago Press, 1907.

Sifton, Elisabeth. *The Serenity Prayer*. New York: W. W. Norton, 2003.

Singer, Irving. *The Nature of Love*. 3 vols. 2nd ed. Chicago: University of Chicago Press, 1984–1987.

———. *The Pursuit of Love*. Baltimore: Johns Hopkins University Press, 1994.

Singer, Peter. *The Life You Can Save*. New York: Random House, 2009.

Slote, Michael. *Goods and Virtues*. Oxford: Clarendon Press, 1983.

Smith, Adam. *An Inquiry into the Nature and Causes of the Wealth of Nations*. 2 vols. R. H. Campbell and A. S. Skinner, eds. Indianapolis, IN: Liberty Fund, 1981.

Smith, Johanna M., ed. *Frankenstein, Case Studies in Contemporary Criticism*. 2nd ed. Boston: Bedford/St. Martin's, 2000.

Snyder, C. R., ed. *Coping with Stress: Effective People and Processes*. New York: Oxford University Press, 2001.

Snyder, C. R., and Shane J. Lopez, eds. *Handbook of Positive Psychology*. New York: Oxford University Press, 2002.

Snyder, M., and A. M. Omoto. "Who Helps and Why? The Psychology of AIDS Volunteerism." In S. Spacapan and S. Oskamp, eds., *Helping and Being Helped*. Newbury Park, CA: Sage, 1991. Pp. 213–239.

Solnick, S. J., and D. Hemenway. "Is More Always Better?: A Survey on Positional Concerns." *Journal of Economic Behavior and Organization* 37 (1998): 373–383.

Solomon, Andrew. *The Noonday Demon*. New York: Scribner, 2001.

Solomon, Jeffrey. "A Balancing Act: How Physicians and Teachers Manage Time Pressures and Responsibilities." In Howard Gardner, ed., *Responsibility at Work*. San Francisco: John Wiley and Sons, 2007. Pp. 107–132.

Solomon, Robert C. *About Love*. New York: Simon and Schuster, 1988.

———. *The Passions*. New York: Anchor Books, 1977.

———. *Spirituality for the Skeptic: The Thoughtful Love of Life*. New York: Oxford University Press, 2002.

Spiegelman, Willard. *Seven Pleasures*. New York: Farrar, Straus and Giroux, 2009.

Stanley, Thomas J., and William D. Danko. *The Millionaire Next Door*. New York: Pocket Books, 1996.

Stebbins, Robert A. *Between Work and Leisure: The Common Ground of Two Separate Worlds.* New Brunswick, NJ: Transaction Publishers, 2004.

———. *Serious Leisure.* New Brunswick, NJ: Transaction Publishers, 2007.

———. "Serious Leisure, Volunteerism, and Quality of Life." In John T. Haworth and A. J. Veal, eds., *Work and Leisure.* New York: Routledge, 2004. Pp. 200–212.

Steinhauer, Harry. "Afterword" to *Johann Wolfgang von Goethe, The Sufferings of Young Werther.* Harry Steinhauer, trans. New York: W. W. Norton and Company, 1970. Pp. 101–125.

Sternberg, Robert. *Wisdom, Intelligence, and Creativity Synthesized.* New York: Cambridge University Press, 2003.

Stout, Jeffrey. *Ethics After Babel.* Princeton: Princeton University Press, 2001.

Sumner, L. W. *Welfare, Happiness, and Ethics.* Oxford: Clarendon Press, 1996.

Swanton, Christine. *Virtue Ethics: A Pluralistic View.* New York: Oxford University Press, 2003.

Swift, Jonathan. *A Tale of a Tub.* In Carl Van Doren, ed., *The Portable Swift.* New York: Viking Press, 1958.

Swiss, Deborah J., and Judith P. Walker. *Women and the Work/Family Dilemma.* New York: Wiley, 1993.

Tatarkiewicz, Wladyslaw. *Analysis of Happiness.* Edward Rothert and Danuta Zielinskn, trans. The Hague: Martinus Nijhoff, 1976.

Taylor, Charles. *The Ethics of Authenticity.* Cambridge, MA: Harvard University Press, 1991.

Taylor, Shelley E. *Positive Illusions: Creative Self-Deception and the Healthy Mind.* New York: Basic Books, 1989.

Telfer, Elizabeth. *Happiness.* New York: St. Martin's Press, 1980.

Thaler, Richard H., and Cass R. Sunstein. *Nudge: Improving Decisions About Health, Wealth, and Happiness.* New Haven: Yale University Press, 2008.

Thoits, Peggy A., and Lyndi N. Hewitt. "Volunteer Work and Well-Being." *Journal of Health and Social Behavior,* Vol. 42 (2001): 115–131.

Thoreau, Henry David. *The Journal of Henry D. Thoreau.* Bradford Torrey and Francis H. Allen, eds. Vol. 5. Boston: Houghton Mifflin Company, 1949.

———. *Walden.* Princeton: Princeton University Press, 2004.

Tiberius, Valerie. *The Reflective Life: Living Wisely with Our Limits.* New York: Oxford University Press, 2008.

———. "Value Commitments and the Balanced Life." *Utilitas,* Vol. 17, No. 1 (2005): 24–45.

Tiberius, Valerie, and Alexandra Plakias. "Well-Being." In John M. Doris and the Moral Psychology Research Group, eds., *The Moral Psychology Handbook.* New York: Oxford University Press, 2010. Pp. 402–432.

Tolstoy, Leo. *Anna Karenina.* David Magarshack, trans. New York: Signet, 1961.

———. *The Death of Ivan Ilych.* Aylmer Maude, trans. In Randall Jarrell, ed., *Six Russian Short Novels.* New York: Anchor Books, 1963. Pp. 237–300.

———. *The Death of Ivan Ilyich.* Lynn Solotaroff, trans. New York: Bantam, 1981.

Twitchell, James B. *Lead Us into Temptation: The Triumph of American Materialism.* New York: Columbia University Press, 1999.

Veenhoven, R. "Happiness as a Public Policy Aim: The Greatest Happiness Principle." In A. Linley and S. Joseph, eds. *Positive Psychology in Practice.* Hoboken: Wiley, 2004. Pp. 658–678.

Wallerstein, Judith S., and Sandra Blakeslee. *The Good Marriage.* New York: Houghton Mifflin Company, 1995.

Warr, Peter. *Work, Happiness, and Unhappiness*. Mahwah, NJ: Lawrence Erlbaum Associates, Publishers, 2007.

Watkins, Philip C. "Gratitude and Subjective Well-Being." In Robert A. Emmons and Michael E. McCullough, eds., *The Psychology of Gratitude*. New York: Oxford University Press, 2004. Pp. 167–192.

Watrous, Malena. "Terminal Bliss." *New York Times*, July 19, 2009, p. 9.

Welty, Eudora. *One Writer's Beginnings*. Cambridge, MA: Harvard University Press, 1984.

White, Nicholas. *A Brief History of Happiness*. New York: Blackwell Publishing, 2006.

Wike, Victoria. *Kant on Happiness in Ethics*. Albany: State University of New York Press, 1994.

Williams, Bernard. *Ethics and the Limits of Philosophy*. Cambridge, MA: Harvard University Press, 1985.

Wilson, Eric G. *Against Happiness*. New York: Farrar, Straus and Giroux, 2008.

Wilson, Timothy. *Strangers to Ourselves: Discovering the Adaptive Unconscious*. Cambridge, MA: Harvard University Press, 2002.

Wolfe, Alan. "Joy to the World," (review of Derek Bok's *Politics of Happiness*). *New York Times Book Review*, February 21, 2010, p.16.

———. *One Nation, After All*. New York: Penguin, 1999.

Woolf, Virginia. *To the Lighthouse*. San Diego: Harcourt Brace Jovanovich, 1955.

World Health Organization. Preamble to the Constitution of the World Health Organization. *Official Record of the World Health Organization*. Geneva: World Health Organization, 1946. Vol. 2.

Wuthnow, Robert. *Acts of Compassion*. Princeton: Princeton University Press, 1991.

Yglesias, Rafael. *A Happy Marriage*. New York: Scribner, 2009.

Zagzebski, Linda Trinkaus. *Virtues of the Mind*. New York: Cambridge University Press, 1999.

Zuzanek, Jiri. "Work, Leisure, Time-Pressure and Stress." In John T. Haworth and A. J. Veal, eds., *Work and Leisure*. New York: Routledge, 2004. Pp. 123–144.

INDEX